FIELD-PROGRAMMABLE GATE ARRAYS

FIELD-PROGRAMMABLE GATE ARRAYS
Reconfigurable Logic for Rapid Prototyping and Implementation of Digital Systems

John V. Oldfield
Syracuse University

Richard C. Dorf
University of California, Davis

A Wiley-Interscience Publication
JOHN WILEY & SONS, INC.
New York / Chichester / Brisbane / Toronto / Singapore

This text is printed on acid-free paper.

Copyright © 1995 by John Wiley & Sons, Inc.

All rights reserved. Published simultaneously in Canada.

To order books or for customer service please, call 1(800)-CALL-WILEY (225-5945).

Library of Congress Cataloging in Publication Data:
Oldfield, John V., 1933–
    Field-programmable gate arrays : reconfigurable logic for rapid
prototyping and implementation of digital systems / John V. Oldfield,
Richard C. Dorf.
        p. cm.
    "Wiley-Interscience publication."
    Includes index.
    ISBN 0-471-55665-3 (cloth)
    1. Field programmable gate arrays. 2. Programmable array logic.
I. Dorf, Richard C. II. Title.
TK7895.G36043 1995
621.39′5—dc20   94-20839

10 9 8 7 6

To John Gray, Irene Buchanan,
and Tom Kean, pioneers
of reconfigurable logic

CONTENTS

*Advanced topic to be omitted on first reading.

*Advanced topic to be omitted on first reading.

FOREWORD

Not much has changed in computing in the last 40 years.

Most computers still use the Von Neumann stored program model with serial execution of instructions, centralized main memory, and a bus tying it all together. We write algebraic formulas and symbolic constructs and surround them with various loop structures to sequentially process an array of data items. Language statements are translated into a fixed set of machine instructions which are then executed one (or perhaps two or three) at a time. Strange errors of unknown origin frequently occur, and even stranger incantations are often necessary to recover from them.

To be sure, the price and performance of computing hardware have improved dramatically over the years, on a curve of steepness and length that may never be equalled in any man-made technology. Computers have gotten dramatically easier to use, largely because user interfaces have become two-dimensional. Instead of typing arcane commands, we now merely push the mouse to a button displayed on the screen and click.

But the way in which computers are built and programmed hasn't changed all that much. It can be argued that languages, compilers, CAD/CAE tools, and so on have improved significantly, but *our underlying models of computation have remained basically unchanged since the earliest days of computing*.

The reasons for this are simple: Hardware is difficult and time-consuming to build and to change. Serial instruction execution is a simple, very general paradigm. Parallel architectures can be more powerful, but are less general. A special-purpose circuit can always outperform a microprocessor-based implementation (assuming the same integrated circuit technology is used for both) *for a small class of problems.* Usually the higher performance is achieved through parallelism, either spatial (replication) or temporal (pipelining). The very specialization which provides this parallelism also necessarily limits the range of its application.

I first became aware of a way in which things could be different in 1968, when I came upon Sven Wahlstrom's article in *Electronics* magazine entitled "Programmable Logic Arrays—Cheaper by the Millions." Wahlstrom, Spandorfer, and other pioneers in this area (see references herein) had come up with a radical idea: instead of relying on permanent fuses or 'cutpoints' to customize an array of integrated circuitry, one could simply include additional gates to do the job. The result would be special-purpose hardware which was easily changed as well.

This idea was somewhat heretical when gates were precious, but most people knew this would not always be the case. I became sufficiently excited about this direction to adopt it as my doctoral dissertation research at Carnegie-Mellon University, and completed the thesis in early 1970. At my thesis oral defense, one committee member asked how long it might be before programmable logic would be a reality and in common use in computing hardware. I thought it might be 5–10 years, given that the first microprocessor was already dimly visible in the integrated future. I suspended work in this area awaiting levels of integration which would make my thesis practical.

Graduate students are often known for their great optimism, but they are by no means unique in this regard. In fact it was nearly 15 years before even the first real FPGA was introduced into the marketplace. Today, nearly 28 years after Wahlstrom's first patent was filed (1966), FPGAs are just beginning to have a significant impact. Two application areas seem to dominate their use so far: random 'glue' logic, and emulation of new integrated circuit designs.

But the real impact of FPGAs—*restructurable hardware*, more to the point—is yet to be felt. As the present authors duly point out, the ability to reconfigure hardware on the fly will have vast ramifications. Once suitable design tools and automatic methods become available, designers and programmers will be able to create custom hardware circuitry and pipelines to suit the problem at hand. I like the term "soft hardware," as it suggests that hardware will become as readily created and malleable as software. In a practical sense, this means that the turn-around time for custom hardware will be just as short as software development is today—seconds or minutes, instead of weeks or months.

And the greatest effect of this will be the freedom to think in terms of highly-concurrent hardware structures which implement the desired computation literally, in many cases directly, rather than by emulation or simulation. Von Neumann architectures will be used only when appropriate, and more organic, customized architectures can begin to flourish. The computer will *be* the computation desired at that moment.

Programmable logic is not just a better way to do conventional designs, but a doorway to whole new domains.

RICHARD G. SHOUP

Interval Research
Palo Alto, California
June 1994

PREFACE

The field-programmable gate array (FPGA) is a relatively new type of component for the construction of electronic systems, particularly those using digital, or more correctly *logical*, circuit principles. It consists of an array of functional blocks along with an interconnection network, and as the name implies, its configuration can be determined in the field, that is, at the *point of application*. The specific function of each block and the connections between blocks are prescribed by the user. For the most part we will be concerned with *reprogrammable* FPGAs in this text, since they offer more flexibility than fuse-programmable devices. This choice is not a matter of taste. Already the FPGA market has a wide range of architectures and alternative ways of controlling configurations. We do not dismiss fuse-programmable architectures, which clearly already provide fast, economical, and compact implementations for logic designs. But it is almost like comparing a ROM-based computer with the more-general RAM-based one. Moreover, this field is at such an early stage of development that no one yet knows the most appropriate design methodologies and run-time environments. The FPGA takes its place in the continuing evolution of very-large-scale integrated (VLSI) circuit technology toward denser and faster circuits. It already provides, for many applications, an adequate number of transistors in a single chip package for the functional blocks, switches for the routing network, and the memory capacity to control both. The prospects for further increases in both circuit density and speed of operation are excellent, since VLSI circuit density continues to double every 2 to 3 years or so. Indeed, billion-transistor (10^9) chips are anticipated by the turn of the century.

Clearly, the ability to reconfigure an electronic component, either to correct an error, or to change an application, has economic benefits, but we suggest that the impact of the FPGA concept is much more profound, in that a logic system may be *dynamically* reconfigured to match changing circumstances. This is a new computing paradigm whose potential is far-reaching. Although present-day FPGA components have only a few thousand or tens of thousands of gates, future ones will have hundreds of thousands or eventually millions of gates. We may expect to see the development of pipelined and parallel processing in which the system configuration changes dynamically. For example, a graphic processing operation might use three processors for three-dimensional calcula- tions and switch to two processors for screen-related calculations. An image processing system could divide computations into parallel tasks for a large number of processors realized within the same FPGA chip. While such schemes may seem futuristic, they suggest that the FPGA should not be thought of as just a VLSI component that replaces others, but as a concept with distinctive new possibilities.

Returning to present-day realizations, the FPGA has significant advantages for the development of prototype systems and their early introduction to the market. The benefits are similar to those associated with the introduction of the microprocessor in the late 1970s, such as programmability and adaptability, but with additional advantages in speed, compactness, and design protection. From an educational viewpoint, designing with FPGAs requires computer assistance at almost every stage of design, including detailed specification, simulation, placement, and routing, and calls for an overall systematic *design methodology*. We consider this to be an important aspect in the education of future engineers, which should improve both the performance and the quality of the systems they produce. At the same time, the increase in designer productivity makes it pos- sible to consider alternative implementations at a higher level than previously, and should not cramp the creativity of a system designer.

ABOUT THE BOOK

The book is intended to serve the needs of several constituencies:

- As a text to accompany an undergraduate course in which students are introduced to FPGAs for the first time, and in which laboratory work is a likely accompaniment.

- As a graduate-level text, with introductory aspects as well as more advanced applications and interest in the underlying VLSI structures of FPGAs, computer-aided design (CAD) algorithms for functional and physical layout.

- For the professional engineer who wishes to obtain an appreciation of FPGA principles and prospects.

In all cases, we assume a familiarity with the basic principles of logic circuits and their realization as digital systems with commonly available components. We have paid more attention than is customary to the nature of the emerging industry and business aspects, since we believe that these should be of interest to all of the preceding categories of reader. VLSI technology has been an exciting business to be in during its formative years, and technical considerations cannot be divorced from financial and marketing aspects.

Chapter 1 discusses the alternative ways in which a logic system can be realized, and the variety of technologies available for the purpose. It considers the design process itself as worthy of study, and highlights various design methodologies that have emerged. Chapter 2 is mostly a review of logical and electrical aspects of digital systems with which the reader should already be familiar, with additional material on implementing state machines so as to take advantage of common FPGA properties. Chapter 3 reviews the architecture of FPGAs, along with the options and trade-offs for different approaches. While the industry is still in its formative years, radically different directions have been taken in setting up the underlying structures, and new architectures will continue to emerge. The chapter concludes with a discussion of appropriate benchmarks for FPGA comparison. Chapter 4 is concerned with CAD for FPGA applications, and attempts to give a comprehensive, manufacturer-independent view of the place of CAD tools, as well as some elementary and specific examples for two particular systems. In Chapter 5 there are a number of case studies of small- and modest-scale designs implemented on different FPGA architectures, along with a substantial example of a parallel controller that stretched the limits of an FPGA architecture and its supporting CAD software. Chapter 6 is concerned with advanced applications of FPGAs, including several large-scale examples in which the FPGA is used as a novel computing structure. The term "custom computing machine" has been coined to describe such systems, and a number of illustrations already exist to show the enormous potential of arrays of FPGA chips for some of the present-day "Grand Challenge" problems, such as high-speed string comparison for the Human Genome Project. Business issues are the focus of Chapter 7, and include a perspective on the start-up and growth of new companies in this field, as well as the relevance of market factors to FPGA applications in the context of other ways of implementing digital systems. The chapter concludes with a short review of intellectual property aspects—how to protect one's own or one's company's ideas in a highly competitive environment. The FPGA has interesting new possibilities for design protection, and can be made extraordinarily secure compared with other VLSI technologies. Chapter 8 was added to the text as late as possible and reviews some recent developments. Much of this chapter has been contributed by the manufacturers concerned, and we appreciate their cooperation. There is a Glossary containing explanations of the technical terms, particularly acronyms, used in the field.

Readers should be aware that we have not included full details of FPGA technical data, nor specific information on particular CAD support software. This decision is based on the fact that well-written technical handbooks are available from the FPGA manufacturers and CAD software vendors, and also recognizes that the publication cycle of a text is long, compared with ever-changing computer software and the intervals between announcements of new FPGA families and devices. For the most part our examples are from Xilinx Inc. and Algotronix Ltd., and readers should contact their nearest distributor for technical information.

A few months before the manuscript was completed, Algotronix Ltd. was acquired by Xilinx Inc., and in the new circumstances two of the original authors, John Gray and Tom Kean, had to withdraw. We believe that the pioneering work they carried out on fine-grain FPGA structures will be recognized as a valuable and complementary alternative to more widely accepted methods used in the industry.

BACKGROUND AND APPLICABILITY

As mentioned earlier, we assume that the reader is already familiar with logic circuits, including the concepts of state machines and their realization. A university-level introductory course should be adequate, and even better if supplemented by laboratory experience, for example, with a logic breadboarding system. Chapter 2 provides relevant review material. In considering using this book as a text, it is worth giving thought to the long-term impact of this technology on both undergraduate and graduate education, since FPGAs could be relevant to a *sequence* of classes related to digital design and computer architecture.

This book could be used as a text for an introductory undergraduate- or graduate-level class on field-programmable logic arrays and their applications. This might be offered in electrical engineering, computer engineering, or computer science. It should be combined with exposure to a practical FPGA system, including supporting CAD hardware and software. It is planned to produce an Instructor's Manual which will include suggestions and advice, as well as worked examples, suggestions for projects, and solutions. This manual will also suggest useful sources of information. The previously listed classes could focus on one particular FPGA architecture, but should include comparisons with other architectures, if at all possible. We recommend that the broader aspects, including design methodologies and business issues, be included in such courses.

The material in the text can be usefully linked to an introductory VLSI design class. Often such courses emphasize full-custom design, and already include most of the basic elements found in an FPGA. While the underlying architecture is highly proprietary, many of the issues in full-custom design, such as global and local communication, memory, input/output pads, general-purpose logic blocks, are particularly relevant. The FPGA also allows much faster turnaround than for full-custom design, and exposure to this material gives students a more balanced perspective on digital system implementation.

The book could be used in conjunction with a project-oriented class, particularly for computer engineering or computer science students. Assuming that adequate CAD support is available, FPGAs should contribute to a considerable increase in student productivity, compared with traditional digital breadboard systems. An added advantage is the emphasis on a systematic approach to engineering design, and the high-quality design documentation that is readily produced from the CAD system. This is highly relevant to the emphasis placed on design by the U.S. Accreditation Board for Engineering and Technology (ABET), which defines "engineering design" as [ABET90]:

> . . . the process of devising a system, component, or process to meet desired needs. . . . Among the fundamental elements of the design process are the establishment of objectives and criteria, synthesis, analysis, construction, testing, and evaluation. The engineering component of a curriculum must include at least some of the following features: development of student creativity, use of open-ended problems, development and use of design methodology, formulation of design problem statements, consideration of alternative solutions, feasibility considerations, and detailed system descriptions. Further, it is essential to include a variety of realistic constraints such as economic factors, safety, reliability, aesthetics, ethics, and social impact.

We submit that FPGAs can provide an outstanding *design* environment for engineering education.

Computer architecture courses are often accompanied by the use of a simulator for trying out proposed architectures. The FPGA and its CAD simulators should be very attractive for such courses, with the added advantage of implementation at speeds much nearer to those of a real system than the slowness of a software simulator. For some of the less-complex FPGA architectures, it is possible to independently develop CAD software, including simulators, and much exploration can be done without the actual hardware parts. The demise of Algotronix as a source of parts should not discourage exploration of this and other novel architectures by simulation. We have already found such a simulator useful for debugging purposes, and they are easy to develop for fine-grain architectures.

At the graduate-level, FPGAs can provide useful target architectures for classes in CAD for digital systems. These include physical design issues such as partitioning, placement, and routing, along with logic simplification and simulation. Clearly, simpler architectures are to be preferred to more complex ones, and it may be necessary to approach the manufacturer for details of CAD file formats, and so forth. Even outside the classroom context, students should be encouraged to develop software aids for FPGAs. These goals would be easier to attain if FPGA vendors actively encouraged more open design systems for their products.

A superficial pass through the book may detect more emphasis on *wiring management* and *layout* issues than might be expected for a component that, in an ideal world, would be designed and configured totally automatically. There is a close parallel with full-custom VLSI design and much scope for designer ingenuity by exploiting the inherent massive parallelism, particularly by pipe-lining.

In summary, the FPGA can provide a realistic implementation vehicle for complex digital systems that are beyond the limits of conventional breadboard logic, and where there is insufficient time for full-custom, standard-cell, or even mask-programmable gate array implementation.

ERRORS AND OMISSIONS

Despite the best efforts of the author team, errors will get through to the printed version. We would appreciate being informed of any such errors, and will endeavor to see that they are identified and corrected in subsequent printings.

ACKNOWLEDGMENTS

First we wish to express our sincere gratitude to our former coauthors John Gray and Tom Kean. Without their enthusiasm, experience, and cooperation the book would never have been started. The authors wish to thank a number of indi-viduals who have contributed to the development of this book. Erik Dagless, Jonathan M. Saul, and Tomasz Kozlowski of the University of Bristol provided the material on parallel state machines in Chapter 2, and the two former authors provided the video controller example given in Chapter 5. Christopher Kappler of Syracuse University contributed the sorter design given in the same chapter, and, along with Kang Shen, developed the self-timed approach to genetic string matching described in Chapter 6. Roberto Melo provided the multiplier exam-ples in Chapter 5 as part of a wider study that included standard-cell designs. Fred Furtek kindly agreed to the insertion of his original and thought-provoking approach to motion estimation that is reprinted, with permission, at the end of Chapter 6. Ted Hagelin of the Syracuse University College of Law provided much of the background on intellectual property issues in the latter half of Chapter 7, and Harold Burstyn made some important corrections to one of the author's interpretations. Amr Mohsen, Wayne Luk, Steven Sillich, and Steven Trimberger were very helpful in commenting on draft versions of the text. Ed Sibert of Syracuse University devoted countless late hours in the production of the final manuscript in Latex. Mary Haas-Wendel became involved in the development of the manuscript at a late stage. She made significant contribu-tions to the business issues chapter based on her experience in the corporate world as well as providing much editorial help. Finally, there are a host of per-sons in both academia and industry who have encouraged the authors directly and indirectly, through papers and discussions.

The authors are of course solely responsible for the views expressed in this book.

BIBLIOGRAPHY

[ABET90]   *Criteria for Accrediting Programs in Engineering*, United States Accrediting Board for Engineering and Technology, Inc., New York, 1990.

[NSF92]   Committee on Physical, Mathematical, and Engineering Sciences Federal Coordinating Council for Science, Engineering, and Technology Office of Science and Technology, "Grand Challenges: High Performance Computing and Communications," National Science Foundation, Washington, D.C., 1992.

ACRONYMS

ABEL	Proprietary language for describing state machines
ABET	Accreditation Board for Engineering and Technology
A/D	Analog-Digital
ALU	Arithmetic-logic unit
ASIC	Application-specific integrated circuit
AT	IBM type of Personal Computer
CAD	Computer-aided design
CAE	Computer-aided engineering
CAL	Configurable Array Logic
CBIC	Cell-based integrated circuit
CHS	Configurable Hardware System
CLB	Configurable Logic Block
CLS	Configurable Logic Software
CPLD	Complex programmable logic device
CMOS	Complementary metal-oxide semiconductor
CUPS	Cell updates per second
D/A	Digital-analog
DES	Data Encryption Standard
DIL	Dual in-line
DRAM	Dynamic random-access memory
DSP	Digital signal processor

ECAD	Electronic computer-aided design
EDIF	Electronic Design Interchange Format
EEPROM	Electrically-erasable programmable read-only memory
EPLD	Electrically-programmable logic device
EPROM	Erasable programmable read-only memory
ESD	Electrostatic discharge

FET	Field-effect transistor
FPGA	Field-programmable gate array
FPCB	Field-programmable circuit board
FPIC	Field-programmable interconnect component
FPID	Field-programmable interconnect device
FPLA	Field-programmable logic array
FSM	Finite-state machine

GAL	Generic Array Logic

HDL	Hardware definition language
HP	Hewlett-Packard

IC	Integrated circuit
IOB	Input/output block
IOE	Input/output element
IP	Initial permutation
ISA	Industry-Standard Architecture

JTAG	Joint Test Action Group

LAB	Logic array block
LCA	Logic cell array
LE	Logic element
LED	Light-emitting diode
LFSR	Linear feedback shift register
LPM	Library of parameterized modules
LSI	Large-scale integration

MCUPS	Millions of cell updates per second
MIPS	Millions of instructions per second
MOS	Metal-oxide-semiconductor
MOSFET	MOS field-effect transistor
MPGA	Mask-programmable gate array
MIS	medium-scale integration
MUX	Multiplexer

NRE	Non-recurring engineering
NTSC	National Television Systems Committee
PAL	Phase alteration (each) line (chapter 7)
PAL	Programmable array logic (other chapters)
PCB	Printed-circuit board
PE	Processing element
PGA	Pin-grid array
PIP	Programmable interconnect point
PLA	Programmable logic array
PLD	Programmable logic device
PLICE	Programmable Low-Impedance Circuit Element
PMS	Processor-memory-switch
PREP	Programmable Electronics Performance Corporation
PNAC	Princeton Nucleic Acid Comparator
PROM	Programmable read-only memory
QFP	Quad flat pack
RAM	Random-access memory
R&D	Research and development
RISC	Reduced-instruction set computer
ROI	Region of interest
ROM	Read-only memory
RS-232	Data transmission standard
RT	Register transfer
SBA	Small Business Administration
SBIR	Small-business innovation research
SRAM	Static random-access memory
SSI	Small-scale integration
SECAM	Sequential color and memory
STEP	Self-timed environmental prototype
STTR	Small business technology-transfer program
TTL	Transistor-transistor logic
UGF	User-gullibility factor
UV	Ultraviolet
VHDL	Very high-level description language
VLSI	Very large-scale integration
VME	Standard computer bus

TRADEMARKS AND PROPRIETARY NAMES

Name	*Company*
ABEL	Data I/O Corp.
ActionProbe	Actel Corp.
Altera	Altera Corp.
Cache Logic	Atmel Corp.
Configurable Array Logic, CAL	Algotronix Ltd.
Configurable Logic Block	Xilinx Inc.
FastTrack	Altera Corp.
FPCB	Aptix Inc.
FPIC	Aptix Inc.
FPGA Foundry	NeoCAD Inc.
GAL	Lattice Semiconductor Corp.
IBM	IBM Corp.
LCA	Xilinx Corp.
Logic Cell	Xilinx Corp.
Logic Cell Array, LCA	Xilinx Corp.
MAC+PLUS	Altera Corp.
NeoCAD	NeoCAD Inc.
NeoCAD Epic	NeoCAD Inc.
NeoCAD Prism	NeoCAD Inc.
ORCA	AT&T
OrCAD	OrCAD Systems Corp.

Name	*Company*
PALASM	Advanced Micro Devices
PLICE	Actel Corp.
Programmable Array Logic (PAL)	Advanced Micro Devices
SPARC	Sun Microsystems
Sun	Sun Microsystems
Timing Wizard	NeoCAD Inc.
Transputer	Inmos Ltd.
Tri-state	National Semiconductor Corp.
ViewLogic, ViewSim, ViewGen, ViewLogic	ViewLogic Systems Inc.
Windows	Microsoft Corp.
Workview	ViewLogic Systems Inc.
XACT	Xilinx Inc.
Xilinx	Xilinx Inc.

CHAPTER 1

SYSTEM IMPLEMENTATION STRATEGIES

The purpose of this chapter is to:

- Describe common implementation styles
- Describe common design styles
- Show where the FPGA fits into these frameworks
- Define the scope of engineering with FPGAs
- Emphasize the importance of a high level, architectural view in design

1.1 THE FPGA PARADIGM

Since the beginning of digital electronics, engineers have sought to design circuits that do useful work on data. To achieve this goal circuits were composed from three key elements:

- Data operators: Gates that implement useful functions by transforming input states to output states.
- Storage elements: Latches, flip-flops, that save state, store operands, and so forth.
- Wires: Point-to-point wires, busses, that communicate values between and among storage elements and data operators.

Indeed, the history of semiconductors can be viewed as the delivery of these simple resources in various conceptual and/or physical packages. Whole industries have evolved around the delivery of a single one of these resources, for example, dynamic random-access memory (DRAM) businesses supplying the components of primary memory to computer manufacturers and the application-specific integrated-circuit (ASIC) vendors, supplying logic resources in the form of gate arrays to systems businesses.

In earlier times, engineers had direct access to these three resources and were able to breadboard systems from gates and flip-flops, or convenient aggregations of them, on simple printed circuit boards (PCBs), by directly wiring them together. However, when integrated circuits evolved, the engineer lost direct access to these resources and was required to use encapsulations of them in logic families [TTL88]. More recently the engineer regained intimate access to the resources with the commercial availability of parts in which functions and wires could be "programmed" during manufacture, that is, as application-specific integrated circuits, albeit at a high cost and long lead time.

It is a truism that an electronic engineer works in an environment defined by progress in components, which in turn evolve from progress in base technologies and manufacturing processes. Progress, however, can be viewed as driven by two forces [Bell78]: *technology push*, improvements in manufacturing, inventions, and so forth, and *market pull*, the quantifiable need for specific products. These forces both act on an engineer and delineate a space for creative activity in systems building. Technology push has driven component density increases in semiconductors and given rise to well-known standard part catalogs. Market pull, on the other hand, has defined specific functionalities and shortened product development cycles, raising the need for nonstandard, or application-specific parts. In this sense the two forces act on opposition, forcing engineers to choose between standard parts or application-specific parts in systems design.

In very recent times, field-programmable gate arrays (FPGAs) have evolved. These components deliver the three elementary resources: storage, logic, and wires in a standard part that can be programmed, at time of use, to make an application-specific circuit. FPGAs thus resolve the conflict between standard parts and ASICs and provide the engineer with intimate and immediate access to all resources for systems building. In this sense they are a fundamental innovation in electronics. A summary of these systems building choices would be:

- Standard part solution: Delivers supplier-defined functionality at low cost.
- ASIC solution: Delivers user-defined functionality at high cost.
- FPGA solution: Delivers user-defined functionality at low cost.

Conceptually a reprogrammable FPGA is a very simple structure as shown in Figure 1–1. It has a control store in the form of static RAM (SRAM). Function units and wires are programmed by writing to the control store, to set up specific gates, storage elements, and interconnect paths. FPGA families are

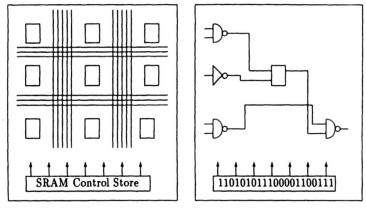

Figure 1-1. Conceptual structure of FPGAs.

differentiated by their chip-level architecture, by the granularity of the function unit and intra- and interchip wiring organization. The simplest paradigm for FPGA use is a (silicon) "sand box" in which systems structures can be built in the time it takes to write to a RAM, and with complexity levels defined by the chip architecture. Because actual circuits are defined by the contents of a volatile SRAM control store, FPGAs address applications in new ways:

Instantaneous implementation as memory-wiring times are usually short, designs can effectively be implemented "instantaneously." This is in sharp distinction to conventional VLSI design where there are usually many weeks from design to manufacture. This feature also creates an opportunity for new methodologies to emerge in design.

Dynamic reconfiguration with some architectures part of the FPGA can be reprogrammed at run-time, that is, in the application situation. Therefore, chip resources can be reused for different functions as time progresses. Circuits could, in principle, even be self-modifying.

Design security: An FPGA's configuration disappears when the chip is powered down. There is a range of applications where this additional level of design security is important.

Field programmability systems built around FPGAs can be upgraded in the field, either by an operator or by telemetry, to correct bugs, recover from damage, or add new functionality.

1.2 DESIGN AND IMPLEMENTATION USING FPGAs

A design exists separately from its mapping into its implementation as one or more FPGAs. Often an individual design is part of a larger system's design.

Designing, in any medium is the most compelling part of engineering, and designing with FPGAs is particularly challenging because the technology is progressing so rapidly, while "manufacturing" times are so short. Unfortunately, designing is not necessarily simple and can require a great deal of creative effort. Standard textbook treatments of design usually focus on some tractable subproblems in designing, such as logic minimization or state machine design. Or they attempt to reduce design to a mathematical formulation, in which there is a perfect solution to an idealized problem. To clarify the situation, it may be better not to strive for a definition of design [Bell72], but to make a distinction between *design* and *implementation*. Within this view, a design is an abstract collection of connected elements, each of which has a defined performance. Elements may of course be recursively defined and may be assemblies of other elements. This structural view of a design is common to all branches of engineering. In electronics, gate elements are connected by wires; in mechanics, beams are connected by fasteners.

For a design to be realized, however, the abstract elements in its structural definition must be mapped onto physical elements that actually exist in some medium. Once this has been achieved an implementation exists. At this point, it is possible to determine quantitative properties of the design to ascertain its "goodness." There are some obviously important properties:

Space: How many components, how much board space, and so on? Space is clearly a key determinant of manufacturing cost, along with production volume.

Speed: How fast does it run? There are normally several performance requirements for a design.

Energy and power demand: Working on data generates waste heat which must be removed with a possible impact on the space measures.

Timeliness: Have all of the above been achieved consistent with some time measure such as total time-to-market?

In product development, engineering is the *management of time and space*.

A diagrammatic form of this view of the world is shown in Figure 1–2. This flowchart clearly separates a technology-independent design phase from a technology-dependent implementation phase. It also suggests an oversimplified view of the world in which a design is implemented in a single FPGA, gate array, cell-based ASIC, and so forth. In real-world implementations, designs are partitioned across a number of parts and a number of levels of physical hierarchy, as shown in Figure 1–3. This figure shows two levels, semiconductor components and printed circuit board assembly. Some products, for example, supercomputers, may be partitioned across as many as eight levels of hierarchy [Bell78].

The simplified view of the process tends to be presented dogmatically, since it provides protection against designs being taken hostage by implementation

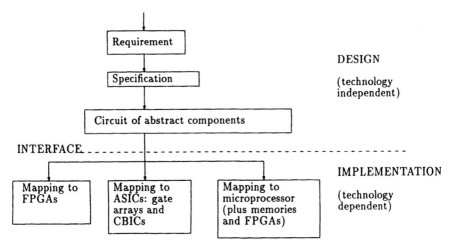

Figure 1-2. Design and implementation.

style, and hence by supplier. But recognizably great designs exhibit a nebulous elegance due to some technology dependence, that is, the engineer has usually exploited some technology-specific feature to meet or exceed required measures in an economic way. This implifies information flow across the interface from implementation to design whether by formal or informal means. It may be in

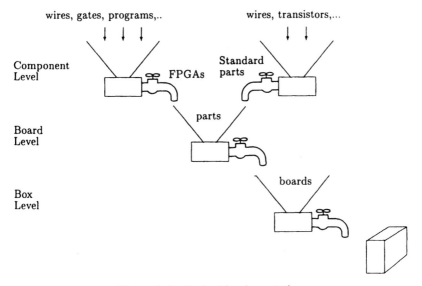

Figure 1-3. Product implementation.

the form of design rules, recommended practice, and so on, but is more likely to consist of knowledge from design experience and practice.

1.3 IMPLEMENTATION STYLES

Although implementations of electronic systems can span a number of levels of physical hierarchy, in reality implementations in semiconductor components and boards dominate. Most of designing leads to PCBs populated with standard components. Progress in component and board technology has spawned particular implementation styles. These may be classified as in Table 1–1, which shows the SSI/MSI, LSI and VLSI eras corresponding very roughly to the last three decades.

1.3.1 Era of Early Logic Families

This era ran through the 1960s and into the 1970s. It was typified by Texas Instruments and transistor–transistor logic (TTL) [TTL88], and National Semiconductor's 4000 series, popularly called small-scale integration (SSI) and medium-scale integration (MSI). Each provided logic in the form of gates, flip-flops, register transfer components, counters, and arithmetic-logic units (ALUs), at the chip level. At the board level, these components were used in relatively small numbers on relatively small boards to provide datapath-sized, for example, 8-bit, quantities of a particular resource, such as immediate storage (registers). Typical early logic era components are shown in Figure 1–4.

TABLE 1-1. Component Eras

	1960s SSI/MSI	1970s LSI	1980s VLSI	1990s
Components	Logic, RT elements	P_μ(8 bit), memory	P_μ(32 bit), gate arrays, CBIC	PALs, FPGAs
Complexity level (Number of gates)	$\approx 10^2$	$\approx 10^4$	$\approx 10^5$	$\approx 10^4$
Pervasive components	TI TTL, National Semi 4000 series	Intel 8008, 1103, AMD 2900	Motorola 68k, gate arrays	
Board sizes in^2	< 10	< 200	< 200	< 200

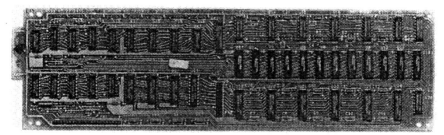

Figure 1-4. Typical early logic era components. (Photograph courtesy of P. Crockett.)

1.3.2   Era of LSI and VLSI Components

The 1970s opened with the invention of the Dynamic RAM, Intel 1103, and microprocessor, Intel 4004, and closed with the 32-bit microprocessor as a common component, for example, Motorola 68000. So technology progress spawned two major market areas, and a larger number of market segments, for example, SRAM, microcontrollers, and so forth. The logic components of the previous era continued to be used in large quantities to "glue" together the larger function chips. Boards became larger so they could accommodate a whole system on a single board, reduce cost, and eliminate the pin/wiring constraints imposed by PCB edge connectors. Figure 1-5 shows a typical subsystem of this era.

1.3.3   Era of ASICs

By the 1980s the twin drives of increasing density [Bell91] and increasing difficulty in identifying standard products redirected attention to using manufacturing technology to make ASICs. If a thousand or more gates of random logic on a chip could be wired in a cost effective way, then the "glue logic" for a system could be provided more effectively. Mask-programmable gate arrays, cell-based ICs (CBICs), and the first programmable components, programmable array logics (PALs) and field-programmable logic arrays (FPLAs), emerged during this decade as ASIC solutions. Boards remained large but delivered more function, since the "real estate" freed up from glue logic was available for primary memory or other functions. Figure 1-6 shows a typical board including microprocessor, memories, ASICs, and the first appearance of programmable components in quantity.

Taxonomy of ASICs   Basically there are three varieties of ASIC: gate arrays, CBICs, and programmable logic devices (PLDs). FPGAs fall into the last of these categories. ASICs only evolved commercially in the 1980s decade as shown in Figure 1-7, which also identifies the companies that played strong parts in establishing the different product types. These companies were mostly

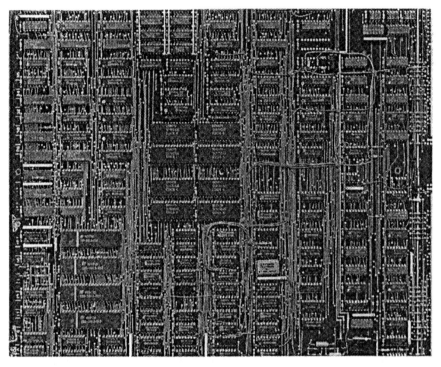

Figure 1–5. Typical large-scale integration/very-large-scale integration (LSI/VLSI) era components. (Photograph courtesy of P. Crockett.)

start-ups, although there was, in the case of gate arrays, an early commercial product from Ferranti, and an internal product at IBM.

Each variety of ASIC is differentiated both by architectural features and by manufacturing process requirements. In consequence, a user may obtain a certain amount of custom logic in a given lead time. For example, CBICs require all the steps of an IC production process, and therefore take the longest time. Gate arrays require only the metalization steps of a production process and have a shorter lead time at a particular cost. PLDs are "manufactured" on the bench or in the application by loading bits into a control store or blowing antifuses. Figure 1–8 shows the relative times and approximate costs. Symbolic representations of the architectures are shown in Figure 1–9.

Gate Arrays Early gate arrays favored a channeled architecture in which rows, and sometimes columns, of gates were separated by wiring channels of a fixed capacity. Density levels were of the order of a few thousand gates, and this was sufficient to implement control structures and glue logic, which tend to appear random in structure. As the requirement grew to implement more regular logic structures, for example, data paths and memories, gate arrays evolved into

Figure 1-6. Typical ASIC era components. (Photograph courtesy of P. Crockett.)

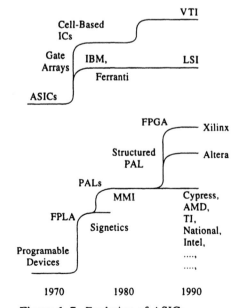

Figure 1-7. Evolution of ASICs.

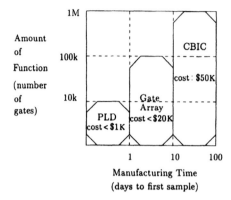

Figure 1-8. ASIC differentiators.

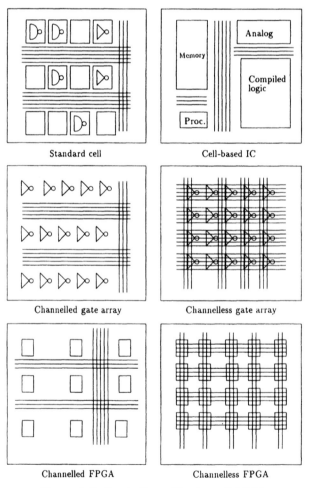

Figure 1-9. Symbolic architecture of ASICs.

channelless or "sea-of-gates" forms. Multilevel metalization capability and the demand for more wires, also influenced this architecture, which allows arrays of uncommitted gates to be overlayed with multiple levels of wire.

Cell-based ICs   Cell-based design provides the user with a library of proven cells, usually of fixed height and varying width, depending on the function performed. By the 1980s, standard cell families had evolved to provide highly complex functions, and silicon compiler technology [Gray79, Gajski88] also increased the availability of function block designs. Fabrication requires a full set of masks and processes, but these circuits provide the most dense and highest performance form of ASIC.

Programmable Logic Devices   The creation of the PLD can be attributed to Monolithic Memories, which introduced the first PAL in 1978. There were early programmable products such as FPLAs [Cavlan75], but these have not been the most successful form of two-level logic product. By the late 1980s the conceptually simple PLDs were complemented by the emergence of complex PLDs in the forms of FPGAs [Xilinx92] and structured PALs [Altera87].

Growth Trends   As VLSI feature sizes have been progressively reduced, the well-known rules of scaling in process technology [Mead80] have provided exponential increases in density and linear reductions in delays. The number of transistors per chip has doubled every 12 to 18 months since 1963 (Moore's First Law). These raw transistors are used to make products such as memories, microprocessors, gate arrays, and FPGAs. The densities of these devices, measured as bits, gates, and cells per chip, have also grown exponentially (see Figure 1–10). This chart shows progress tracking Moore's law for different products. It is interesting to note that sustainable businesses seem to emerge from getting 1000 or more useful elements, bits, gates, and cells, on a chip. For example, the commercial gate array market was pioneered by Ferranti during the 1970s with chip parts containing hundreds of gates, but it was not until a decade later that a billion dollar business developed from companies such as LSI Logic with products containing a few thousand gates per chip.

1.3.4   Era of Programmable Logic

With the emergence of complex programmable components, especially FPGAs, we can expect the typical systems PCB to resemble Figure 1–11. In this, a traditonal microprocessor is complemented by a number of SRAM-programmed FPGAs, memory parts, and possibly a special-purpose processor. The Von Neumann engine supports general-purpose computation as well as the programming of the FPGAs which, in turn, support time-multiplexed special-purpose computation.

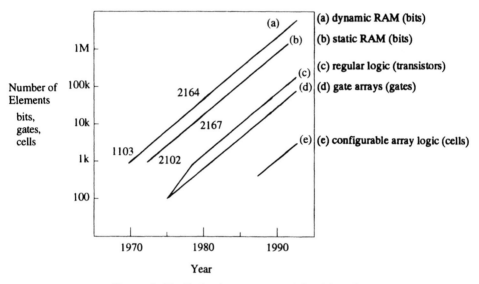

Figure 1–10. Technology progress (after Moore).

Figure 1–11. Typical components of the PLD era. (Photograph courtesy of P. Crockett.)

1.4 DESIGN STYLES

Returning to Figure 1–2, how can the *design* phase be addressed? The task, grossly simplified, is the creation of a *circuit of abstract components* that converts a specification to an implementation. Since we are concerned with digital systems, the specification is likely to be a formal or informal description of an *algorithm*. The *interpretation* of the algorithm effects some useful work on data. An algorithm can be thought of as a set of rules or a set of processing steps, for transforming data and executing a computation. The algorithm is a static description which needs to be interpreted by a machine to perform the work. The circuit of abstract components is this machine. So the design task begins by choosing a set of relevant elements, hardware and software, and interconnecting them. This process defines a systems *architecture*. Historically, there have been two generic architectural styles: the software paradigm based on the Von Neumann model of computation and the hardware paradigm. All design architectures, including those using FPGAs, fall into one of these two classes or are made up of elements that fall into these classes. Under the software paradigm, an algorithm is mapped into *code* that is interpreted by a *processor*. Figure 1–12 shows an outline of a Von Neumann engine, with a memory (M), various registers (memory address, memory data, program counter, etc.), and an arithmetic-logic unit. Under the hardware paradigm, an algorithm is mapped into storage and function units that are isomorphic with the computation. Figure 1–13 shows a hardware application-specific processor for an encryption processor which is further discussed in Chapter 6. It is important to understand the trade-offs in architectural choice. Form and function are largely determined by architectural choice in this branch, as well as other branches, of engineering. Furthermore, at this, the highest level of design abstraction, it is possible to make the greatest gains in a design's performance or spatial demands. As more of a design is instantiated, the design process moves to lower levels where smaller improvements in measures are the rule. For example, choosing a *pipelined* architecture may gain hundreds of percent improvement in the performance of a system, while a choice of circuit technology may only deliver improvements of the order of tens of percent.

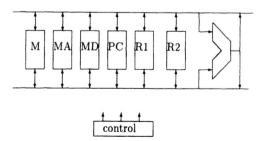

Figure 1–12. Von Neumann engine datapath.

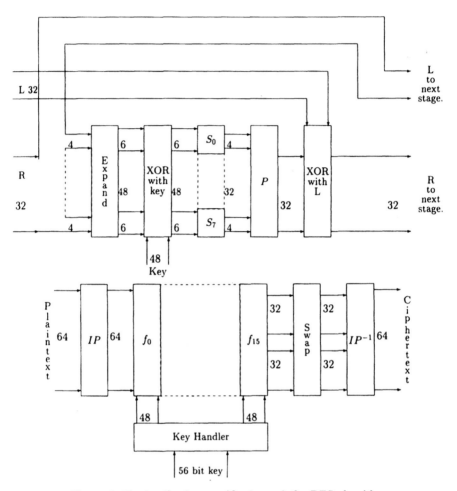

Figure 1-13. Application-specific datapath for DES algorithm.

To expose the two architectural styles let us consider two simple designs for a vector product algorithm,

$$\sum_{i=0}^{n-1} a_i * b_i$$

1.4.1   The Software Paradigm

Under the software paradigm the design task is to write a *program* for this algorithm, such as,

```
sum=0
for i=0 to n-1 do
   sum=sum + a[i]*b[i]
```

and compile this for a Von Neumann computer. Using the one in Figure 1–12, let us assume a simple base and displacement addressing scheme and a register assignment: R1 is the accumulator and R2 is the base register. So the memory layout is:

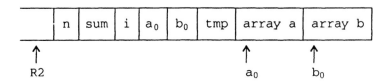

Then the program to compute this function is as shown in Figure 1–14.

1.4.2   The Hardware Paradigm

Under the hardware paradigm, a design could be based on the interconnection of two hardware stacks, two function units, and two registers, as in Figure 1–15. The data could be represented in bit-serial or bit-parallel form and the hardware stacks, of finite size, would be separately loadable. This design could be built from standard parts at the MSI level.

1.4.3   The Configurable Hardware Paradigm

Even with this simple example, the features of the two architectural styles can be distinguished by examining the datapaths and control structures of each design. With the software model, a very simple computer of primary memory, register file, and ALU, was animated by a complex control part manifested in the compiled code. With the hardware model a more complex datapath of six elements was complemented with a simple, sequencer type of control structure. The trade-offs in complexity of data and control structures are summarized in Figure 1–16. The design under the hardware model is an *application-specific machine* or *custom computer* that would execute the algorithm at high speed at the cost of building at least one implementation of the hardware. In contrast, the software model would yield a low-performance solution. The program has to be interpreted, which costs time, but the solution would be cheaper since computers are mass-produced, reusable commodity products. With the advent of reprogrammable FPGAs, general-purpose reusable machines can be built from mass-produced commodity components. So a *con-*

```
        CLR    R1
        STR    R1,R2,2   sum=0
        STR    R1,R2,3   i=0

loop    LOAD   R1,R2,4   R1=a₀
        ADD    R1,R2,3   R1=a₀ + i
        LOAD   R1,R1,0   R1=a[i]
        STR    R1,R2,6   tmp=a[i]

        LOAD   R1,R2,5   R1=b₀
        ADD    R1,R2,3   R1=b₀ + i
        LOAD   R1,R1,0   R1=b[i]

        MLT    R1,R2,6   R1=b[i]*tmp
        ADD    R1,R2,2   R1=sum+ditto
        STR    R1,R2,2

        LOAD   R1,R2,3   R1=i
        ADDIM  R1,1      R1=R1+1
        STR    R1,R2,3

        CMP    R1,R2,1   compare i:n
        BNE    loop      branch if i ≠ n
```

Figure 1-14. Program for Von Neumann computer.

figurable hardware paradigm for computation can be supported in which the performance benefits from mapping algorithms directly into hardware can be combined with the price benefits of commodity products. An overview of the competitive features of all three paradigms is shown in Table 1-2. It should be noticed that although the presentation here suggests that architectural choice is

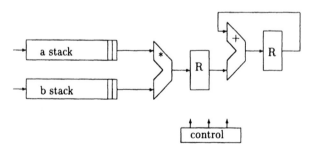

Figure 1-15. Vector product processor.

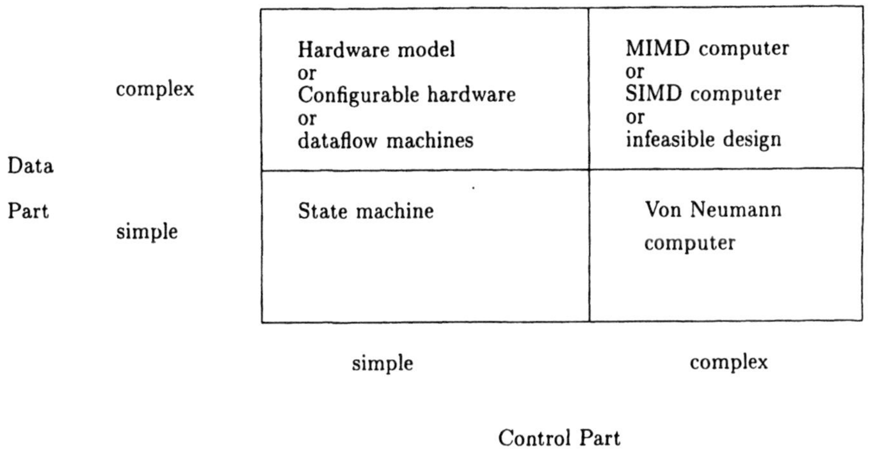

		Hardware model or Configurable hardware or dataflow machines	MIMD computer or SIMD computer or infeasible design
	complex		
Data			
Part	simple	State machine	Von Neumann computer

                         simple   complex

                              Control Part
              Figure 1-16. Complexity trade-offs.

about selecting a hardware or software model, in real situations the "best" architectural solution may include modules taken from each model. An application for a simple ASIC replacement would be addressed with an FPGA design under the hardware model. A cellular automation algorithm might be addressed with an FPGA implementation of an automaton rules processor coupled to a state memory, the Von Neumann model. In between, a software solution to an appli-

TABLE 1-2. Comparative Features of the Three Paradigms

Feature	Software	Hardware	Configurable Hardware

Instruction
  interpretation
	Integral number
	  of cycles
		None	None

Gate delay	Low	Low	High
Spatial demand	PCB	IC	PCB
Cost (1 off)	Commodity	High NRE	Commodity
Architectural efficiency	Fixed	Tailored architectures	Tailored architectures
Execution efficiency	Fixed units	Tailored execution units	Tailored architectures
Bit efficiency	Fixed	Variable word size	Variable word size
Data representation	Fixed	Variable word size	Variable word size
Reusability	Yes	No	Yes

cation might be accelerated with a hardware model, a coprocessor coupled to the bus architecture of a host computer.

Model Software			Hardware
Application Von Neumann computer	Virtual cellular automaton	Coprocessors Systolic m/c	ASIC

1.5   DESIGN METHODOLOGIES

1.5.1   Describing a Design

There are many ways of describing a design and confusion over what a design description is. Diagramming templates and drawing boards have been replaced by electronic computer-aided design (CAD) products. Technology progress and the resultant increases in design complexity have extended simple circuit descriptions in terms of transistors, resistors, and capacitors to data bases that can include hierarchical schematics, hardware description language programs, simulation models, layout artwork, test patterns, and so on. This plethora of design data can be understood more clearly by separating *design description* and *notation*. To describe a design unambiguously, data must be created, or generated, in three domains of description: structural domain, behavioral domain, and physical domain. Figure 1–17 shows a Venn diagram representation and identifies the elements of design description in each domain. At the logic level a structural description could be a logic diagram, a behavioral description could be a set of logic equations, and a physical description could be a standard cell layout for an ASIC (or a fuse map for a PAL). Appropriate *notations* are used to create these descriptions, while different notations may be used to create different fragments of design. A read-only memory (ROM) will appear as a block in a logic schematic with its contents in a truth table.

In addition, complex designs are created by building up design descriptions over a number of levels. Traditionally, engineering design has involved a *divide and conquer* approach in which conceptually large modules are partitioned into smaller units repeatedly until suitable for implementation at some (physical) level of design abstraction. Conceptual levels of design abstraction include circuit, logic, register transfer, and processor-memory-switch (PMS) [Bell71]. Physical levels of abstraction include semiconductor components, printed circuit boards, and card cage backplanes. So the one-dimensional view of design descriptions (Figure 1–17) is too simple and should be modified to allow for

Structural Description

Components: modules, symbols
Connections: lines, names
Notations: schematics, HDLs

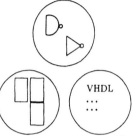

Physical Description   Behavioral Description

Components: blocks, cells   Components: modules
Connections: wires   Connections: names
Notations: artwork, fuse maps   Notations: languages

Figure 1-17. Domains of description.

descriptions at different levels, each single domain becoming a multiple number of sheets. An elegant method of visualizing this, and any design process flow (see Chapter 4), has been suggested [Gajski88] in which a relational graph with three axes, a "Y", is used for the three domains of description (Fig. 1–18). Each axis is scaled for level of design. With this diagram, design process steps can be represented by transitions (arcs) from a point on one axis to a point on another axis, such as creating a layout for a logic diagram. Design process flows thus appear as spiral paths toward the origin of the graph, as design process steps progressively refine behavioral, to structural, to physical design descriptions.

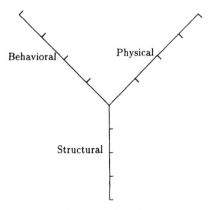

Figure 1-18. Gajski–Kuhn diagram.

Structural Design Structural design simply connects elements together. It is common to most branches of engineering. Wires connect active and passive components in electronics, rivets and fasteners connect structural elements and beams in bridge building. In both cases, the structural composition defines an architecture that imbues the system it defines with certain desirable characteristics: performance, structural integrity, and so forth. A fuzzy, rather than precise objective in structural design, is to create an *elegant* architecture that addresses cost and performance objectives of the specification in a simple but effective way. With FPGAs, structural design is achieved with a schematic drawing tool.

Physical Design Physical design involves producing sufficient data for a design to be manufactured, including testing. With FPGAs, physical design requires the definition of functions for the logic blocks and routing paths for the interconnections. This is analogous to producing a layout in VLSI design. The manufacturing data are held in a binary file for programming the part. Tools used for physical design include symbolic editors, generators, automatic place-and-route software.

Behavioral Design Behavioral design is creating a description of the way in which the design functions. It may be embodied in a simulation model, a hardware description language program, a set of logic equations, or simply a truth table. Logic diagrams can become behavioral descriptions with the use of simple drawing conventions. PAL implementations are often developed by writing behavioral descriptions in proprietary hardware description languages.

1.5.2 Hierarchical Design

Hierarchical, or structured design, was rediscovered by hardware designers in the late 1970s, when the increasing complexity of full-custom design for products such as microprocessors created serious bottlenecks. Prior to this, software engineers had adapted traditional "divide and conquer" engineering methods in building complex software products. Ideas such as modularization, information hiding, stepwise refinement were recast to help VLSI design tasks. In effect, programming techniques were applied to VLSI layout design because programming language constructs allowed crisp descriptions of artwork, particularly when it contained iterated or conditional features. Whole software design products, including silicon compilers and generators, evolved at this time. The complexity levels of present-day FPGAs match the custom designs of that period, so that the ASIC design methods developed then remain highly relevant.

Figure 1–19 shows two hierarchical decompositions of a simplified datapath that could form part of a Von Neumann computer. The drawing could be expanded to a more detailed set of schematics which, at the lowest level, would show circuit or logic diagrams of cells. Both partitionings are valid design descriptions and they differ by choice of partitioning scheme: horizontal, emphasizing bit slice designs, or vertical, emphasizing functional unit designs.

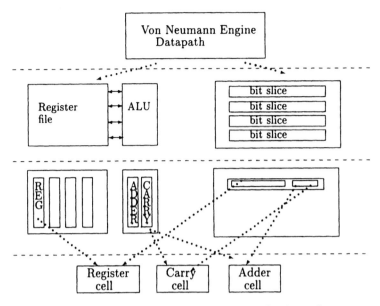

Figure 1-19. Hierarchical partitions of a datapath.

Just as there is a choice of partitioning scheme, there is also a choice in the expression of a wiring scheme. In this example, there would normally be bussed, that is, global, wires to communicate operands and results between the register file and the ALU. A true hierarchical design would partition pieces of these wires into the underlying cells, introducing a potential complexity in getting at connectivity data for simulation. There is an analogy here to the use/danger of global variables in software design.

1.5.3 Technology-independent Design

Technology-independent design asserts that it is desirable to design only at a high level, using a hardware description language (HDL), and have this converted automatically by synthesis software to an intermediate form that can be targeted to different implementation styles and different suppliers. It is analogous to high-level language compiler technology where code generators work from an intermediate form to create code for specific machines. The arguments for technology-independent design include increases in design productivity from working at a high level, and increases in optimality by having the broadest choice of supplier and ASIC solution, not to mention the avoidance of being in thrall of a single supplier. Arguments against technology-independent design include loss of efficiency in mapping a high-level design to an implementation and the associated loss of direct control of time and space in a design, both of which may be key to a winning implementation. The current battle-ground for these arguments is the FPGA marketplace. Technology-independent and gateless design are possible with the appropriate toolset. Decisions relative to the cost in space and speed are left to the design engineer responsible for the application. In engineering in general, irrespective of the level of design, it has always been the case that great designs can be an order of magnitude better than average designs, most usually because of the creative insights of an engineer with an understanding of the underlying technology, that is, technology *dependence*.

1.5.4 The Mead–Conway Design Method

In 1980 a text appeared [Mead80] that described a methodology for VLSI design down to the silicon artwork level. The techniques advocated have been widely adopted in the design of large silicon structures. The described methodology is state of the art and is embodied in software products for design. Mead–Conway (for lack of a more descriptive name) is a hierarchical design method that places emphasis on managing the communications (wiring) complexity in a design. This is important, since the cost of moving data around a VLSI circuit is at least as large as the cost of working on it. Mead was one of the first to understand this and propose efficient design techniques, which include:

- Wiring management as a key objective in high levels of design.
- Use of simple design rules to abstract away detail.
- Use of building blocks as in data paths and PLAs (two-level logic blocks) that have "naturally" elegant wiring structures (see Table 1–3).

This methodology places emphasis on structural and physical aspects of design in transforming architectural specifications like Figure 1–13 to clean imple-

TABLE 1–3. Natural Wiring Forms

Module	Natural Form
Logic function	Two-level logic block (PLA, ROM)
State machine	Two-level logic block (PLA, ROM)
Register file	Data path
ALU	Data path
Multiplier	Combinatorial array

mentations as in Figure 1–20. There are obvious isomorphisms in the descriptions. In fact, the Mead–Conway methodology normally keeps the structural and physical descriptions isomorphic, thus avoiding the complexity pitfall in hierarchical design of having separate structural and physical hierarchies. Using a program to generate both hierarchies, for example, a silicon compiler, is a convenient way of keeping descriptions consistent.

With FPGAs, all of these techniques can be applied, provided the FPGA delivers a homogeneous implementation medium for building circuits. In this respect, the fine-grain FPGA architectures, like the Configurable Logic Array with its cellular array of gate level elements, are a better match to a homogeneous environment than coarse-grain channeled architectures. The former can be expected to provide alternative implementation options for VLSI designers.

1.5.5 Temporal Design

With FPGAs, or any implementation medium, there are decisions to be made about the time domain aspect of the design. These decisions are largely in the area of choice of timing discipline and design for performance. The provision

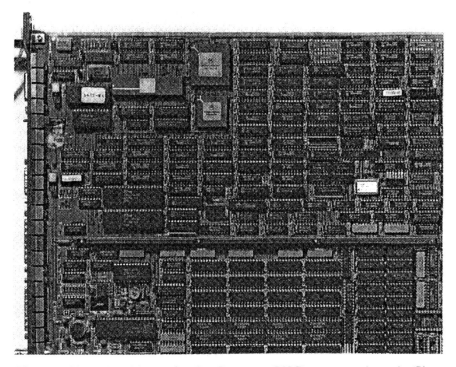

Figure 1–20. Reduced Instruction Set Computer (RISC) processor datapath. (Photograph courtesy of P. Crockett.)

of specific types of storage elements in the basic cell of the FPGA may restrict the choices open to the designer.

Clocked   In this discipline the actions of individual cells are synchronized to a system clock. It helps to consider a circuit as a sequence of register transfer computations, as in Figure 1–21. Timing disciplines impose a regulated data flow through the system so that intermediate results are held safely in registers after being computed by one stage of combinatorial logic and before being passed on to the next stage of combinatorial logic. The usual analogy is between this model and the locks of a canal. If two consecutive registers/"lock gates" are open in the same period of time, data/"water" will "flood" through the system. Problems can arise when delays on the wires distributing the clocks *skew* these signals and shift the register operations in time. Some FPGAs provide special global, low-delay wires to ensure synchronous operation.

If FPGA cells are to be used as "smart-memory" within a computer system, then a clocked scheme may be the technique of choice, since it allows a microprocessor to read and write to internal nodes of a circuit implemented by the cells without disturbing a computation being performed by the cell array. Note that the choice of a clocked system does not relieve the user of responsibility for removing timing hazards.

Single-phase clocking: One way to ensure correct operation is to use edge-triggered master–slave storage elements and a single-phase clock (clocks 1 and 2 in Figure 1–21 would be the same signal). This discipline, defined in the TTL era, is supported by such storage elements in FPGA families.

Two-phase clocking: Another method of ensuring correct operation is to use two-phase nonoverlapping clocks with storage latches. This would apply in Figure 1–21, and the lack of overlap between clock 1 and clock 2 prevents data moving more than one stage per clock cycle. This timing discipline was popularized during the VLSI era and is described in [Mead80]. In some situations, for example, if the FPGA provides latches with true and complement clocks, it is possible to avoid the extra wire overhead and use a single clock feed.

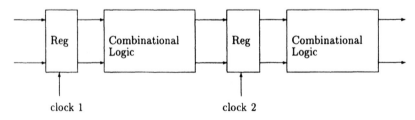

clock 1   clock 2

Figure 1–21. Register transfer model.

Self-timed   In this discipline, described by Seitz in [Mead80], each cell generates explicit "go" and "done" signals which are routed in parallel with the data signals. An edge transition, up or down, is a handshake signal, and any time may elapse between transitions. This discipline is very attractive since it relieves the user of most of the timing problems associated with logic design. However, if one were to build a purely self-timed FPGA there could be an area cost, since the cell logic is more complex than for a synchronous methodology. The "go" and "done" signals take routing resources, and fairly large "consensus" gates are required where wires split at multiplexors and where functions are being computed to provide the necessary control.

In the case of self-timed micropipelines there can be efficient FPGA implementations with conventional cell resources. Chapter 6 gives two examples.

1.5.6   Pipelined

This is an extension of the clocked design methodology and offers some exciting possibilities. If all transfers within and between cells are synchronized to a single, fast system clock and additional buffer storage is provided at each selection position, then the system can be pipelined at a very low level. The storage requirement does not imply an unacceptable overhead because of the storage by the gate capacitance of the buffering inverters.

1.5.7   Unsynchronized

In this case, users are provided only with logic gates and take full responsibility for timing themselves. This flexibility is necessary for cells that are to be used as PLDs.

PROBLEMS

1. How big should a PCB be?

2. What is best way to make wiring capacity match wiring demand, for example, with a PCB?

3. Structure a "flat" design in two different ways.

4. Structure/partition a design for FPGA implementation.

5. Do a design selecting components from a library selection and then in free form.

6. What happens to global wires in a hierarchical design? What implications does this have for different design processes including: schematic design, layout, and simulation?

BIBLIOGRAPHY

[Altera92] *Data Book*, Altera Corporation, 1992.

[Bell71] Bell, C. G., Newell, A., *Computer Structures: Readings and Examples*, Addison-Wesley, 1971.

[Bell72] Bell, C. G., Grason, J., Newell, A., *Designing Computers and Digital Systems Using PDP-16 Register Transfer Modules*, Digital Press, 1972.

[Bell78] Bell, C. G., Mudge, J. C., McNamara, J. E., *Computer Engineering: A DEC View of Hardware Systems Design*, Digital Press, 1978.

[Bell91] Bell, C. G., McNamara, J. E., *High-Tech Ventures—The Guide for Entrepreneurial Success*, Addison-Wesley, 1991.

[Cavlan75] Cavlan, N., Cline, R., "Field-PLAs Simplify Logic Design," *Electronic Design*, pp. 84–90, September 1975.

[Chan94] Chan, P. K., Mourad, S., *Digital Design Using Field Programmable Gate Arrays*, Prentice-Hall, 1994.

[Fawcett92] Fawcett, B. K., "Taking Advantage of Reconfigurable Logic," *The Programmable Gate Array Data Book*, Xilinx, Inc., San Jose, pp. 7-24–7-32, 1992.

[Gajski88] Gajski, D. D., *Silicon Compilation*, Addison-Wesley, 1988.

[Gray79] Gray, J. P., "Introduction to Silicon Compilation," *Proc. 16th Design Automation Conference*, pp. 305–306, June 1979.

[EDN92] Anon., "High-Density PLDs," *EDN*, pp. 76–88, January 2, 1992.

[Laws90] Laws, D. A., "Programmable Logic Is In!" *Electronic Engineering Times*, p. 52, August 20, 1990.

[Mead80] Mead, C. A., Conway, L. M., *Introduction to VLSI Design*, Addison-Wesley, 1980.

[Patter93] Patterson, W., "A Flood of New Programmable Logic Devices," *Xcell*, No. 9, pp. 3–5, 1993.

[Swager92] Swager, A. W., "Choosing Complex PLDs and FPGAs," *EDN*, pp. 74–84, September 17, 1992.

[TTL88] *TTL Logic Data Book*, Texas Instruments, 1988.

[Xilinx92] *The Programmable Gate Array Data Book*, Xilinx, Inc., 1992.

CHAPTER 2

REVIEW OF LOGIC DESIGN AND ELECTRICAL ASPECTS

The purpose of this chapter is to:

- Review the principles of combinational logic circuits

- Review the principles of sequential circuits, including state machines

- Review relevant electric circuit aspects of field-programmable gate array (FPGA) technology

In understanding the basic structure of an FPGA, or in mapping a problem onto an FPGA, one must be familiar with certain key aspects of logic design. The terms *logical design* and *digital design* are often used as synonyms for logic design. Fortunately, all FPGA design systems include computer-aided design (CAD) programs to take care of the more tedious aspects of logic manipulation, including extensive optimization. You will be glad to know that the regularity of FPGAs removes some of the agony of choice you may have experienced with transistor–transistor logic (TTL), for example, "which primitive gate should I use from the variety available?" But we must be at home with the fundamental concepts of logic design for combinational and sequential circuits. There will be an emphasis on systematic ways of logic design for FPGA applications. Although many FPGAs can be reprogrammed to correct an error, the time and effort in rerunning CAD programs can be excessive.

2.1 COMBINATIONAL CIRCUIT DESIGN

Combinational logic circuits have outputs that are strictly functions of their inputs, and have no memory, that is, state. The sequence of steps in synthesizing a design is as follows:

Problem definition: The required circuit may be described informally, in English sentences, or as an actual schematic diagram, as a truth table, or formally by a high-level definition language.

Boolean equations: The description is converted into a set of equations in terms of Boolean variables.

Simplification: The set of equations may often be simplified, for example, removing redundant terms.

Minimization: The equations may be manipulated further, depending on the eventual implementation technology, and the aims of minimization, such as maximum speed or minimum resource use.

Technology mapping: The equations are implemented in a particular technology. The set of primitive elements will vary between technologies, and for FPGAs, from one architecture to another. A complex equation might require several basic elements, while a simple one might share a basic element with another equation.

2.1.1 Boolean Algebra

Boolean algebra is concerned with variables that only have two states—true or false—and with expressions formed from such variables. While computer aids are often available, it is useful to be fluent in manipulating Boolean equations, usually to simplify them.

A number of alternative notations are in use for functions of Boolean variables, of which we will use the first given in each instance:

Negation, for example, $\overline{A}$, $\sim A$, A', $NOT(A)$

Disjunction, for example, $A.B$, $A \cap B$, $A * B$, $AND(A, B)$

Conjunction, for example, $A + B$, $A \cup B$, $OR(A, B)$

There are a number of useful theorems including the following:

commutativity: the order of terms in a logical sum or product is of no consequence

$$A + B = B + A$$

$$A.B = B.A$$

associativity: the order of evaluation of the same function is of no consequence

$$(A + B) + C = A + (B + C)$$

$$(A.B).C = A.(B.C)$$

distributivity:

$$A.(B + C) = A.B + A.C$$

$$A + B.C = (A + B).(A + C)$$

DeMorgan:

$$\overline{A + B} = \overline{A}.\overline{B}$$

$$\overline{A.B} = \overline{A} + \overline{B}$$

Example   The following equation is in sum-of-products form. Simplify it and convert to product-of-sums form:

$$F = X.Y.Z + X.\overline{Y} + X.Z + Y.\overline{Z}$$

It can be expanded to the canonical form:

$$F = \overline{X}.Y.\overline{Z} + X.\overline{Y}.\overline{Z} + X.\overline{Y}.Z + X.Y.\overline{Z} + X.Y.Z$$

The last four terms include all combinations of Y and Z, so the expression can be simplified and reordered:

$$F = X + \overline{X}.Y.\overline{Z}$$

Applying the second distributivity theorem, we obtain:

$$F = (X + \overline{X}).(X + Y.\overline{Z})$$

The first term is always true, so we can eliminate it. Applying the theorem a second time, we obtain the product-of-sums form:

$$F = (X + Y).(X + \overline{Z})$$

For the most part, equation manipulation can be left to CAD programs. FPGAs vary considerably in the basic blocks that are used to implement combinational logic. The technology mapping process is discussed later, and depends on the number of signals that may fan-in to a block, and the generality or specificity of the function generated.

2.1.2 Multiplexers and Boolean Function Evaluation

Some circuit technologies, such as complementary metal-oxide semiconductor (CMOS), provide excellent electrically controlled switches. These can be easily connected to form multiplexers (MUX), which allow the selection of one from 2^n inputs. For example, with a 4 : 1 MUX, controlled by two variables A and B, we can implement any of the 16 possible Boolean functions of them, as shown in Figure 2–1, by choosing appropriate Boolean values for the inputs C_0, C_1, C_2, C_3.

For example, the values 0, 1, 1, 0 provide the exclusive-OR function. By linking these inputs to FPGA configuration memory, we obtain a space-efficient and flexible means of evaluating Boolean functions. As the size of the multiplexer increases, the number of possible functions increases extremely rapidly. With a 32 : 1 MUX, which has five control inputs, we can generate any function of five-variables, of which there are 2^{2^5} possibilities, that is, over 4 billion.

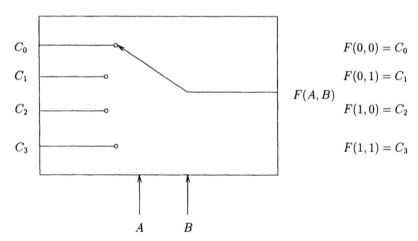

Figure 2–1. 4 : 1 MUX for Boolean function of two inputs.

2.2 SEQUENTIAL CIRCUITS

Combinational logic produces outputs that are strictly functions of the inputs. But many computations and digital systems require the storage and reuse of information as part of a sequence of operations. The behavior of a sequential circuit depends on its initial state and the sequence of inputs it has experienced. Sequential circuits have state memory as well as combinational logic. For the most part, we only consider synchronous sequential circuit examples, that is, in which they are clocked by a regular clock, and whose inputs must be stable at the time of a clock edge transition. This method or discipline is much easier to implement and check out in practice, but we must be aware that externally applied signals may not always conform. We take up this point later in the chapter.

2.2.1 Latches and Flip-Flops

Sequential machines require memory to hold their current state. The latch is the most elementary form of memory, and is illustrated in Figure 2–2. If the CONTROL input is true, the output OUT becomes the same as input IN. If CONTROL goes false, OUT retains its previous value. This is often referred to as a *transparent latch*, because of the direct connection between input and output, and is *level-sensitive*. It is in fact a basic element in the Algotronix architecture, but limited in utility, because the transparency allows signals to pass through. If we take two latches in cascade, we can form an *edge-triggered* D-type flip-flop, as shown in Figure 2–3. While CLOCK is true, the master latch is transparent, and keeps note of the latest D input. As soon as CLOCK goes false and propagates through the inverter, the mater latch value is asserted as the output of the slave latch, which maintains this value until the next time CLOCK goes from FALSE to TRUE. Changing state takes time, and there is a minimum time—*setup time* for an input to be stable prior to the CLOCK going false. Edge triggering allows us to guarantee single actions following an event. The D (delayed) flip-flop is a basic element of a number of FPGA architectures, including the Xilinx family.

It is very straightforward to construct other types of flip-flops from these primitive types. For example, a toggle flip-flop changes state every time it is

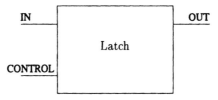

Figure 2–2. Transparent latch.

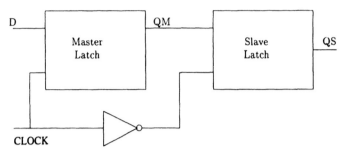

Figure 2-3. D-type flip-flop.

clocked, and this can be arranged simply by feeding the inverted output of a D flip-flop back to its D input. Some flip-flops can be cleared or set at any time, independent of the clock, and such facilities are referred to as *asynchronous* clear or set. Other forms for memory include static serial- or random-access memory (RAM) used to hold configuration information. This is referred to in the next chapter.

2.3 STATE MACHINES

State machines provide a formalism for sequential logic. Finite state machines (FSM), as the name implies, have a finite amount of memory. The next state of any FSM depends on its present state and its inputs. There are two types: the Moore, or *state output* machine, in which the output depends strictly on the present state, and the Mealy, or *transition output* machine, in which the output depends on both the current state and the inputs. A well-known example, the traffic light controller [Mead80], is useful in bringing out the distinction.

A farm lane intersects a busy highway. There is a sensor to detect the presence of vehicles on the lane and traffic lights control both lane and highway. Figure 2-4 shows the state diagram. Assuming there has been no farm traffic for a while, the detection of a vehicle on the lane will cause the highway traffic lights to switch from green to yellow, staying in yellow for a short time—say 5 seconds. Then they will change to red, while the farm lane lights display green. After a longer time—say 30 seconds—or if no cars are detected, the lights will show yellow for a short time to the farm lane while maintaining red to the highway traffic. Finally, the cycle completes by presenting green to the highway again. A longer time-out—30 seconds—prevents the cycle being repeated too frequently. The two time-outs, short and long, are produced by a separate timer. Note that it is started as a result of a transition, rather than presence in a state, and so the FSM is of the Mealy type. The outputs controlling the lights are directly associated with state, that is, they are of Moore-type, but overall the FSM is a Mealy machine.

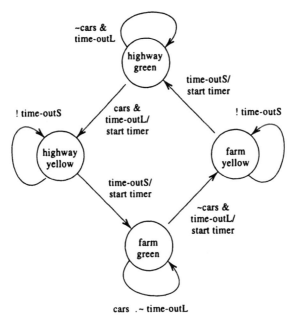

Figure 2–4. State diagram for traffic light controller.*

2.3.1 Encoded State Machines

If a state machine has *n* states, we need a minimum of $\lceil \log_2 (n) \rceil$ bits to hold the current state. There are a variety of ways of encoding state, that is, assigning bit patterns for each state. Once assigned, we can determine the logic for determining the next state in terms of the present state and the inputs.

Example A state machine has two input channels, *X* and *Y*, and an output, *Z*. It is required to output "1" whenever a multiple of three 1s have been received on either or both inputs, otherwise the output must be "0." Figure 2–5 shows a suitable state diagram for this Moore-type FSM. Figure 2–6 shows the state assignments and logic equations.

2.3.2 "One-hot" State Machines

Encoded-state implementation is optimum in state storage, but since many FPGA architectures have a generous supply of flip-flops, other factors need to be considered. FPGAs may have limited fan-in to the associated combinational logic, and need extra space for decoding state. We can often reduce the amount of combinational logic and improve the speed of operation at the same

*Carver A. Mead and Lynn Conway, *Introduction to VLSI Systems* (pg. 85), ©1980 by Addison-Wesley Publishing Company, Inc. Reprinted by permission of the publisher.

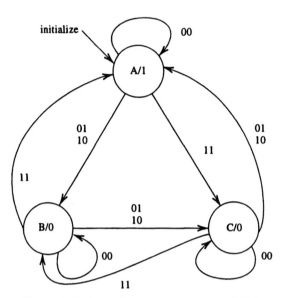

Figure 2–5. State diagram—Moore–type FSM.

time. In addition, the design procedure is very straightforward. This discussion is based on [Knapp90].

One-hot coding uses one bit per state, that is, there is no encoding. Figure 2–7 shows a flip-flop for a particular state. The D input is driven from an OR-gate, which combines inputs for:

1. *Previous states:* Any state that can transition into this state, such as P1

			XY				
state	Q2	Q1	00	01	11	10	OUT
	current state		next state				
A	0	0	00	01	10	01	1
B	0	1	01	10	00	10	0
C	1	0	10	00	01	00	0

$$D1 = \overline{Q1}.\overline{Q2}.(\overline{X}.Y + X.\overline{Y}) + Q1.\overline{Q2}.\overline{X}.\overline{Y}. + \overline{Q1}.Q2.X.Y$$

$$D2 = \overline{Q1}.\overline{Q2}.X.Y + Q1.\overline{Q2}.(\overline{X}.Y + X.\overline{Y}) + \overline{Q1}.Q2.\overline{X}.\overline{Y}$$

$$OUT = \overline{Q1}.\overline{Q2}$$

Figure 2–6. Encoded state machine.

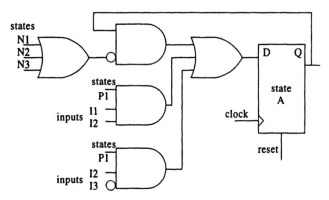

Figure 2–7. State flip-flop circuit for "one-hot" coding.

or P2 in Figure 2–8, provides an input. If it is unconditional, just the state signal is sufficient. If conditional, we create an AND gate for the combination of state and conditioning signals, for example, P1 with I1 and I2.

2. *Default condition:* If there is a default condition in which the state machine remains in this state provided the exit conditions are not satisfied, we provide another AND gate fed by the state itself and the inverted OR of the exit conditions. The upper left OR gate would be fed by logic corresponding to the conditions for exit to N_1, N_2, or N_3.

Some FPGA architectures have a global reset signal that resets all flip-flops. This can be used to advantage, but since the initial state must be asserted, we

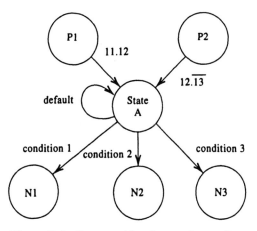

Figure 2–8. State machine for one-hot coding.

state	Q3	Q2	Q1	00	01	11	10	OUT
					X	Y		
	current state			next state				
A	0	0	1	001	010	100	010	1
B	0	1	0	010	100	001	100	0
C	1	0	0	100	001	010	001	0

$$D1 = Q1.\overline{X}.\overline{Y} + Q2.X.Y + Q3.(\overline{X}.Y + X.\overline{Y})$$

$$D2 = Q1.(\overline{X}.Y + X.\overline{Y}) + Q2.\overline{X}.\overline{Y} + Q3.X.Y$$

$$D3 = Q1.X.Y + Q2.(\overline{X}.Y + X.\overline{Y}) + Q3.\overline{X}.\overline{Y}$$

$$OUT = D1$$

Figure 2-9. One-hot state coding.

use an inverter on the output of the flip-flop concerned, thus maintaining the "one-hot" basis. Since the number of possible states could considerably exceed the number of valid states, there is a risk of the state machine entering an invalid state, whereupon it would remain there indefinitely. While the risk is small, it is straightforward to arrange for a presence in one state to reset the flip-flops of others. For example, State A may reset the flip-flop for State B, provided A is not the immediate predecessor of B.

Figure 2-9 shows the state assignments and equations. Extensive studies have been carried out for a set of benchmark circuits [Schlag91], and have confirmed the benefits of this form of implementation for at least one popular FPGA architecture.

2.4 PETRI NETS FOR STATE MACHINES*

The finite state machines described earlier are *sequential* machines: only one state can be active at a time. This makes it difficult to design an FSM that is required to control parallel processes. One approach is to divide the specification into a number of sequential machines, which are linked together to implement a parallel controller. However, this does not explicitly represent the concurrency, and so makes it difficult to detect synchronization errors such as deadlock (when two processes are waiting for each other). A more satisfactory method of representing the concurrency is to use a single parallel controller that

*Section 2.4 was contributed by Erik L. Dagless, Jonathan M. Saul, and Tomasz Kozlowski.

can have several states active simultaneously. Such a parallel controller can be represented using a *Petri net* model. This gives a clear specification of the parallelism in the design. The specification can then be analyzed for correctness, and used as a basis for the implementation.

2.4.1 Basic Concepts

A Petri net is a directed graph comprising nodes of two kinds—places and transitions—and directed arcs that connect places to transitions and vice versa. Places are commonly represented by circles and transitions by bars. A place can contain a token, which is depicted as a black dot. A marking of a Petri net is a mapping of a set of tokens to places in the net. The behavior of the system represented by the Petri net is defined by the movement of tokens. A simple Petri net is shown in Figure 2–10.

In the general case, arcs can be labeled with integer numbers that describe how many tokens are carried through a particular arc when the tokens move around the net. Petri nets involving arcs that are able to carry only one token at a time are called *ordinary Petri nets*. The following sections are restricted to the consideration of ordinary Petri nets.

Tokens can proceed through a Petri net according to a certain rule called a *transition firing rule*. To define this rule some other definitions have to be introduced.

The *input places* of a transition are the places that are connected to the transition by arcs leading from those places to the transition. Similarly, the *output places* of a transition are the places connected to the transition by arcs leading from the transition to those places. A transition is enabled if each of its input places contains at least one token. If a transition is enabled, it may fire. A firing of a transition removes a token from each of its input places and adds a token

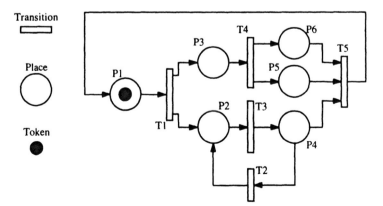

Figure 2–10. Simple Petri net.

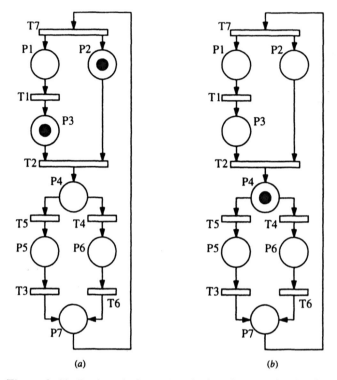

Figure 2-11. Petri net before (*a*) and after (*b*) transition T2 fires.

to each of its output places. Figure 2–11 shows a Petri net before and after the firing of transition T2.

All enabled transitions fire asynchronously, subject to the rule presented previously with the restriction that tokens are indivisible. In Figure 2–11*b* both transition T4 and transition T5 are enabled, but only one of them can fire since they share an input place holding a token. Firing either of them disables the other. Such a situation is called a conflict. When a conflict arises in a net, the choice of which transition to fire is arbitrary. If a system that is represented by a Petri net is to be deterministic, all conflicts must be removed from the net.

2.4.2 Basic Properties

A Petri net representation of a system can be used as an input for analyzing behavioral properties of the system [Murata89]. Two properties are essential to ensure that a system described by a Petri net is to work correctly. The properties are liveness and boundedness (or safeness). Both liveness and boundedness are strictly connected not only with a structure of a net but also with an initial marking. A Petri net with a marking is called a *marked Petri net*.

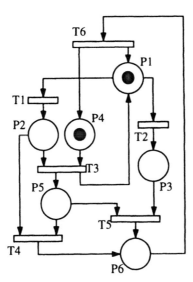

Figure 2-12. Nonlive Petri net.

When describing the properties just mentioned, marked Petri nets will be considered.

A Petri net is said to be live if for any marking reached from the initial marking it is possible to fire any transition of the net by progressing through a firing sequence. If a Petri net representation of a system is live, it means that there is no deadlock in the system. The Petri nets shown in Figures 2-10 and 2-11 are live. Figure 2-12 gives an example of a nonlive Petri net.

It is nonlive because when P1 and P4 have tokens and T2 fires no further firing is possible. The net would be live if it could be guaranteed that whenever the marking is P1, P4 only T1 could fire.

A marking M is said to be reachable in a Petri set N with the initial marking M0 if there exists a firing sequence that transforms M0 to M. A Petri net is said to be bounded (or k-bounded) if the number of tokens in each place does not exceed a finite number (a finite number k) for any reachable marking [Murata89]. Safeness is a special case of boundedness. A Petri net is said to be safe if the number of tokens in each place never exceeds one. Figure 2-13 shows Petri nets that are safe, 2-bounded, and unbounded, respectively.

Some bounded although nonsafe, or even unbounded Petri nets can be considered as bounded ones when some restrictions are imposed on the transition firing rule.

2.4.3 Extended Petri Nets for Parallel Controllers

To describe digital controllers using the Petri net model, each place is used to represent a local state in the controller. The marking, or global state, is obtained

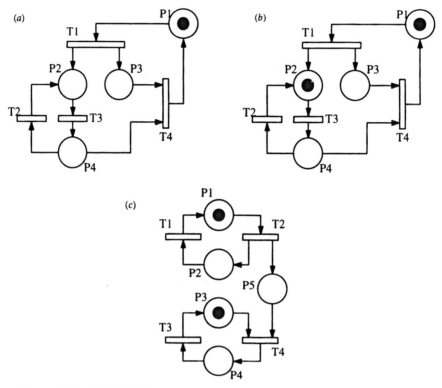

Figure 2–13. Safe (*a*), 2-bounded (*b*), and unbounded (*c*) Petri nets [Murata89].

by concatenating these local states and mapping them onto the controller's state register. Transitions map onto the combinatorial logic block. Resetting the controller returns the Petri net to its initial marking. The model is extended in the following three ways:

1. Transition enabling is modified by optionally attaching a predicate to each transition, where each predicate is a Boolean function of the controller's input signals. A transition is now enabled if all of its input places are marked and its predicate, if present, is asserted.

2. The Petri net is synchronously clocked so that its marking is only updated at the start of each clock cycle. Transitions fire when the clock is active provided the inputs and other conditions enable the transitions to fire. This will then create a new marking in the net.

3. The controller's output signals are attached to selected nodes in the Petri net, and are asserted whenever any of their associated places are marked (for Moore outputs) or transitions are enabled (for Mealy outputs).

This model of the Petri net provides all the features needed to allow the representation of digital controllers. However, for complex designs the net can be simplified by using enabling or inhibiting arcs. These are additional predicates on a transition that originate from a place somewhere else in the net. When a transition has an enabling arc attached to it, it can only fire when the place connected to the enabling arc contains a token. The token does not move as a result of the transition firing. When a transition has an inhibiting arc attached to it, then it can only fire when there is no token present on the place connected to the inhibiting arc. An illustration of the use of enabling and inhibiting arcs is given in the frame-store example discussed in Chapter 5.

Adding enabling or inhibiting arcs makes the net less easy to test, since it can introduce deadlocks not detectable by the normal liveness tests. Transformation techniques exist to turn a net with enabling/inhibiting arcs into a near-equivalent standard Petri net form, sufficiently good to allow liveness tests to be carried out.

2.4.4   Simple Example—A Traffic Light Controller

A traffic light controller*can be described using the Petri net notation and more naturally allows the description of the controller function. Consider a crossroads with lights N-S and E-W. The light colors are red, amber, and green. The N-S flow and the E-W flow are controlled by lights with the same pattern. Thus the normal sequence would be:

$$R_N G_E \rightarrow R_N A_E \rightarrow R_N R_E \rightarrow R_N A_N R_E \rightarrow$$
$$G_N R_E \rightarrow A_N R_E \rightarrow R_N R_E \rightarrow R_N R_E A_E \rightarrow \text{start again.}$$

The sequence is described by the central pattern in the PN of Figure 2–14. The lights are defined by the places P_1 to P_8. The transitions T_1 to T_8 would be enabled by timers designed to give the required interval for each light phase. While this core sequence can be described by an ordinary FSM technique, the power of the PN becomes apparent if a more complex specification has to be realized. For example, the lights can be allowed to remain green until traffic is detected on the other road. The loops $P_9 : T_9 : P_{10}$ and $P_{11} : T_{10} : P_{12}$ deal with this situation. Places T_9 and T_{10} are enabled by a sensor detecting a vehicle in the east–west and north–south roads, respectively. Only when a token reaches P_{10} and P_{12} will the light sequence continue, provided that the time-outs for T_5 and T_1 have finished.

An even more exotic arrangement could count the vehicles, perhaps to allow a longer time period when a high flow rate is detected. The two loops $P_{13} : T_{11}$ and $P_{16} : T_{12}$ count vehicles; T_{11} and T_{12} are enabled when the sensor detects a vehicle, and P_{13} and P_{16} increment a counter. The counting process is stopped

*This example is based on traffic signaling practice in the United Kingdom.

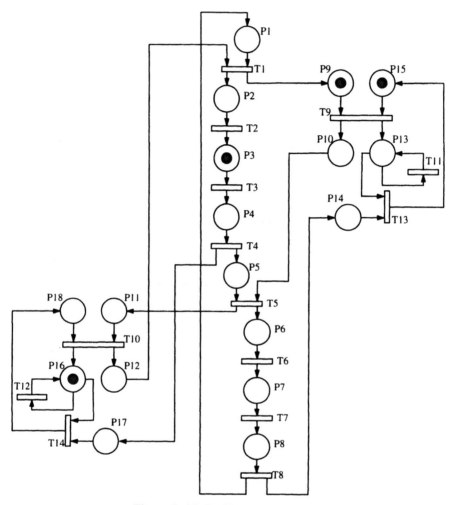

Figure 2-14. Traffic light controller.

when the corresponding road gets a green light, that is, T_8 or T_4 fires. This causes P_{14} and P_{17} to acquire a token, which allows T_{13} and T_{14}, respectively, to fire, removing the token from P_{13} and P_{16} in the counting loop. The action places tokens in P_{15} and P_{18}, allowing the counting sequence to be reenabled for next time.

The initial marking is important and not obvious. Clearly it is desirable to start on $R_N R_E$, that is P_3 or (P_7). (From here on, the items in parentheses are an alternative marking.) The other markings must ensure that the counting nets are live. By inspection, it is clear that a token needs to be available to allow T_{14} (T_{13}) to fire when P_{17} (P_{14}) receives a token from T_4 (T_8), so a token in P_{16} (P_{13}) is necessary.

Also, if the E-W (N-S) counting sequence is to be activated, then there need to be tokens in P_9 (P_{11}) and P_{15} (P_{18}). (There may be other initial markings that are perhaps simpler, but they will not ensure a safe starting point for the traffic on the junction: for example, a more logical initial marking would be $P_1 : P_{12} : P_{15}$.)

2.4.5 Implementation of Petri Net Description

The implementation of the Petri net can take one of many forms. There are three currently developed methods that yield good results. One technique is to identify partitions of the net, which become linked finite state machines. Each state machine may then be implemented using the methods described earlier. Another approach is to identify sequential portions of the machine as macro places or macro transitions, thereby reducing the net to its parallel constituents only. These parallel states are then allocated unique state variables. The rest of the places are coded using the states of the macroplace and sufficient new state variables to encode the places uniquely. This approach results in an efficiently implemented design using a small number of flip-flops.

The most straightforward approach, however, is to assign one flip-flop to every place in the net. This is analogous to the one-hot encoding for FSMs described earlier in the chapter. For a design to be implemented in an FPGA with plenty of flip-flops, such as a logic cell array (LCA), this is an acceptable approach [Schlag91]. All flip-flops are cleared at power-up. The ones with an initial marking have inputs and outputs inverted, so their outputs are asserted at the outset. The basic features are (1) feedback around each flip-flop for it to retain its token, and (2) a previous synchronous reset fedback to all preceding flip-flops to clear tokens as they move across a transition.

The example in Figure 2–15 shows a small part of a net together with its implementation. The net consists of initially marked place P1, normal place P2, and transitions T1 and T2. Input A to T1 and input B to T2 are from other places in the net.

The flip-flop for place P2 can be seen to be set, on "DC," when the output from T2 is high. It remains set as the bit is recirculated, until the reset signal from the subsequent place is asserted (by which time the output from T2 will be low again). Place P1 is similar, but with the flip-flop input and output inverted to implement the initial marking. Since transitions fire when all input conditions are satisfied, they are simply AND gates when there is more than one input, as for T2, or nothing, as for T1.

This form of implementation is very straightforward and can be easily automated. Furthermore the simplicity of the circuitry is well-suited to small combinational blocks of logic, such as the configurable logic blocks (CLBs) inside an LCA. In most cases, a flip-flop and the preceding Boolean expression fit into one CLB. An implementation with more economical flip-flop usage would result in many more high fan-in logic functions, which would have to be split between multiple CLBs and could potentially slow the machine down.

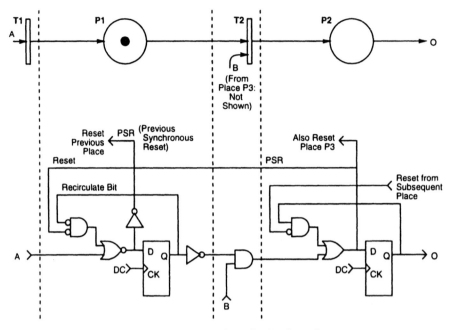

Figure 2–15. Implementation of a Petri net fragment.

A small amount of minimization can be done where a small net of two states exists. These can be readily implemented by a single flip-flop rather than two.

2.5 ELECTRICAL ASPECTS

While from many points of view we may regard FPGAs as consisting of idealized logic elements, in practice we need to be aware of the ways in which they are realized as electrical circuits, and their operation as analog circuits.

2.5.1 Complementary MOS Circuits

Almost all FPGAs use CMOS integrated-circuit technology. It uses two types of MOS transistor, referred to as N- and P-type. N-type transistors employ electrons as mobile charge carriers, while P-type transistors use holes instead. Figure 2–16 shows a complementary pair connected to form an inverter. Since we know that holes will move toward a lower potential and electrons toward a higher one, we can label the source (S) and drain (D) terminals as shown. The N-type transistor conducts if the voltage between its gate (G) and source

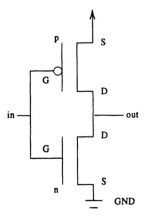

Figure 2-16. CMOS inverter.

exceeds a small positive threshold voltage. The P-transistor conducts if its gate-to-source voltage is more negative than a small (negative) threshold voltage. So if the input voltage to the inverter is zero (logic false), the P-transistor conducts, while the N-transistor does not. This causes the output voltage to be raised to the supply voltage Vdd, by charging the output capacitance. If the input voltage is high, corresponding to logic true, the N-transistor conducts, discharging the output capacitance and producing a logic false value. CMOS output voltages swing between the full range of the supply rail voltages, and can tolerate significant deterioration in input logic levels. As a result CMOS circuits have excellent noise margins.

Either type of transistor may be used as a voltage-controlled switch, referred to as a pass transistor. While conduction can take place in either direction, since the roles of source and drain reverse, an N-transistor will only conduct while its gate–source voltage exceeds its built-in threshold voltage, and similarly the P-transistor in the complementary sense. Accordingly, an N-transistor can be described as a "good conductor of 0s, but a poor conductor of 1s," and vice versa for its P-type counterpart. Degradations in signals are corrected with active logic such as the inverter just described. While pass transistors take little space, they introduce significant capacitance to ground and have finite series resistance, for example, 1–10 kilohms when conducting. The effect on signal propagation speeds is discussed later in this chapter.

2.5.2 Voltage Levels and Loading

FPGAs may be used with other CMOS circuits and also TTL circuits. The power supply voltage is 5 V, and so CMOS output voltages swing from 0 to 5 V. TTL circuits have a smaller output voltage range, typically from 1 to 2.5 V.

Some FPGA pad circuits can be configured for this range of input signals as well as for CMOS.

Inside an FPGA, circuit loads consist of capacitances that are charged and discharged. There is very low power dissipation when there is little activity, a particularly strong feature of CMOS circuits. As clock frequencies are increased, the power dissipation may become quite significant.

2.5.3 Three-state Outputs

A three-state driver circuit* is controlled by two signals—an enable/disable signal that allows the other signal—high or low, to be applied to the output being driven. If disabled, the output is effectively disconnected from the input, and may float or be driven to a logic high or low level by an enabled driver connected to the same output, typically a bus connection. The third state is referred to as the high-impedance state. As well as providing three-state pad drive capabilities, some FPGAs contain internal three-state buses, which allow many-input AND functions.

2.5.4 Signal Propagation in CMOS

Modern CMOS processes provide a number of alternative conductors for interconnections. Typically there are two, or sometimes three metal layers, which have low series resistance and low shunt capacitance to the substrate. These are excellent for propagating signals over (relatively) long distances, for example, a clock that must feed many different parts of an FPGA with very little skew, that is, variation in arrival times. To provide flexibility in interconnection, reprogrammable FPGAs use MOS transistors as switches between conductors, each controlled by a static RAM bit. The transistor introduces much more resistance and capacitance, as well as degrading the signal somewhat. In consequence, complex connections may have significant amounts of resistance and capacitance distributed along their length. The resulting circuit may be analyzed as an R–C transmission line [Weste93]. For a truly distributed line, a partial differential equation known as the diffusion equation applies. Analysis shows that signal propagation times increase as the square of line length. In consequence, FPGAs often use buffer amplifiers to break such interconnections into sections with short delay. Provided the buffer delays are small, the overall delay can actually be reduced, but this adds a further complication in that connections are no longer bidirectional, and buffers must be configured to take into account signal direction.

---

*The term Tri-State is sometimes used instead. Tri-State is a trademark of National Semiconductor Corporation.

2.5.5 Electrostatic Precautions and ESD Protection

Particularly in dry climates, it is easy to generate voltages of the order of several thousand volts by electrostatic effects, such as friction with an insulator. If handled carelessly such voltages may be applied to an integrated circuit chip and cause it to fail. Fortunately, FPGA chips are equipped with electrostatic discharge (ESD) protection circuits, which limit the effect of such voltages. Despite these protection mechanisms, users should employ electrostatic discharge mats and wrist ground straps when handling FPGAs or any CMOS integrated circuit.

2.5.6 Switch Debouncing

Mechanical switches are not ideal in their behavior. For example a single-pole, single-throw switch such as in Figure 2–17, will exhibit contact bounce when operated, that is, the moving contact will momentarily be connected and within milliseconds be disconnected, possibly making several brief contacts before settling down. Logic circuits are so fast that they don't distinguish switch bounce from deliberate user actions. The circuit shown in Figure 2–18 uses a set–reset flip-flop to "remember" the first connection, and provided the switch doesn't make contact with the upper contact again, will cause the signal OUT to make a single transition from ground to Vdd.

2.5.7 Power Supply Regulation

FPGA chips usually have multiple numbers of Vdd and ground connections, to ensure that power supply voltage levels are maintained inside the chip. Switching rates are often so high that quite large instantaneous currents flow in the power supply connections, both on- and off-chip. Although inductive effects

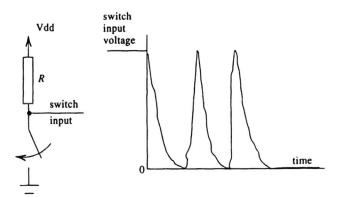

Figure 2-17. Switch contact bounce.

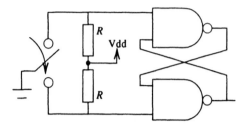

Figure 2-18. Debounced switch circuit.

are negligible inside the chip, the small inductance of the circuit package and connecting wires or traces can lead to significant voltage drops in power supply connections. Some FPGA output circuits can be configured to be *slew-rate limited*, provided the associated signals do not have to be fast changing for the application. This can have beneficial effects, both on power supply regulation and in reducing noise.

2.5.8 Metastability Characteristics

The theory of synchronous sequential circuits assumes that all signals, whether external or internal, are stable during a "decision window" around the time of clock transitions. The manufacturer of any flip-flop specifies setup and hold times before and after the clock edge, as illustrated in Figure 2-19, during which the input signals, such as D, should be stable, along with a propagation delay for any output change, Q. Many systems have to cope with real-time inputs that are not synchronized to the system clock, and so this requirement cannot be guaranteed. If an input changes within the decision window defined by these values, the effect may be to cause the flip-flop to change state, but with insufficient energy to make a complete transition. If a partial transition takes the flip-flop output voltage to a central region midway between the supply rail voltages, there may be little or no feedback to complete the transition or return to the previous state.

Consider the experiment suggested by Figure 2-20. The logic threshold voltage V_{inv} is that for which the input and output voltages are identical. Given identical inverters, if we set the upper input voltage to V_{inv} and closed the switch before removing the voltage source, the circuit would remain poised at V_{inv} forever! This only appears to be a stable state, since the slightest disturbance is reinforced by positive feedback around the loop and drives the circuit voltages to stable values, high or low. Accordingly the third state is referred to as *metastable*. The longer we wait after a clock edge, the more likely the output will have reached one of the true stable states, but we can only express this in terms of probability. Theoretical and experimental studies have confirmed this phenomenon and related it to parameters that can be determined for any flip-flop.

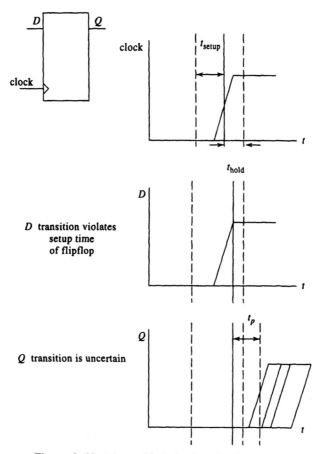

Figure 2-19. Metastable behavior of a flip-flop.

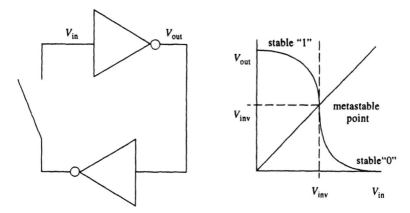

Figure 2-20. Metastable operation.

Assume that the clock rate is f_c and the D input experiences asynchronous edge transitions uniformly distributed over the clock period at a lower frequency f. We will not see any change in the flip-flop output until the nominal propagation delay t_p is over. If we wait a given time t_r (measured from the rising clock edge), we will occasionally find that the Q output is neither a good "0" nor a good "1," that is, it is metastable. The mean time between such events will be

$$t_m = \frac{e^{t_r/\tau}}{T_0 f f_c}$$

where T_0 and τ are constants for the flip-flop concerned, assuming operation at f, f_c. Figure 2–21 shows the improvement brought about by a few nanoseconds of extra delay for an internal flip-flop of a particular FPGA. It is based on [Alfke92] and includes the nominal propagation delay. Fortunately, the small size and high speed of flip-flops realized internal to FPGAs has considerably improved the situation, compared with earlier small-scale integration (SSI) parts.

Although metastability cannot be eliminated for synchronous systems subject to asynchronous inputs, its effects can be reduced by

- keeping clock frequencies as low as possible
- using a synchronizer for each asynchronous input
- using extra clock cycles for resolution

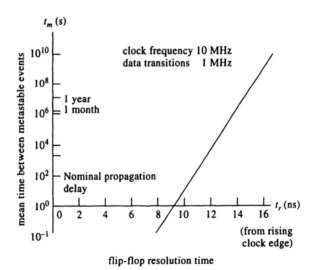

Figure 2–21. Improvement in metastability resolution with added delay.

All these points delay the processing of data slightly, but the alternative of unreliability is unacceptable. Reference [Shear92] discusses some improved synchronizers.

PROBLEMS

1. You have been given a state diagram for a sequence checker, whose output will be 1 whenever the sequence 0101 is detected. Develop a one-hot design that takes advantage of possible simplifications. Specify the state transition table. The design should use D flip-flops and combinational logic restricted to NANDs, NORs, and inverters.

BIBLIOGRAPHY

[Alfke92]   Alfke, P., Wu, P., *"Metastable Recovery," The Programmable Gate Array Data Book*, Xilinx, Inc., pp. 6-16–6-17, 1992.

[Dingman91]   Dingman, S., "Determine PLD metastability to derive ample MTBFs," *EDN*, pp. 147–154, August 5, 1991.

[Hill93]   Hill, F. J., Peterson, G. R., *Computer Aided Logical Design With Emphasis on VLSI*, 4th ed., Wiley, 1993.

[Johnson93]   Johnson, H. W., Graham, M., *High-Speed Digital Design: A Handbook of Black Magic*, PTR Prentice-Hall, 1993.

[Knapp90]   Knapp, S. K., "Accelerate FPGA Macros with One-Hot Approach," *Electronic Design*, September 13, 1990.

[Leach93]   Leach, T., Hackett, B., "Modern Synchronous Design," *ASIC & EDA*, ASIC and EDA, Los Altos, pp. 44 and 50–52, 1993.

[Mead80]   Mead, C. A., Conway, L. M., *Introduction to VLSI Systems*, Addison-Wesley, 1980.

[Murata89]   Murata, T., "Petri Nets: Properties, Analysis and Applications," *Proc. IEEE*, Vol. 77, No. 4, April 1989.

[Peterson81]   Peterson, J. L., *Petri Net Theory and the Modeling of Systems*, Prentice-Hall, pp. 195–196, 1981.

[Petri87]   Petri, C. A., *Concurrency Theory: Petri Nets: Central Models and Their Properties*, Advances in Petri Nets 1986, Part 1, W. Brauer, W. Reisig, and G. Rozenberg, Eds., Springer, pp. 4–24, 1987.

[Schlag91]   Schlag, M., Chan, P. K., Kong, J., "Empirical Evaluation of Multilevel Logic Minimization Tools for an FPGA Technology," FPGAs, Edited Papers from the International Workshop on Field Programmable Logic and Applications, W. Moore and W. Luk, Eds., pp. 201–213, Abingdon EE & CS, 1991.

[Shear92]   Shear, D., "Exorcise Metastability from Your Design," *EDN*, Vol. 37, No. 25, pp. 58–64, December 10, 1992.

[Shoji92]   Shoji, M., *Theory of CMOS Digital Circuits and Circuit Failures*, Princeton University Press, Princeton, 1992.

[Unger86]   Unger, S. H., Tan, C. J., "Clocking Schemes for High-Speed Digital Systems," *IEEE Transactions on Computers*, Vol. C-35, No. 10, pp. 880–895, October 1986.

[Wakerly90]   Wakerly, J. F., *Digital Design Principles and Practices*, Prentice-Hall, 1990.

[Weste93]   Weste, N., Eshraghian, K., *Principles of CMOS VLSI Design*, 2nd ed., Addison-Wesley, 1993.

CHAPTER 3

INTRODUCTION TO FPGA ARCHITECTURE

This chapter is intended to provide an introduction to field-programmable gate array (FPGA) architecture from the systems engineer's rather than the very-large-scale integration (VLSI) designer's point of view. After reading this chapter you should have an understanding of the main FPGA families and be able to make an informed choice of a suitable FPGA for a particular application. The following topics are covered:

- Background to the FPGA concept
- The main classes of FPGA devices
- Important components of FPGA architectures
- Programming technologies
- Techniques for benchmarking FPGA architectures
- A brief history and bibliography of the development of FPGAs

3.1 BACKGROUND TO THE FPGA CONCEPT

3.1.1 History

During the 1960s digital systems were built from small-scale integrated circuits and transistors interconnected on a printed circuit board (PCB). These transistor–transistor logic (TTL) components were small enough that their functions were applicable to almost all digital designs (e.g., it is hard to think of a digital system that could not make use of a 7400 quad NAND gate). This meant that it was commercially attractive to provide a library of such components that were electrically compatible and could be connected to build the target system. As the number of transistors per chip increased, manufacturers realized they had a problem on their hands: the so-called "part-number" problem. With increasing transistor count, logic parts became more specialized and hence usable in fewer systems—for example, an LSI part like the 74LS275 Wallace Tree Multiplier is not useful in most systems. At the same time, the design and manufacturing cost of the parts increased with transistor count. For this reason catalog logic families stalled at the LSI level. Newer structures were required to take advantage of VLSI—there were three approaches:

1. *Microprocessors/memories:* Microprocessors and memory chips are attractive to the component manufacturer as catalog items since they can be used for *programmable systems* resulting in high volume sales. However, microprocessors are fundamentally unsuited to many traditional logic applications where instantaneous computation of simple functions is required.

2. *Programmable read-only memories (PROMs) and programmable array logic (PALs):* Any combinational logic function with a fixed number of inputs and outputs can be implemented as a lookup table of outputs against inputs in a PROM. Many architectural variants for implementing combinational logic have grown up around this simple idea.

3. *Application-specific integrated circuits (ASICs):* ASIC technology recognized that because the functionality of a VLSI logic device is application specific, there will necessarily be a large number of such devices. This implied that ASIC design must be done by systems engineers with *applications* knowledge rather than IC designers employed by the manufacturer with detailed knowledge of the technology. The key step in accomplishing this transfer was to provide systems engineers with the same model of design they were used to—libraries of simple primitive devices interconnected on a substrate—and make designing ICs as close as possible to designing PCBs. This led to the channeled gate array architecture, which although relatively inefficient in its use of silicon, is close to the PCB model of design. By limiting use of the underlying technology, it becomes possible to produce correct designs on first-silicon, thus avoiding costly redesign cycles. This architecture provides an array of identical basic logic building blocks with wiring channels that can be selectively connected to implement desired functions.

FPGA technology can be seen as a logical extension of these three approaches made possible by improvements in the performance and density of VLSI technology. The three main classes of FPGAs are as follows:

1. *Computational logic arrays:* These devices extend the processor/memory paradigm by implementing algorithms at the gate level in a reprogrammable structure.

2. *Structured PALs:* These devices extend the PROM/PAL paradigm by using the density of VLSI to create a more general-purpose device capable of implementing the functionality of several simple PALs interconnected on a PCB.

3. *Channeled FPGAs:* These devices extend the ASIC paradigm by producing a field-programmable structure with similar capabilities and user interface to that for gate arrays, but avoiding the costly and time-consuming design cycle required for a custom chip.

These three families of devices are synthesized from a relatively small toolkit of primitive circuit elements, and so there is, despite their different philosophies, a strong similarity between them and a clearly identifiable FPGA or configurable logic product class.

We now examine the three classes of configurable logic devices in turn.

3.2 CHANNEL-TYPE FIELD-PROGRAMMABLE GATE ARRAYS

The first class of FPGA devices represents a straightforward attempt to bring the advantages of field programmability to gate array technology, by supporting an essentially unchanged design paradigm (netlist of library parts) from early PCB technology, and hence appeal to practicing systems engineers. The two key commercial examples of this class of device are the Xilinx and Actel FPGAs.

3.2.1 Distinguishing Architectural Features

The distinguishing architectural features of today's FPGAs are:

1. Gate-array-like wiring channel and logic block structure: logic and communication resources are clearly separated and distinct. This is reflected in the CAD system where placement of logic blocks on the logic array and routing between them are treated as separate phases of design.

2. Support for bidirectional and multiple source wires. Bidirectional wires are problematic in RAM programmed structures because the fundamental switching elements have a high impedance and intermediate buffering is required. They are, however, commonplace in PCB and gate array design styles where they are efficiently supported primitives. Designers of FPGAs include them in their architectures to maintain continuity with previous technology.

3. Function units with many inputs. Large function units with many inputs are provided which can implement entire blocks of logic. Making the

logic blocks more complex than those in conventional gate arrays reduces the number required and, more importantly, the number of wiring segments required between them to route the design. This is of key importance for RAM-based FPGAs where wiring channels are expensive both in terms of area and delay.

4. Programming interfaces are optimized for low board-level overhead rather than rapid reconfiguration. This is a natural outcome of the target market: ASIC replacement.

5. Conventional CAD Software. This is not itself an architectural feature but it is nonetheless a key reason behind many of the architectural decisions.

3.2.2 Scaling with Technology Improvements

A typical RAM-programmed FPGA, such as the Xilinx 3000 series, has five wiring tracks per wiring channel, and 4- or 5-input programmable logic blocks. In contrast, typical channel-type mask-programmed gate arrays (MPGAs) have around 20 tracks per channel and 2-input fixed-function logic blocks. As we noted before, the reason for using larger logic blocks in the RAM-programmed devices was to reduce the area and delay penalties of the inefficient wiring resources. As process technology improves it will be feasible to create larger FPGA devices, which should in turn allow larger user designs to be implemented. One problem with this approach is that larger designs will not only have more nets but the average length of net will increase as well. This implies that the width of the wiring channels may have to be increased, as will the size of the array. Another reason for increasing the number of routing resources is to reduce the time required for placement and routing, particularly for larger designs. As wiring channels become wider, the switch boxes become more complex: delay and area costs may increase more than linearly with wiring channel width.

To reduce the effect of scaling devices on routing capacity, FPGA designers may choose to increase the complexity of the logic blocks. There is a clear limit to this technique. Since 2^n bits of RAM are required to implement all functions of n input variables, adding an extra input variable doubles the amount of control store required. The example of the Xilinx FPGAs is of interest in this context: there are now three generations of this family—the 2000, 3000, and 4000 series: each generation has increased the width of wiring channels and the size of function units as well as the number of blocks provided by the highest density member of each generation.

Another question mark over the scalability of channeled FPGAs to support large user designs comes from the observation that large ASICs are normally partitioned into subsystems that can have very different wiring and logic requirements: some areas of the ASIC may be devoted almost completely to wires (e.g., wide busses), some to very dense structured logic blocks (e.g., datapaths), and some to mixed wire and logic (e.g., random-logic control). Sea-of-gates MPGAs have largely replaced channeled arrays for high-end ASIC applications because, not having separate wiring and logic areas, the balance can be varied according to need rather than being fixed in advance by the base array designer. A similar trend can be expected in field-programmable devices.

3.2.3 The Xilinx 3000 Series

The Xilinx 3000 series is without a doubt the most commercially successful FPGA architecture to date, but is quite complex to understand. In this section we can only provide an overview of the architecture: for full details you are referred to the manufacturer's literature.

Figure 3–1 shows the underlying structure common to all the Xilinx Logic Cell Array (LCA) devices. Programmable input–output blocks (IOBs) at the perimeter of the device provide off-chip interconnections. The core of the device consists of an array of configurable logic blocks (CLBs) embedded in routing resources. Logically separate from these resources but physically intermingled with them is the RAM control store memory. The number of CLBs provided ranges from 64 for the XC3020 to 320 for the XC3090.

The interconnect structure of the Xilinx array is shown in Figure 3–2: the CLBs are surrounded by 5-track-wide wiring channels connected together by switching matrices in a gate-array-like arrangement. The small dots represent programmable interconnection points where CLB inputs and outputs can be connected to the wiring areas. Not all the dots are coincident with the wiring channels because the array provides two other classes of routing resource:

1. *Direct Interconnect:* Direct-interconnect resources can be used to route CLB outputs to inputs of adjacent CLBs without passing through switch matrices. Because of the programmable interconnect circuits that allow control over the CLBs input sources, the delay is higher than for a direct metal connection. Direct interconnect offers relatively high-speed local connections. The CLB ".x" output (terminal names are as in Figure 3–3) can be routed to inputs on the neighboring CLB to its left (".c" input) or right (".b" input) and the CLB ".y" output to the neighboring CLB above (".d" input) and below (".a" input). At the edge of the array, direct interconnect is provided between CLBs and IOBs. Direct Interconnect on the Xilinx architecture is similar to the neighbor interconnect of the sea-of-gates FPGAs introduced later in this chapter, but considerably less flexible.

2. *Long Lines:* Long Lines bypass the switch matrices and provide low delay paths for signals that must travel long distances. There are three Long Lines in each column and two along each row of the device. Long Lines can be driven by adjacent IOBs or CLBs, and can be used to implement three-state busses and wired logic functions.

Figure 3–3 shows the Xilinx CLB. This complex structure is composed of three resources: the combinatorial function unit, the data flip-flops, and the

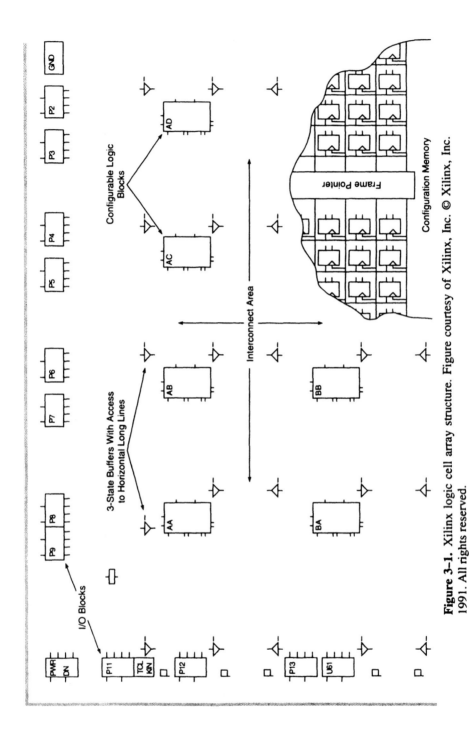

Figure 3–1. Xilinx logic cell array structure. Figure courtesy of Xilinx, Inc. © Xilinx, Inc. 1991.

58

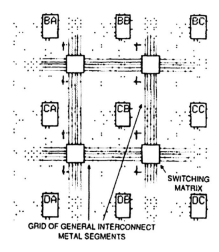

Figure 3-2. Xilinx 3000-series routing. Figure courtesy of Xilinx, Inc. © Xilinx, Inc. 1991. All rights reserved.

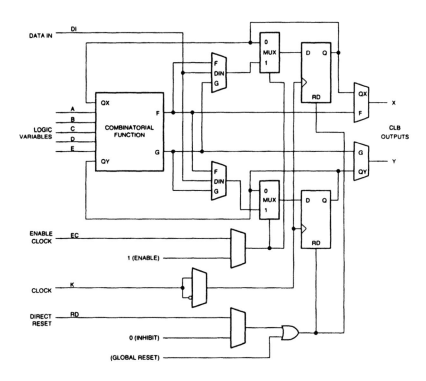

Figure 3-3. Xilinx 3000-series configurable logic block. Figure courtesy of Xilinx, Inc. © Xilinx, Inc. 1991. All rights reserved.

function selection multiplexers controlled by the device configuration. Inputs and outputs from the CLB are connected to the programmable interconnection points (PIPs) of the routing resources described earlier. The program-controlled multiplexers in Figure 3–3 are concerned with choosing appropriate inputs for the flip-flops and selecting between the flip-flops and combinatorial logic outputs for connection to the CLB outputs. The combinatorial function unit is composed of a 32-bit lookup table memory to allow it to implement any function of five variables. Additional program-controlled multiplexers within the combinatorial function unit provide for implementing a small number of functions of six or seven variables and partitioning the lookup table to implement any two functions of four input variables. There are restrictions on which of the inputs to the combinatorial function (QX, QY, .a, .b, .c, .d, and .e) can be used in each of these modes. This structure allows many common macro functions familiar to TTL designers to be implemented in a single CLB. The CLB flexibility is paid for by routing delay in the internal programmable multiplexers.

3.2.4 The Actel ACT 2 Family

The Actel ACT 2 FPGA family (Figure 3–4) is very close architecturally to an MPGA. The reason for this is that the small size and relatively low *on* resistance of the antifuse switching elements allow the use of conventional wide wiring channels (36 tracks/channel horizontally and 15 tracks/column vertically). The resistance of the antifuse is around ten times higher than that of a contact in a mask-programmed technology. For this reason the ACT 2 wiring channels are designed to minimize the number of antifuses per routing path. No connections are allowed with more than four antifuses and most are implemented with two or three (Figure 3–5). This limit will further reduce area efficiency compared to an MPGA. The ACT 2 function (Figure 3–6) unit is significantly more complicated than a single gate on a conventional gate array, but much less complex than the Xilinx CLB. The additional complexity is required to optimize performance for common logic macrocells, given the speed penalties of the antifuse switches. In addition two special signals are provided for high-speed, low-skew clock distribution.

The gate-array-like architecture of the Actel device allows conventional fully automatic placement and routing tools to be used. Users of the Actel system are isolated from the underlying architecture to a much larger extent than those of RAM-programmed FPGAs. Realistic benchmarking of the Actel architecture against low-end mask-programmed devices is possible: comparison with RAM-programmed FPGAs is much more problematic.

Antifuse-based FPGAs offer inherently better density, lower cost, and delay characteristics than RAM-based FPGAs in classic channeled architectures, given comparable process technology.

1. RAM-programmed devices have managed to stay one generation of process technology ahead of antifuse-based devices. The reasons for this

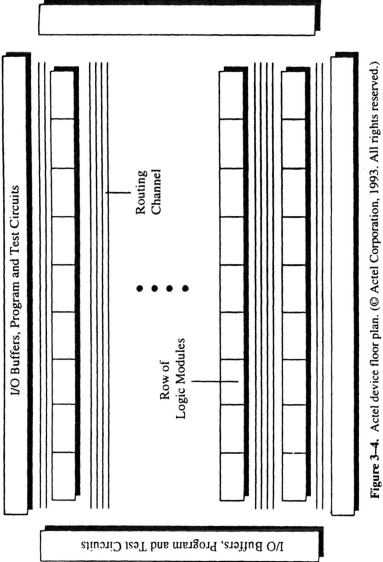

Figure 3–4. Actel device floor plan. (© Actel Corporation, 1993. All rights reserved.)

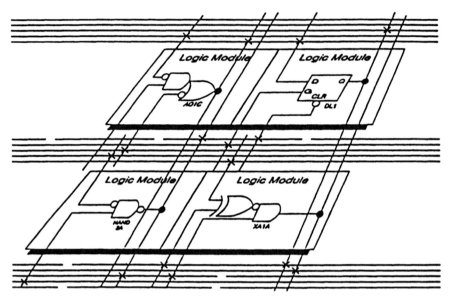

Figure 3-5. Actel routing, detailed view. (© Actel Corporation, 1993. All rights reserved.)

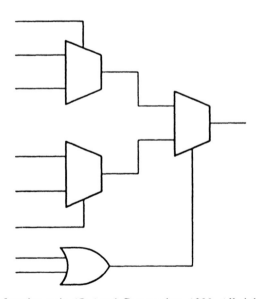

Figure 3-6. Actel function unit. (© Actel Corporation, 1993. All rights reserved.)

are in part commercial and in part technical: static random-access memories (SRAMs) are often used to drive process improvements and are usually the first parts available with a new fabrication process. SRAM-based FPGAs can therefore be introduced relatively quickly on a new process technology. Antifuse devices, on the other hand, require special processing of the antifuse elements, which adds complications to a standard complementary metal-oxide semiconductor (CMOS) process. Thus, after a geometric shrink on the base CMOS process, about one additional year is required for the antifuse process development. In 1992, the largest RAM-based FPGA from Xilinx, the XC4010, had a chip area of 196 mm^2 on 0.8-μm two-layer metal technology. The largest antifuse-based FPGA, the ACT1280, had a chip area of 112 mm^2 on 1.0-μm two-layer metal technology. Due to the larger chip area, the XC4010 was at the time 2.5 times more expensive than the ACT1280, based on quantities of 100.

2. It is certainly true that an antifuse is very much smaller than a transistor–RAM cell combination, and has a much lower "on" resistance and capacitance than a minimum-sized transistor.

- Antifuses are programmed by higher-than-operating voltages, which are routed via programming transistors. These programming circuits take up a relatively small area, and the programming transistors add significant capacitance to the wiring tracks. Architectures that attempt to minimize the overhead of these circuits increase programming time and can make it impossible to test that antifuses have operated correctly on the device programmer. In this case, the user would have to write test vectors for the design, just as in the case of an MPGA.

- Pass transistors on RAM-programmed FPGAs are not necessarily minimum-sized devices: by using wider transistors one can obtain lower "on" resistances, but with higher capacitive loading.

3. RAM-based FPGA devices have moved further away from the masked gate array model than antifuse-based devices. This has allowed them to improve speed and density at the expense of compatibility with previous technology.

At the time of writing Actel devices have higher performance characteristics (according to Programmable Electronics Performance Corporation (PREP) benchmarks up to 30%) than Xilinx devices: the greatest advantage of the Actel parts is that the wide wiring channels result in much better results from automatic place-and-route tools, with more predictable performance and capacity.

The disadvantage of antifuse technology over RAM-based FPGAs is simple: when the configuration needs to be changed, you write a check, not a RAM!

3.3 STRUCTURED PROGRAMMABLE ARRAY LOGIC

Before examining structured PALs, we will look at a simpler concept, the programmable read-only memory (PROM) as applied to two-level programmable logic. The idea is simple: a lookup table with n inputs, m outputs, and 2^n rows. The PROM is attractive because:

1. Given the number of inputs and outputs, one can specify a given device *before* determining the actual logic function to be implemented. This is a powerful capability since it allows the PCB design to be started before the logic design is completed. It also allows for PROM design upgrades after the PCB design is finalized.

2. The delay through the programmable device is constant and independent of the logic function implemented: again this is a powerful property, allowing the separation of timing verification from logic design.

3. The function of the device can be specified at a high level as a series of logic equations or as a truth table, allowing rapid design.

There are two major drawbacks with the PROM architecture that have prevented it from becoming dominant in the marketplace:

1. Silicon area, and hence cost, and sometimes more importantly, package and board area, is determined by the number of product terms. There are 2^n product terms in an n input PROM.

2. Delay through a PROM is proportional to the number of product terms, and hence scales badly as the number of inputs increases.

For these reasons PROMs are only suited for those functions where it is necessary to completely decode the input signals: a good example might be a lookup table for converting character codes from one set to another.

In full-custom design, programmable logic arrays (PLAs), for which both AND and OR planes are programmable, are the dominant method of implementing medium-to-large-size arbitrary logic functions. The programmable equivalent of these devices have, however, failed to penetrate the programmable logic market to a significant extent. This is because the extra layer of programmability increases delay, while programmable PLAs no longer provide the property of PROMs that all functions of n variables can be implemented. Instead a fixed smaller number of product terms must be chosen *a priori* by the device designer, with the consequence that devices can no longer be selected solely on the basis of the number of input and output variables. Similarly any change to the function to be implemented may result in it no longer fitting the chosen device.

By far the most common architecture in the programmable logic market today is the PAL, where the AND plane is programmable but the OR plane is fixed, with a small number of product terms contributing to each output variable. Figure

3–7 shows a simple commercial device, the 16L8, so-called because there are 16 inputs to the AND plane and 8 outputs from the OR plane. Some of the device pins are dedicated inputs and some are programmable input outputs ($I/O_2..I/O_7$). OR plane outputs on $I/O_2..I/O_7$ can also feed back into the AND array.

This PAL architecture is predicated on the observation that a large class of real designs require relatively few product terms per output. The key advantage of this architecture is that speed can be high because there are no longer wide wired ORs in the OR plane. One important disadvantage when compared to PLAs is that product terms are now dedicated to a particular output pin, and so multiple copies of particular product terms may be required. A design can fail because a particular output does not have enough product terms, despite the fact that the total number of product terms required is smaller than those provided. It can be painful when a proposed change to logic within a PAL on an existing PCB requires more product terms on a particular output than the chosen device supports!

One obvious question from the preceding discussion is why are PALs not the solution to all programmable logic needs? Why not just go out and buy a 50L50 device to do any reasonable design with up to 50 inputs and 50 outputs? There are at least two problems:

1. Delay is also influenced by the AND plane, both in terms of the length of wires required to reach individual product terms and the width of each product-term-wired AND area (twice the number of inputs because both true and complement forms of input variables are required). Thus in equivalent technology, a 50-input PAL might be three times as slow as a 16-input PAL: so if your particular application could be implemented in a small number of 16L8s or a single 50L50, you might well choose the 16L8s.

2. If one implements a large logic function using several small PALs, one can choose each PAL from a catalog providing a range of options in characteristics such as number of inputs, number of outputs, and number of product terms per pin. Thus, it may be appropriate to choose a PAL with eight product terms per output for some output variables and one with two product terms per output (but more outputs) for others. One can also use the routing flexibility of the PCB to route different input variables to different PALs and to use outputs from one PAL as inputs to another. A straightforward extension of the PAL architecture in which every output had the same number of product terms, all input variables were fed to all output product terms, and all outputs had feedback terms, would be much less efficient in terms of the total number of fuses required.

Structured PAL designs address these efficiency problems by simply extending the basic PAL architecture while preserving its speed and ease of use. The key commercial examples of structured PALs are the Altera devices. We

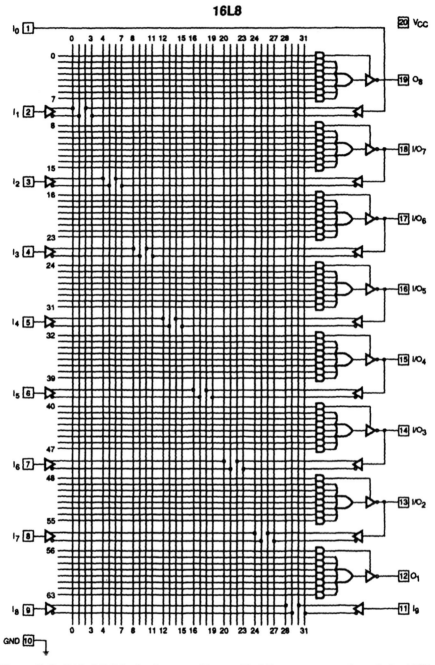

Figure 3-7. PAL 16L8 logic diagram. (*Notes:* (1) All unprogrammed or virgin AND gate locations are pulled to logic "1." (2) Programmable connections.) Copyright © Advanced Micro Devices, Inc. 1993. Reprinted with permission of copyright owner. All rights reserved.

now briefly consider the Altera EP1810: this device has been chosen because it illustrates the main components of the structured PAL architecture, while still being simple enough to serve as an introductory example. State-of-the-art structured PALs offer more of the same.

3.3.1 The Altera EP1810

Figure 3–8 shows the basic architecture of the device. There are two varieties of macrocell (corresponding to OR plane outputs in the 16L8); Figure 3–9 shows

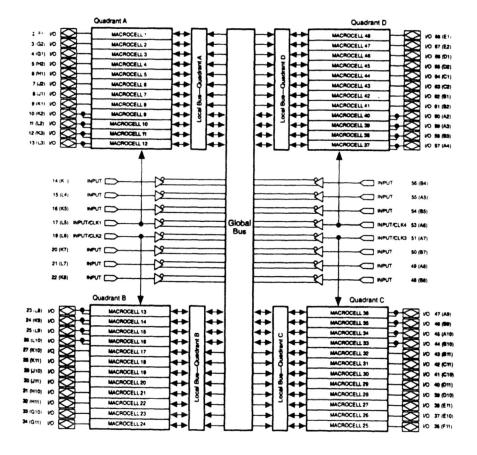

Figure 3–8. EP1810 block diagram. (Reprinted with permission from Altera Corporation)

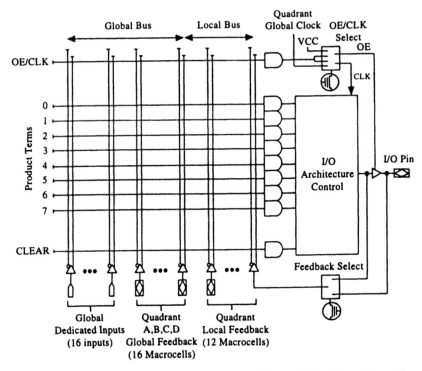

Figure 3–9. EP1810 local macrocell. (Reprinted with permission from Altera Corporation)

a "local" macrocell; and Figure 3–10 a "global" macrocell. Note the architecture is very similar to that of the classic 16L8 device, except that there are now two classes of product terms: local and global. This difference is motivated by the realization that many nets in most designs do not have to be routed to every gate! For roughly the same silicon area there are four times as many local nets as possible global nets, so larger designs can be implemented. The price for this is that one has introduced a simple placement and routing problem. One has to select where to place a particular piece of logic on the device with regard to its connectivity and one can no longer guarantee that a design will fit on the device, given the number of output macrocells and input variables required.

The box labeled IO Architecture Control provides additional flexibility in the use of the output pin: for example, conditional inversion, along with input and output latching. There is considerable flexibility in the choice of clocking scheme applied to these registers. The ability to conditionally invert the output can allow functions to be implemented using fewer product terms. For example, the function $f = X_0 * X_1 * X_2 * X_3$ requires a single product term, while the function $\overline{f} = \overline{X_0} + \overline{X_1} + \overline{X_2} + \overline{X_3}$ requires four. This facility can make the difference between a function fitting in a single macrocell and overflowing.

Although in this device all macrocells have the same number of dedicated

3.4   COMPUTATIONAL LOGIC ARRAYS

It is becoming apparent that the best method of increasing the speed of computation as we approach the speed limits of silicon technology is to increase parallelism. One problem with increasing parallelism is that computing structures consist of more than one resource. There are three classes—processor, memory, and communications. Different algorithms require different amounts of each resource, but to guarantee n times speedup, an n processor parallel computer must provide n times the limiting resource, that is, not only n processors but n times the memory and communications as well. While VLSI technology can provide increases in density each year it is not feasible to expect to increase performance on each of three independent axes while maintaining constant price. Parallel supercomputers will always be expensive.

Systolic and other VLSI design styles where processors are tailored to particular applications offer a way out of this problem. Since processors are specialized they can be much simpler and hence smaller and faster than general-purpose processors: thus one can have more of them at the same cost. Similarly memory and communication resources can be tailored for a given algorithm. Reconfigurable VLSI devices have the potential to provide the benefits of special-purpose processors to general-purpose computing devices.

Computational logic arrays consist of an array of rectangular cells covering the plane provided by the underlying silicon. In their purest form there are only connections to their nearest neighbors. This architecture has the following features:

1. Regularity and symmetry. The regularity and symmetry of the cellular array is attractive from the point of view of the CAD tool author, since there are fewer special cases to take account of in the choice of algorithm. When combined with a hierarchical design style, these properties allow subcircuits to be placed and routed independently, then rotated and reflected within larger blocks to optimize the floorplan. By contrast, most channeled architectures start off by flattening the netlist to eliminate hierarchy. Hierarchical place-and-route schemes can be much faster and more area-efficient than ones based on a flat netlist, particularly for well-structured regular designs.

2. The cells within the array implement a small, carefully chosen set of primitives. There is no support for constructs from previous technologies that do not map efficiently onto the programmable architecture. This allows designs created with this technology in mind to be implemented efficiently, but makes direct transfer of designs done using primitives from previous technologies costly.

3. The single resource of the cellular array scales well with improvements in technology. Instead of trading wiring channels for cells, as in a channeled architecture, one simply provides more cells. Cellular arrays can be

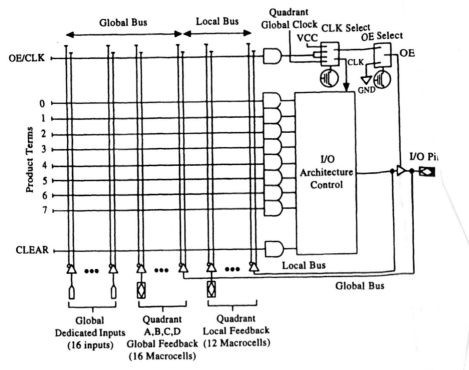

Figure 3–10. EP1810 global macrocell. (Reprinted with permission from Altera Corporation)

product terms, in some structured PALs different macrocells have different numbers of product terms. This can result in more efficient mapping of user designs, avoiding unused product terms in some macrocells, and the need to cascade macrocells to build more complex functions in other places. Anothe capability of some devices is that some product terms can be shared betwee adjacent macrocells programmably connected to the OR planes of both, so th they can be assigned to one or the other, depending on the demands of t design.

As can easily be surmised from the preceding description, use of comp PLDs is dependent on "fitter" software, which attempts to match the req' ments of the user's design with the resources supplied by the PLD. As as logic minimization, the software must match the number of product and input variables required by an output with those available from ent macrocells. Some degree of intelligence is required by such algo An unavoidable side effect of this approach is that a small change user's input specification could result in a design no longer fitting i ular device or requiring pinout changes resulting from changes in n assignments. Either of these outcomes is undesirable if PCB design completed.

designed to scale across chip boundaries without the chip boundary being apparent to the user.

4. Cellular arrays can be embedded in a static RAM in a manner that allows random access to the control store. This in turn allows rapid reprogramming, partial reprogramming of sections of the device, and access to internal state within circuits implemented by the device. This sort of access is harder to achieve in channeled structures with multiple classes of resource, because of discontinuities in the layout of the control store.

5. Cellular arrays accumulate delays through neighbor connections. This fact, coupled with their target application areas, has led to design styles that emphasize the use of pipelining to maximize throughput at the expense of latency. Pipelining is supported efficiently by cellular architectures that offer latches or flip-flops as cell functions.

As an example of a cellular array, we will consider the Algotronix Configurable Array Logic (CAL) devices [Kean89]. Other examples include the Atmel 6000 series, described in Chapter 6, and the Pilkington Micro-electronics architecture described in Chapter 8.

3.4.1 The Algotronix CAL1024

The Algotronix device consists of an array of cells with nearest-neighbor connections as shown in Figure 3–11. Each of these cells contains a function unit

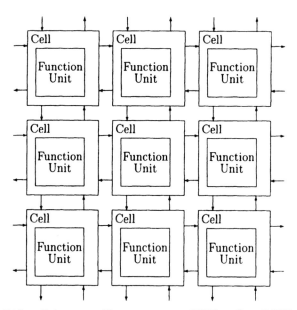

Figure 3–11. CAL cellular array. Figure courtesy of Xilinx, Inc. © Xilinx, Inc. 1991. All rights reserved.

capable of implementing any of the 16 possible combinational functions of its two variables (labeled X1 and X2), or transparent latches with true or inverted data (X2) and clock (X1) inputs for a total of 20 possible functions. The cell also contains a routing unit (Figure 3–12) which can route any of its neighbor inputs (North, South, East and West) or the function unit output (Self) to any useful neighbor output. Although the multiplexers cannot route signals back to where they came from, for example, North Input to North Output, this configuration would be redundant since the signal will be available on another source within the cell to the north: the user programming model allows these connections, but the CAD system eliminates them prior to programming the physical device. Since each output has its own dedicated multiplexer, routing an input to an output cannot block the use of any of the other outputs (as can happen with switch boxes in channeled arrays). Similarly, the routing function is perfectly symmetrical, allowing rotation and reflection of designs after placement and routing. The two function unit inputs can be taken from any of the neighbor inputs, and in addition, the X1 input can be taken from one of two global signals (G1 and G2) that are fed to all cells on the array. These signals are normally used for clock distribution. The output of the function unit is mapped into the device control store and can be read back using the programming interface. In addition, incremental changes can be made to portions of the control store, and it is possible to clear latches using the programming interface.

The CAL is programmed using a RAM-like interface with address and 8-bit-wide data busses that are not shared with input–outputs from the cell array. This allows the control store to be accessed without affecting computations running on the array. All 32 input and output signals from the edge of the array are brought out, and can be connected to an adjacent chip. This allows chips to be cascaded to support the user programming model of an arbitrarily large cellular array: chip boundaries are only apparent to the user by the increased delay on signals that cross them. This simple programming model makes large multichip structures much easier to design. The cascading of chips is supported

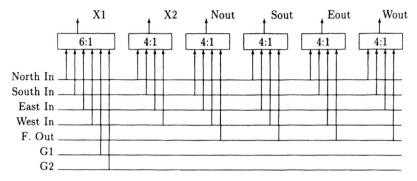

Figure 3–12. CAL cell routing. Figure courtesy of Xilinx, Inc. © Xilinx, Inc. 1991. All rights reserved.

by a proprietary pad architecture, which uses three logic levels to allow an input and an output signal from a chip to its neighbor to share the same physical pad. The pads can also be programmed to interface to normal TTL and CMOS parts.

3.5 VLSI PRIMITIVES

In the previous sections we have considered some important current FPGA devices: many of their key architectural features are predicated on the primitives of the implementation technology.

3.5.1 Function Units

The function units of today's configurable logic devices are based on several techniques:

1. *RAM lookup tables:* In this structure the input variables are used to select values from a RAM memory that has been preloaded with values representing the truth table of the function to be implemented. Thus all possible functions of the input variables can be implemented. Selection can use the RAM addressing mechanism in appropriately structured devices or a separate decoder taking its data inputs from RAM Q outputs. This structure offers area efficiency and predictable delays which scale well as the number of inputs is increased. It is the structure of choice for function units that attempt to implement all functions of four or more variables. An additional advantage is that it is possible with some extra overhead to allow the lookup table RAM to be used as a RAM within a user's design. The disadvantages of this implementation technique are:

   (a) If the RAM addressing mechanism is used to select a lookup table output, it is difficult to organize the control store as a conventional static RAM, as is done in most of the computational logic arrays. Thus the advantages of random access to the control store for partial reconfiguration and access to internal state are lost.

   (b) The large function units are inefficient at implementing common simple logic functions such as two input NANDs. This problem can be tackled by partitioning the RAM into smaller blocks and selectively combining their outputs. This can allow a single function unit to implement two functions of three variables or one function of four. Naturally, the extra multiplexing to provide this flexibility requires additional control memory and adds delay.

2. *Multiplexer based:* This style of function unit is based on the observation that all functions of two input variables can be implemented by a single 2:1 multiplexer by placing appropriate combinations of the input variables, their inverses, and the constants 0 and 1 on its inputs. The

technique can be generalized to allow more input variables and to implement latches. The main advantage of this style of function unit is that it can be implemented using the same primitives as the routing logic: in a cellular array in which function and routing are intermingled this allows for a high density layout. Multiplexer-based function units (Figure 3–13) are used in the Algotronix CAL architecture and in several antifuse programmed FPGAs. The delay through a multiplexer-based function unit is path dependent, and software can be written to optimize user designs so that the fast path through the function unit is assigned to signals on the critical path through logic blocks.

3. *Fixed function:* The function unit provides a single fixed function. The single fixed function has the advantage of simplicity and low delay per stage. The principal disadvantage is that larger numbers of function units are required to implement logic within user designs, and the corresponding cascading of function units and routing delays results in poor overall performance.

3.5.2 Wide Gates and Long Lines

These structures are used in RAM-programmed FPGA technology to provide a low-delay alternative to the more general interconnect resources. The basic resource is a long metal wire that may potentially be connected to cell and IO block inputs and outputs. Long lines normally cross the entire array horizontally or vertically, although variations in which only half the array is crossed are also useful. Connections between long lines and cell inputs are inexpensive, since they require only an additional terminal on a multiplexer (so for the price of one bit of RAM a 4-input routing multiplexer to a function unit input could be

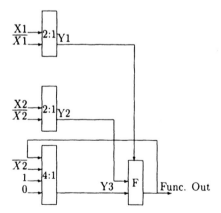

Figure 3–13. CAL function unit. Figure courtesy of Xilinx, Inc. © Xilinx, Inc. 1991. All rights reserved.

expanded to an 8-input multiplexer to select one of four long lines as well). It is common, therefore, for a long line to have input connections to all adjacent cells and I/O blocks. Connections between cell outputs and long lines are expensive because at least one bit of RAM is required to selectively connect the cell output to the long line. Additional flexibility can be provided in the buffer between the cell output and the long line to allow, for example, wired NOR (in conjunction with a programmable pull-up resistor) or threestate (where a second data signal is used to control the buffer) protocols to be used.

The speed advantages of long lines are dependent on switching the relatively large capacitive load of the line quickly. This arrangement requires a large buffer, which implies heavy dynamic power consumption. Static power consumption will also result in the case of wired logic. This power consumption is significant and cannot be safely neglected. When a line can be driven by several large buffers it is important to ensure that there will not be contention between those buffers: in the worst case, damage to the device can occur. This occurs when half the buffers attempt to force the common wire low and the other half attempt to force it high, so the more output connections to the wire the worse things become. The situation is complicated by threestate protocols where *enable* signals are generated by the user's logic, and the need to ensure that contention does not occur when the device control store contains random values prior to configuration. One way of doing this is to provide a global signal, that forces all buffers to the high impedance state. These problems with multiple-source long lines are particularly important with computational devices where the control store is reprogrammed frequently and the device must be as tolerant as possible to incorrect configurations. A computer with a halt-and-catch-fire instruction is difficult to sell!

Multiple-source long lines are relatively expensive resources in terms of device area because of the associated control store and relatively large buffers. For this reason they are usually in short supply. Even though a long line crosses the entire chip, if it is used by logic at one edge of the array, it is not available for use by a different signal at the other side. Providing programmable break points at which the long line can be segmented as required is therefore attractive architecturally. Unfortunately, the only method to achieve this segmentation in a RAM-programmed structure is to place a pass transistor switch between two metal segments of the line. When this switch is *on*, a buffer on one side of the switch must charge or discharge the capacitance on the other side of the switch through its series resistance. This effect rapidly removes the performance advantages of the long metal wire, although it may be tolerable for a single breakpoint.

3.5.3 Switches and Switch Boxes

The switch is the simplest routing function: it may take the form of a pass transistor controlled by a RAM cell, a fuse or antifuse, or an erasable programmable ROM (EPROM) cell, according to implementation technology.

Switches allow signals to pass in both directions, although where the switch has a high impedance (such as a pass transistor) buffering circuits to restore logic levels will often force a direction on signals. A single bit of control store is required to control a switch (since it has two possible states).

Switch boxes are structures used where vertical and horizontal wiring channels cross in RAM-programmed FPGAs to mimic the rich connectivity available in mask-programmed devices. Unfortunately, RAM cells are much bigger than the contacts, vias, and gaps in metal tracks used at the switch positions in the mask-programmed technologies and so some compromises have to be made. Only a small proportion of the possible permutations can be implemented: the fact that one can connect the desired signals to terminals of the switch box is no guarantee that the required connections between them can be made. In fact, routing failures caused by limited flexibility in the switch boxes are relatively common. As an example the routing options offered by the switch boxes in the Xilinx 3000 series device are shown in Figure 3–14.

An additional factor is that pass transistors degrade the signal to such an extent that signals passing through more than a few (approximately three) must have their levels restored. Level restoring buffers are therefore commonly placed at the edge of the switch box. These buffers add delay to the signal, require control store for their own switches, and force a direction on the signal.

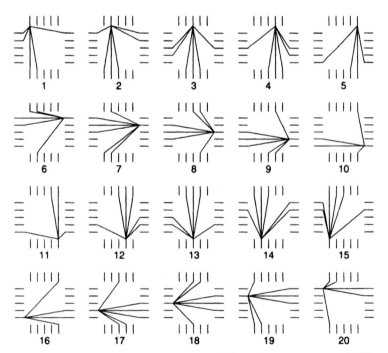

Figure 3–14. Xilinx switch box–routing possibilities. Figure courtesy of Xilinx, Inc.

Thus wires that pass through switch boxes and have their level restored by program controlled buffers cannot be truly bidirectional in the sense of a tristate bus with multiple sources. The accumulated resistance of switches within switch boxes also affects delay: Figure 3–15 shows this effect on the Xilinx 3000 series architecture.

One additional architectural option is to offer metal segments of different lengths within the wiring channels. For example, instead of every metal segment being broken at every switch box, some longer tracks that were broken at every second or third switch box could provide better delay characteristics for longer wires. One problem with this approach is the need to determine the balance between such resources *a priori* before manufacturing the device when user designs will make widely varying demands on the routing resources. Provision of varying length wires also complicates CAD systems that must try to make optimum choices of resource assignments.

3.5.4 Multiplexers

The multiplexer is a common routing structure in RAM-based technologies. The principal advantage of the multiplexer is that it allows a single bit of control store to control several switches and is hence more efficient in its use of RAM. For example, a 4 : 1 selector can be implemented in a multiplexer with 2 bits of RAM. A schematic for this multiplexor is given in Figure 3–16. If the same selector was built using switches, then 4 bits of RAM would be required. There are various area/performance trade-offs possible in the design of multiplexors: in particular not all paths through a multiplexer need have the same delay. For example, in a cellular structure one might notice that long wires are generally straight and optimize the paths corresponding to straight wires in the multiplexers for speed.

3.5.5 Input–Output Pad Design

The design of the input–output (I/O) pads on FPGAs must take into account many, sometimes conflicting, requirements:

1. Support both TTL and CMOS voltage levels on input.
2. Support bidirectional, input, output, open collector and three-statable output modes.
3. Provide high drive current on output to interface with bipolar logic, drive devices such as light-emitting diodes (LED's) directly, and rapidly switch capacitive loads.
4. Limit output drive to reduce power consumption, prevent overshoot, and reduce supply noise. This is particularly important in applications where high pinout FPGAs are used and large numbers of outputs may switch simultaneously.

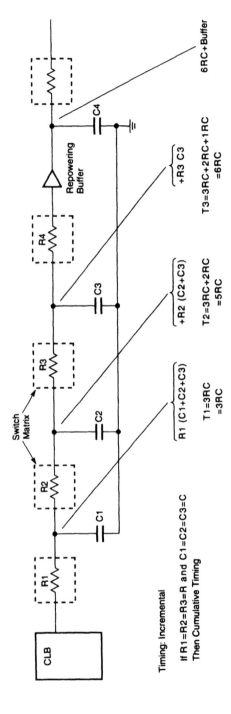

Figure 3–15. Xilinx interconnect. Figure courtesy of Xilinx, Inc. © Xilinx, Inc. 1991. All rights reserved.

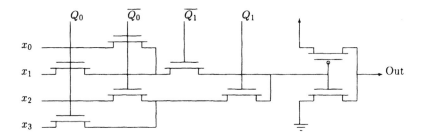

Figure 3–16. Simple pass transistor multiplexer.

5. Interface to crystals to provide clock oscillators, without the need for external specialized chips.

6. Interface to on-chip routing resources. For many FPGA architectures, there are significantly fewer off-chip connections than on-chip routing wires at the edge of the array. The choice of which category of routing resource to connect to the pads has important consequences for the performance and flexibility of the device.

7. Provide simple analog interfacing capabilities. Although no commercial FPGAs currently offer operational amplifiers, digital to analog (D/A) or analog to digital (A/D), as special-purpose resources in the pad ring, this is an obvious extension to the current technology. The programmable hysteresis characteristics and voltage level sensing features of today's devices can be used in subtle circuit configurations to build simple analog functions.

8. Interface efficiently to other FPGA chips from the same manufacturer to allow arrays to be built up from multiple chips.

The provision of a flexible I/O architecture with many I/O connections can have important implications for FPGA performance and reduce the requirement for long lines within the chip. For example, one common technique is to connect a critical input signal to more than one input pad on the device (perhaps on opposite sides of the array) to reduce the length and hence the delay of internal connections between the input and the gates that use it.

The power consumption of FPGA devices is normally largely determined by the use of the I/O pins. When high pin count FPGAs are used it is vital to consider the potential power consumption (transient as well as static) of the proposed I/O configuration as well as the availability of I/O blocks. It is quite possible to melt an FPGA by ignoring this aspect of design, particularly if it is in a plastic pack.

As an example of the programmable I/Os on FPGAs Figure 3–17 shows one of the programmable I/O blocks (IOBs) on a Xilinx 3000 series device. The

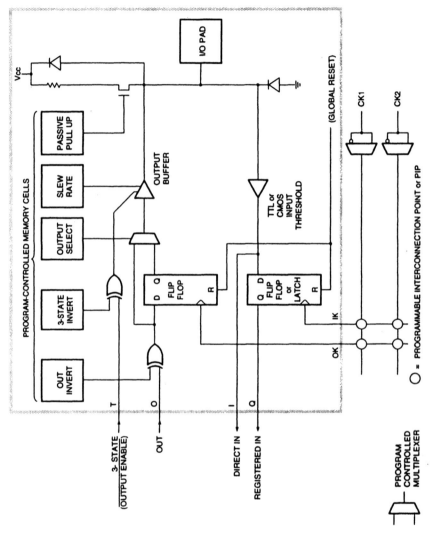

Figure 3-17. Xilinx programmable IOB. Figure courtesy of Xilinx, Inc. © Xilinx, Inc. 1991. All rights reserved.

80

features offered by this IOB are somewhat richer than those offered by most FPGA IOBs.

3.6 PROGRAMMING

3.6.1 Technology

The main technologies used in the control store of FPGAs and programmable logic devices (PLDs) are as follows.

Static RAM   The basic static RAM cell consists of two CMOS inverters connected in a loop to form a bistable device. The state of this device can be overwritten by external signals on the bit lines (marked B in Figures 3–18 and 3–19) via pass devices gated by the word lines (marked W). The sizes of the transistors are chosen to ensure that normal logic values on the bit lines can change the state of the cell (write cycle), but if an intermediate voltage is placed on the bit line, which is then left floating, the RAM cell itself can drive the bit line high or low according to its state (read cycle). In the case of the six-transistor RAM (Figure 3–18) true and complement values are applied to both sides of the RAM (effectively pushing and pulling it during a write), and in the five-transistor RAM (Figure 3–19) only one signal is applied (push only). Five-transistor RAMs are significantly more dense than six-transistor RAMs because less area is required to route bit and word lines through the array: they are also much harder to design and have less noise immunity. As process technology moves below 1 μm and with the move to 3-V power supplies, five-transistor RAM designs are being replaced by the more stable six-transistor cells.

The RAM cell is a storage device only, and in the FPGA application its Q output will control a separate (normally n-type) transistor switch.

EPROM   The EPROM device is based on special metal-oxide semiconductor field-effect transistors (MOSFETs) with floating (unconnected) gates (Figure 3–20). If sufficient charge is trapped on the gate, the channel will conduct. Thus the EPROM transistor can function as a simple switch in the same way

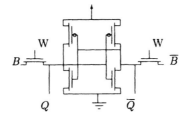

Figure 3–18. Six-transistor static RAM.

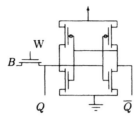

Figure 3–19. Five-transistor static RAM.

as a fuse or antifuse. Charge is injected into the silicon dioxide above the transistor channel in a special programming mode by generating high-energy "hot" electrons within the channel region using higher-than-normal voltages. These electrons are attracted toward the floating gate by capacitive coupling. When the high programming voltage is removed, the electrons are trapped in the floating gate. Ultraviolet light is used to erase the device by giving the trapped electrons sufficient energy to escape from the gate dielectric. Programming and erasing of EPROM-based devices normally take place outside the target system and require special equipment. In addition, erasing devices is a relatively slow process, taking about 15 to 20 minutes.

EEPROM The electrically-erasable programmable ROM (EEPROM) transistor (Figure 3–21) is similar to the EPROM transistor, but a second polysilicon gate overlapping the first floating gate is added. EEPROM devices are erased electrically by applying a suitable voltage to this second gate to allow elec-

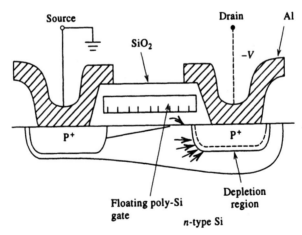

Figure 3–20. EPROM floating-gate MOSFET. Reprinted with permission of McGraw-Hill from Geiger, R. et al. "VLSI Design Techniques for Analog and Digital Circuits," McGraw-Hill © 1990.

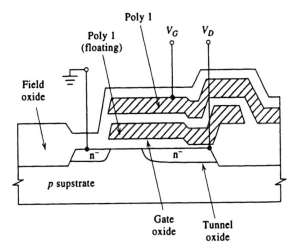

Figure 3-21. EEPROM floating gate MOSFET. Reprinted with permission of McGraw-Hill from Geiger, R. et al. "VLSI Design Techniques for Analog and Digital Circuits," McGraw-Hill © 1990.

trons trapped on the floating gate to be discharged by a tunneling mechanism. EEPROM cells are somewhat less dense than EPROM cells and to date have found application only in relatively simple (GAL) Generic Array Logic devices which are reprogrammable pin equivalents for PALs. GALs are normally programmed out of circuit using special equipment. Most EEPROM technologies have a limit on the number of read/write cycles before the device fails: this limit makes the technology unsuitable for use in computational applications where the device may be reprogrammed thousands of times.

Fuse This technology relies on simple fuses formed from metal links that are forced open circuit by high programming currents. Since the fuses are made of metal they have low impedance in the closed condition and hence can support high-speed operation. Fuses are used on most low-density PAL devices based on bipolar technology: they are not found on any high-density FPGA-type devices. Current technology can guarantee a programming yield of about 97% for fuse-based devices, that is, 3% of devices supplied to customers can be expected not to program correctly.

Antifuse An antifuse is a two-terminal circuit element that normally offers a high impedance between its terminals, but after a programming voltage higher than the operating voltage is applied, the impedance is reduced to a low value permanently. This is the opposite behavior to a fuse where the programming voltage causes the device to enter a high impedance state. Normally-open anti-fuses are more suitable than fuses for use in gate-array-like structures because the metal segments and logic resources of the device can be tested in isolation before any antifuses are programmed. Another advantage is that antifuses are blown where connections are required on the user design, whereas fuses are blown wherever a potential connection provided by the underlying architecture is not required: this implies that in a general-purpose device far fewer antifuses need to be programmed than fuses. There are several antifuse structures in use, of which the most popular is the programmable low-impedance circuit element (PLICE) used in Actel gate arrays (Figure 3–22). When an 18-V programming pulse is applied across the terminals (drawing a current of 10 mA for less than 10 ms) the dielectric is ruptured and the device impedance is reduced from a value above 100 MΩ to a value less than 1 kΩ. These values are guaranteed by the manufacturer. The PLICE antifuse is bidirectional in its low-impedance state. Another important criterion for antifuse-based devices is the range of maximum and minimum resistances within which an antifuse is said to be programmed. Adaptive programming techniques are utilized to program antifuses to final resistances with minimum variations.

Other technologies such as ferric RAM and flash EPROM may be expected to be used in this application in the near future.

3.6.2 Issues

The different classes of FPGA device have different goals and requirements for their programming interface. In the ASIC replacement application, for example, simple low overhead interfaces are required (a real ASIC has no programming overhead), whereas the computational array requires a high bandwidth interface to support rapid reprogramming. The main issues in the choice of programming interface and control store technology are discussed in the following sections.

Overhead Pins Overhead pins to support programming in RAM-programmed FPGAs increase package and hence part costs. Extra data and address busses are expensive at the board level. However, they allow random access to the control store for rapid reconfiguration and access to the state within the user

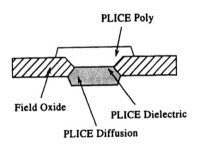

Figure 3-22. PLICE antifuse. (© Actel Corporation, 1993. All rights reserved.)

logic. In some devices, programming and device I/O signals share a physical pad, with a mode control input to select which is active. One disadvantage of this scheme is that if the configuration of the device needs to use the shared I/O pins, control store accesses cannot be made without affecting the computation being implemented by the device.

External Support Circuitry   With RAM-programmed FPGAs it is necessary to load the device configuration into the RAM control store from external non-volatile storage, normally EPROM or ROM. It is desirable that this is done with the minimum of support chips: there is not much point in replacing ten TTL and PAL devices with an FPGA if one needs four TTL devices and an EPROM to bootstrap the FPGA! Thus placing the bootstrap logic on the FPGA itself is highly desirable in stand-alone applications. On the other hand, when the FPGA is to be used in a microprocessor-based system, a straightforward memory-like interface can be attractive; depending on the function of the FPGA, it may be possible for the microprocessor or microcontroller to load its configuration from the system's nonvolatile storage. It is also desirable that when multiple FPGAs are used on a board they can be configured from a single large memory and associated circuits, rather than multiple smaller memories and associated circuits for each FPGA.

Testability   The choice of programming method affects testability of systems using FPGAs in several ways. Use of RAM-based rapidly reprogrammable FPGAs allows special FPGA configurations to be developed for use in system tests. These can be used to test board traces and even adjacent non-FPGA devices as well as the FPGA chips themselves. This technique has the potential to reduce test time for completed assemblies and the need for complex board testers and to allow self-test in the field. This method of testing using FPGAs can be successfully integrated with the JTAG boundary-scan methodology. Note that the reconfigurability of FPGAs allows a special configuration for board testing and can make it unnecessary for the FPGA to provide dedicated hardware resources for JTAG registers. Conversely, use of write-once technologies such as antifuse has adverse implications for tests, in that the configurations of the devices themselves must be verified. In general, it is not always sufficient to rely on the device programmer to check that fuses read back correctly since a partially blown fuse may pass a static read back test but cause the device to fail at operating speed and temperature.

Reliability   There are reliability concerns associated with the configuration store of all FPGA technologies.

Write-once fuse-based devices such as PALs can be sensitive to the calibration of the programming equipment. Pin-equivalent devices from different manufacturers often have different programming algorithms. Failure to observe the manufacturer's specifications exactly may cause higher numbers of devices to fail on the programmer, but more seriously, devices may pass the programmer read back test but fail in the field. Such failures can be intermittent and are often hard to diagnose. It is essential that devices are programmed on a trusted system and that the programmer is well maintained. When this is done field failures are rare although a significant percentage of devices may fail to program correctly—there is no way for a PLD manufacturer to test if a fuse will fuse before it leaves the factory. Another concern for some programming technologies in safety-critical applications is that they have not been in production long enough to verify their long-term reliability. It is impossible to say for certain what percentage of devices will survive ten years when they have only been manufactured for three, although accelerated failure tests can provide enough confidence for most applications.

The reliability concerns with RAM-programmed technologies are centered around well-known effects experienced with commercial SRAM devices. The most serious problem is that alpha-particle radiation can potentially change the state of one of the control RAM cells. This is called a soft error, since the state of the RAM can be restored by writing it again. Extreme doses of radiation can cause unrecoverable failures in all common VLSI technologies, although different technologies have different degrees of radiation hardness. Failures are less likely to occur on FPGAs than normal SRAMs because FPGA RAM cells normally have a higher load capacitance (because they are connected to logic), are accessed relatively rarely (RAM cells are at their most vulnerable to spurious writes during a read cycle when internal voltages are compromised), have better power supply connections (RAM designers can take advantage of the low power consumption of static RAM cells to route power locally on nonmetal layers, whereas FPGA designers will normally route on wide metal tracks to support adjacent logic circuits), and are designed for stability rather than access speed. Choice of packaging technology can also reduce the radiation problem since alpha particles are emitted by the package: plastic packages emit at a rate about ten times lower than ceramic packages. An analysis of the soft error rate caused by this mechanism, based on experiments with radioactive sources placed in direct contact with the die to accelerate soft error rates predicted that a Xilinx XC2064 device would function for about 46,000 years without an error under normal conditions. Similar results are likely for the other SRAM-programmed parts since the memory cells are of the same basic design. As process technology improves and transistor sizes become smaller, RAM cells will become more sensitive to alpha particles. There will be more of them per device, and so the soft error rate is likely to increase.

Although it is impossible in theory to stop soft errors from happening, they can be detected by reading back the control store and comparing against a reference or using parity or other error-detection codes. Checking circuits can be built into devices or be external, as are the parity checkers for computer memory chips. The value of such checking circuits is open to question given the inherent reliability of the static RAM technology used in FPGAs compared to that of the dynamic RAM (DRAM) technology where parity checking is normally applied, the much smaller number of bits of store involved, and the fact that the action of reading the RAM itself could have a negative impact on device reliability. Another approach would be simply to refresh the control store periodically without attempting to determine whether errors had occurred. For some designs, this can be done without disturbing the current computation. This approach has the merit of avoiding the need to read the device control store during operation.

It should also be noted in this connection that soft errors can potentially occur on any bit of state in a digital circuit in all common implementation technologies, including the state of the user's design. Since there are likely to be much fewer bits of state in the user's design than in the configuration store and the structures involved are physically larger than those in a RAM cell, it is much less likely to happen there. Thus it could be argued that if soft errors are of concern in a particular application, it would be more appropriate to use a self-checking design style (e.g., triplication) within the design implemented on the FPGA than to check the FPGA's control store. Such design styles also detect errors immediately and can often compensate for them or fail gracefully; parity checking the control store can do no more than raise a flag that something went wrong at some time in the past *after* incorrect results have been output.

EPROM-based technologies are sensitive to the device the programmer used, as are all fuse-programmed devices. In addition they can be erased by UV light: manufacturer's data gives a figure of about 1 week of exposure to direct sunlight or 3 years exposure to fluorescent room lighting to erase an EPROM if a suitable opaque label has not been fitted. In the context of device reliability we are more concerned with the exposure required to make it probable that a single bit will be erased rather than the time to erase the whole device. Versions of EPROM-based erasable programmable logic devices (EPLDs) in nonwindowed packages are worth considering for high-reliability applications. Given their sensitivity to UV light, use of these devices in environments where they might be exposed to other forms of radiation (e.g., X-Rays) should be considered carefully.

Technologies based on electrically erasable memory may be unreliable if exposed to either radiation or voltage transients on programming pins.

All the programming technologies used in FPGA devices to date have more than adequate reliability for most applications. When considering FPGAs for safety-critical applications or stressful environments it is important to make a thorough study of the reliability of the chosen device. This may involve persuading manufacturers to release proprietary information or running one's own characterization experiments on the device.

Manufacturing Concerns   There are several manufacturing concerns related to the use of write-once FPGA devices: RAM-based devices present no special difficulties. The most obvious concern is that the devices must be programmed during manufacture. This has several consequences.

1. Some devices will fail to program correctly: this must be taken account of

in price comparisons between technologies and in determining inventory levels.

2. Programming the FPGA devices is an additional manufacturing step that must be coordinated with the others and requires its own tooling, which can be relatively expensive. Most complex FPGA antifuse-based devices take a significant amount of time to program and some require that user-supplied test vectors be run.

3. It may be necessary to swap PLDs in the field after design revisions or after a completed board fails the final test. Therefore, it is common practice to use sockets with write-once PLD devices, while other components are normally soldered directly to the board. The cost of sockets can be significant in volume manufacture, and sockets themselves compromise reliability by making the assembly more susceptible to mechanical shocks. If you do not believe this then try mailing a few boards with socketed PLDs overseas! Sockets also involve an extra assembly stage in which the components are inserted; failures can be introduced here by poor connections between device pins and sockets (especially on high pin count devices) and device leads that bend under the device rather than entering the socket (especially dual-in-line (DIL) devices).

4. The fine lead pitch on high pin count surface mount packages can cause handling problems with devices that are programmed out of circuit. The process of inserting and removing the device from the programmer socket may displace one or more leads sufficiently to cause problems when the device is mounted on the board. For this reason, it is likely that in-circuit programming will become the technology of choice for high pin-out devices.

Granularity and Speed of Reconfiguration Granularity refers to the smallest unit of the FPGA that can be reprogrammed. In most cases this is the entire chip. Allowing small changes to the configuration RAM allows dynamic reconfiguration of subcircuits and can be attractive in computational applications. This feature can be used to set the state of latches in the design implemented on the FPGA. This feature is attractive even in logic replacement applications since it can dramatically simplify the circuit to be implemented on the FPGA, for example, by eliminating the need for load and clear functions on a counter.

Access to Internal State Access to internal state is desirable to support design debugging and in computational applications to access results without the overhead of routing them to the edge of the array. There are two main techniques for providing such access:

1. Special output lines, which can be selectively connected to the outputs of internal gates and are available at dedicated pads. This technique allows

real-time monitoring of internal signals using conventional test equipment and is very useful for debugging FPGA designs embedded in board-level systems. Normally there are a very small number of such lines available, so relatively few circuit nodes can be monitored. This technique is used in the "actionprobes" of Actel's FPGAs that allow two internal device nodes to be monitored in real time.

2. Mapping cell outputs to control store RAM. This technique is most useful in devices that allow random access to the control store. Although signals cannot be monitored in real time, any node in the circuit can be watched and no external test equipment is required. This technique is particularly advantageous in computational applications where the clock to the user circuit can be controlled by the host computer performing the accesses to memory. This technique is used in the Algotronix CAL applications.

Design Security Many write-once PLDs have a "security" fuse which when blown, prevents the fuse array from being read back by a device programmer. This feature is intended to prevent competitors from "reverse engineering" the user design, that is, determining the principles of operation. Naturally, it also has adverse consequences for testability and diagnosis of failures in the field. The security fuse on simple PLDs is of no value because the configuration can easily be determined by applying vectors to the device pins. With most complex PLDs based on a PAL architecture, the security fuse would be little more than an inconvenience to the determined. Less obviously, RAM-programmed FPGAs can give design security since the contents of their control store is lost when power is removed. When RAM-programmed FPGAs are used in conjunction with a host microprocessor, extremely secure operation is possible since encryption can be used to protect configurations prior to downloading into the FPGA (configurations for the FPGA can come into a tamperproof module over a communications interface, and so need not be present in nonvolatile store within the tamperproof unit) and the microprocessor can rapidly overwrite the control store or remove power to the FPGA if it detects attempts at tampering.

3.7 BENCHMARKING

One of the problems of the programmable logic area has been the lack of progress in developing credible methodologies for comparing architectures. In the absence of such methodologies, marketing departments have sprung in to fill the gap with a wide variety of benchmarks based around two main numbers, gate equivalents and utilization. This situation mirrors the somewhat checkered history of benchmarking conventional computers. A third class of benchmarks based around the use of silicon area has been proposed by academics, but no comparative data have been published as yet.

3.7.1   Utilization

Utilization is defined as the ratio of resources used to those provided to implement a particular design. For example, a design as implemented on a cellular array may use 50% of the available cell function units. High utilization is seen as a "good-thing," indicating that the architecture efficiently supports the design. The principal advantage of this metric is that it is easy to calculate. There are several serious shortcomings, however.

1. Utilization figures are influenced by the size of the box one draws around the design. If the box is measured in chip units, then the design may use a small percentage of the chip's resources simply because it is a small design. For this reason, one might suggest drawing the bounding box in terms of logic cell units. While this is certainly an improvement, it suffers from the drawback that designs that use special-purpose resources (e.g., long wires) may need to be spread out over the chip to access those resources. Similarly when there is free space, it is often advantageous to spread a design round the periphery of the array to minimize delays caused by routing between the edge of the chip and the logic. Thus even when the bounding box of the design is drawn at the cell level, good architectures that implement designs efficiently using only a small fraction of available resources, may show lower utilization numbers than poorer architectures. It is a hard problem to determine whether a cell is unused because a design did not need to use it (and therefore available for use if the design was expanded) or unused because routing congestion prevented it being reached.

2. Utilization figures are influenced by cell granularity: larger cells will in general result in higher utilizations. To understand this point consider two cellular arrays: one whose function unit could implement any function of up to four input variables and one whose function unit could implement any function of two input variables. There will be many fewer 4-input function units per chip than 2-input function units per chip, given similar implementation technologies. Some of the 4-input function units will be implementing simple functions, such as 2-input gates. These function units will count as fully utilized on a simple cell counting benchmark, but in fact when one considers the amount of control store and other resources assigned to them, their *internal* utilization is low (it requires 4 bits of RAM to control a function unit capable of implementing all functions of 2-input variables and 16 bits of RAM to implement a function unit capable of implementing all functions of four variables). If one wishes to make a valid comparison between the architectures based on the utilization of the underlying resource (RAM cells or silicon area), one must take into account the internal utilization of the larger cells. Furthermore, when one compares well-implemented designs on these architectures, one will normally find that a higher percentage of the larger cells are used than

the smaller cells. One reason for this is that the routing resource on the 4-input cell array will have been designed with enough capacity to ensure that almost all the expensive function units can be used. Where function units are less expensive, it makes sense to trade off the area required by a routing system rich enough to ensure that they could all be used, with the area that is effectively lost in function units that cannot be used because of routing constraints. This trade-off reduces utilization as measured in terms of function units, but increases utilization as measured in terms of the percentage of RAM cells and silicon area that are being usefully employed.

3. Limited architectures and constrained layout styles can lead to high utilization but very low efficiency. As an example, Algotronix developed a simple piece of synthesis software for its array that generates a ROM-like implementation of a truth table. This implementation does not take advantage of the full flexibility of the cell in terms of either routing or function and corresponds to a design done on a much more limited architecture. When one implements a seven-segment decoder using this tool, one requires 80 cells and obtains 100% utilization. An implementation that takes full advantage of the array, on the other hand, requires 44 cells and has 64% utilization. It is also approximately three times as fast.

3.7.2 Gate Equivalents

Gate equivalent figures can be derived in three main ways.

Marketing Gates Marketing gates are calculated by FPGA suppliers using advanced algorithms based on three basic parameters:

1. The highest number of 2-input NAND gates (or some other simple primitive) required to implement any circuit configuration of their device. For example, if a configurable cell can implement a D-latch and it takes five NAND gates to implement a D-latch in a particular gate array vendor's library and there are 4000 configurable cells, then a gate equivalent figure of 20,000 could be quoted. This would correspond to implementing a 4000 stage shift register on the device.

2. The user gullibility factor (UGF) is used to derate the figure calculated in step 1 by a percentage intended to represent the device use by "real" designs, since most people will not believe the figures in step 1.

3. The gate equivalent figures quoted by their direct competitors are used to alter the UGF figure arrived at in step 2 by a sufficient margin to ensure that the current product comes out ahead of all existing competition in any gate equivalent comparisons done in the trade press.

Benchmark Gates Benchmark gates are calculated by running a series of "typical" benchmark circuits through automatic placement and routing systems on the target FPGA. These benchmark circuits have previously been implemented on an industry standard gate array technology using n gate array gates and are classified as having n equivalent gates. From the results of these tests the FPGA is rated as being equivalent to n gates in the gate array technology. This technique is certainly the most credible way of benchmarking FPGAs in common use, but it has several problems.

1. The technique tests not only the underlying architecture but also the entire CAD system. This may be regarded as an advantage, but it is unclear whether benchmark results are more influenced by place-and-route software than by the underlying architecture. Place-and-route systems are generally under continuous improvement, and often have a large number of tuning parameters that can make sizable differences to the final results. Thus benchmarks that rely on place-and-route can generate a lot of heat without throwing much light on the architectural comparison.

2. More seriously, this benchmarking technique will favor architectures that are similar to the gate array, over more radical architectures that may be more efficient in programmable structures. This is because the original designs will have been done with gate array technology in mind and will use primitives that are efficiently implemented on gate arrays.

3. The benchmark circuits chosen are often not representative of those used in the application of interest. Poor performance on benchmark circuits typical of small glue-logic functions is not indicative of performance when implementing highly structured systolic arrays. In this context it is worth pointing out that many standard benchmarks are too small and show only how efficiently particular subcircuits can be implemented. Ideally there should be whole systems composed of many subcircuits, for which serious consideration has been given to floorplanning issues, in order to minimize area and optimize routing.

4. Benchmark circuits are known in advance and are generally small; often they are based on popular TTL parts. This implies that FPGA architectures and CAD systems can be tuned to score well on them, for example, by providing a particular resource useful in the benchmark circuit or by handcrafting a macro to implement a benchmark subsystem.

5. One important architectural trade-off in FPGA design is whether to devote silicon area to special-purpose resources that allow the very efficient implementation of particular common subcircuits or whether to devote it to increasing the quantity or performance of the general-purpose resources provided. As an example, an area devoted to a long line could be used to tune the performance of all the routing multiplexers, and an area devoted to wide gates could be used to improve the performance or increase the number of functions implemented by the cell function units. Small

benchmarks that involve the use of only a small proportion of a device's resources favor architectures that provide special-purpose resources over those that provide general-purpose resources, both in terms of density and performance measures. This is because they do not reflect the normal situation with larger designs where the number and distribution of special-purpose resources over the chip may prevent their use. For example, a 16 : 1 multiplexer may be implemented very efficiently using long lines on a given architecture to reduce delays. When this circuit is placed and routed in isolation there are plenty of long lines to go around. In a more realistic design one might need four or five such multiplexers plus an address decoder and some register files, all of which will compete for the long line resources. The distribution of the long lines on the chip limits where these units can be placed if they are to take advantage of the long lines. Thus, it is unlikely that every subunit on the real design will be able to take advantage of the special-purpose resources. It is also likely that those that do not use the special-purpose resources on an architecture that provides them will be slower and require more area than those on the architecture without special resources. The actual performance of the two architectures on a realistic design is likely, therefore, to be significantly different from that predicted by the benchmark.

A better way of obtaining realistic gate-equivalent numbers would be to specify a set of several applications to be implemented by different FPGAs at a very high level and allow the implementations to be done by experts on those architectures. Unfortunately, the effort involved in implementing realistic applications is likely to rule out this approach.

Real Gates   These are gate-equivalent figures arrived at by users after implementing their applications on a given FPGA. Unfortunately, these numbers cannot be arrived at without spending several months and several thousand dollars on CAD tools. Normally real gate counts are 5 to 10 times smaller than marketing gates, and can be either better or worse than benchmark gates according to how well the application and chosen design style fits the architecture.

3.7.3 RAM- and Area-based Benchmarks

A third class of benchmarks that has found favor mainly in the academic community attempts to quantify architectures based on their use of the underlying resource: silicon area. With RAM-based FPGAs, silicon area scales vary closely with RAM cell count and counting RAM allows a comparison between architectures independent of technology design rules and die size. This style of benchmarking is therefore of most use to those attempting to evaluate architectures rather than those attempting to decide which existing device to buy.

There are two basic ways in which this methodology can be used: the first is to implement a set of benchmark circuits and compare the absolute RAM cell cost of each implementation. As with the gate-equivalent benchmarks, the choice of benchmark circuits is of critical importance. The second is to attempt to make a more mathematical, information-theoretic analysis of the architecture based on the number of distinct circuit configurations it can implement for a particular number of bits of control store. This form of analysis can rapidly become intractable, but it is likely that in the long term fundamental results obtained here will be as important for FPGA designers, as those obtained in computational complexity theory are for algorithm designers.

3.7.4 Benchmarking and Dynamic Reconfiguration

One important area that has not been considered in any of the FPGA benchmark proposals to date is the use of dynamic reconfiguration. Dynamic reconfiguration can allow swapping of large sections of an application into and out of an FPGA. For example, a serial interface may be specified to either be in receive or transmit mode. Using dynamic reconfiguration, an FPGA of sufficient size to implement the larger of the receive and transmit functions could be used: with conventional technology the FPGA would have to be large enough to implement both functions at the same time. The area saving could approach 50%. Should this give the FPGA that supports dynamic reconfiguration as many equivalent gates? Does it have 200% utilization?

Similarly, direct accesses to the control store can be used on smaller logic blocks within a design to implement functions such as clearing or loading registers or customizing adders for a particular constant input: this technique can often halve the gate count and double the speed of a subunit. The ability to read the contents of an internal register through the control store interface might make a large bus to route the value to the chip edge redundant, saving a large amount of space. Should benchmarks take these capabilities into account or should they insist that every architecture implements the same netlist?

3.7.5 The PREP Benchmarks

In 1993, PREP, a nonprofit organization supported by most of the major companies in the programmable logic market, produced a set of nine benchmarks [Prep93]. These benchmarks cover a range of traditional logic functions from state machines to adders and counters. For each benchmark two main numbers are calculated: the number of instances of the benchmark that can be fitted on the device and the maximum clock frequency the benchmark can run at on the device. PREP has a benchmarking methodology and publishes "certified" results so one does not have to trust the device manufacturer's own data. While these benchmarks are far from perfect, they represent the best available source of comparative data on FPGA architectures.

3.7.6 Summary and Health Warning

In conclusion, with the present state of technology, one should treat all benchmark claims with several pinches of salt. If at all possible look for similar applications to yours that have been successfully implemented on the architecture either in manufacturer's applications notes or in published literature. Be aware that there is a high degree of variance in the efficiency with which an architecture may implement different applications; just because it scores well on benchmarks does not mean it is good for your application. Also be aware that to take full advantage of FPGAs, it is necessary to adopt different design styles that match their architectures; if you avoid doing so, performance and resource efficiency will suffer badly. Trying to map an existing TTL netlist onto the FPGA is usually a recipe for disaster. Many new users of FPGAs make purchasing decisions on the basis of the CAD system's ability to support design input in terms of TTL macros to allow easy conversion of existing designs: many quickly become disillusioned with the results, particularly for RAM-programmed architectures. Similarly, benchmarks that do not involve changing design styles will not indicate the full potential of the architectures they measure.

3.8 HISTORICAL BACKGROUND

3.8.1 Early Work

The origins of much of today's FPGA research are in work in the late 1960s and early 1970s on cellular arrays. This work was mainly concerned with improving the fault tolerance of logic structures, thus allowing larger silicon areas or whole wafers to be used to implement logic. The method proposed was to cover the wafer with a regular array of restructurable cells capable of implementing general logic functions. Both fuse- and flip-flop-programmed structures were proposed and investigated. Important early work in this area was done by Manning [Mann77], Minnick [Minn64], Wahlstrom [Wahl67], and Shoup [Shoup70]. A good survey article of the early research appears in [Minn67].

3.8.2 PALs and Structured PALs

The first programmable two-level logic products were PROMs from Harris and Monolithic Memories. Monolithic Memories later introduced field-programmable logic-array (FPLA) devices based on bipolar fusible link technology, and later Birkner and Chua at Monolithic Memories invented the PAL architecture that was to dominate the marketplace, replacing TTL as the method of choice for implementing glue-logic functions.

The PAL concept was further improved with the introduction of GAL devices. These devices were erasable either electrically or by UV light and used low power CMOS rather than bipolar technology. The most popular of these devices, the 22V10 can emulate a wide variety of conventional PALs.

Structured PALs were introduced and popularized by Altera Corporation, which was founded in 1983 to provide a field-programmable alternative to mask-programmable gate arrays.

3.8.3 FPGAs

The Xilinx FPGA architecture was designed by Ross Freeman and introduced in a paper in the 1986 Custom Integrated Circuits Conference [Carter86].

The Actel FPGA architecture [Actel90] and antifuse technology was designed by a team led by Amr Mohsen and Abbas El Gamal, and was described in a series of papers early in 1988 [Mohsen88], [El-Ayat88].

3.8.4 Computational Arrays

The Algotronix CAL device [Algo91] was introduced in a paper presented at the Decennial Caltech Conference on VLSI in 1989 [Gray89], based on an architecture developed in 1985 as part of Tom Kean's Ph.D. research [Kean89]. Concurrent Logic [Conc91] introduced the CFA600 Series in 1991 as the result of long-term work on cellular arrays by its founder Fred Furtek. The Pilkington Microelectronics "sea of gates" architecture was designed by Kenneth Austin and licensed to GEC/Plessey as the electrically-reconfigurable architecture (ERA) [Pless91].

3.8.5 VLSI Primitives and Programming

A more detailed but less current treatment of the VLSI design issues of FPGA architectures is presented in [Kean89]. Textbooks on CMOS design are [Weste85] and [Glass85]. These books also provide good introductory treatments of RAM cell design. A useful survey article of nonvolatile MOS memory technology, including newer flash memory technology, appeared in [Pash89].

The PLICE antifuse technology is described in [Osann88]. An antifuse allowing metal-to-metal connections with much lower resistance than the PLICE technology is the basis of a more recent FPGA family [QL91].

Studies on soft error rates in Xilinx FPGAs are contained in [Xilinx92]. A description of an FPGA that continually checks its control store is in [Felton91].

3.8.6 Benchmarking

The first serious attempt to benchmark FPGA circuits against traditional gate arrays was done by Actel Corporation [Osann88]; [Wein91] gives a comparison of Xilinx and Actel devices over a set of benchmark circuits. Various academic groups have used benchmark circuits to evaluate commercial FPGAs and suggest architectural improvements [Rose92] or to support novel architectural ideas [Walkup92].

SUMMARY: HOW TO CHOOSE AN FPGA

Let's assume that you have to select an FPGA for a new project and have received literature from about 20 possible contenders. Where do you go from here?

Stage 1. Elimination Trials

In this stage you should eliminate any architectures that cannot meet the following criteria (at this point you should believe manufacturers' claims since the objective is to weed out "no-hopers" before doing more detailed analysis).

1. Does the part appear to be reasonably priced?
2. Does the part have reasonable density and performance (PREP numbers)?
3. Has the part been in production for more than a year? If it hasn't been, then you probably won't be able to get one, and if you do, it could have unforeseen glitches.
4. Can you see at least ten realistic designs done using this architecture either in the manufacturer's literature or published elsewhere? If the part fails this criterion, then you should ignore any benchmark claims and reject it. Note that this point refers to the architecture: a new part based on an established architecture is worth considering.
5. Do you think the manufacturer will still be making them next year? This point refers both to large corporations that may leave the FPGA business or completely change their architecture by licensing another product, as well as to small start-ups that might go bankrupt.

Under exceptional circumstances (e.g., if only one supplier can offer a required feature) an architecture which fails here may go forward into the next round.

Stage 2. Comparative Evaluation

At this stage you should be left with at most five strong contenders, all of which are probably capable of doing the job. You should evaluate them based on the following criteria:

1. *Start-up Costs.* There are time and money costs associated with introducing a new FPGA. CAD software in particular is expensive, complex, and requires time to learn. Programmers, in-circuit emulators, and other development hardware also cost money. If you or someone within your organization has used a particular device before, are happy with it, and have the support technology on hand, then you should probably go with it.
2. *Generality.* It is usually worth choosing an FPGA that is more general-

purpose over a specialized one more suited to your application because the more general device could be used in other projects within your organization. This means you get more value for the time and money invested in getting started with the new device.

3. *Speed and Density for Your Application.* You should be able to estimate these elements using a pencil and paper. If you cannot do so, then this is a black mark against the architecture. Naturally, the technology must be able to meet your speed and density requirements. If your application cannot fit on a single chip, then you must evaluate how easy it is to split designs over multiple chips. If your design is relatively small, then you should evaluate the range of parts available to ensure that you can buy one that fits your application for a reasonable price (rather than just a large, high-priced part).

4. Can you see an example of the device being used successfully in a similar application to yours? If so, then this is a very good reason for going with the device.

5. *Board Level Costs.* You should evaluate the extra circuitry required at the board level (if any) to support the FPGA.

6. *Heat and Power.* With the exception of bipolar PAL devices, which can have extreme power requirements, heat and power requirements of programmable devices are moderate. However, a battery-based application might provide a strong reason for choosing one architecture over another.

7. *Manufacturing Costs.* You should evaluate any additional costs associated with manufacturing boards that use the FPGA (e.g., FPGA programming costs).

8. *Reliability.* You should ensure that the FPGA meets the reliability standards required by your application.

9. *Technological Leadership.* It is often worth choosing a device based solely on its technological leadership; this can translate to technological leadership for your product. Working with leading-edge technology is rewarding if you are prepared for and can afford the inevitable glitches.

PROBLEMS

These questions are intended to bring out real-world issues covered in the chapter. There are no right or wrong answers. The material in the body of the chapter should be helpful in tackling the questions, but your own background knowledge and experience is equally important. Some of the questions are included because the writer would like to know the answers!

1. Dynamic RAM technology offers considerable density improvements over the static RAM used in FPGAs. What are the main obstacles to its use in

this application and how can they be overcome? (*Hint:* Consider the refresh cycle, a background in VLSI design may be helpful.)

2. How well-suited are the following classes of logic block for implementation in a structured PAL: 16-bit adder, multiplier, address decoder, DMA request/acknowledge, and control logic? Where appropriate suggest an alternative, more effective implementation.

3. The following benchmark has been proposed for a comparative evaluation of the density afforded by various FPGA devices:

   (a) Identify product die size and technology.

   (b) Identify the largest and smallest macro that will fit in a single logic cell. Size is measured using a table of equivalent gates required to implement the macro in a gate array technology (e.g., XOR scores 3, 2-input AND scores 1). Average the result to yield the average gate count per logic cell.

   (c) Multiply the average gate count per cell by the number of cells per device.

   (d) Derate the result by a utilization factor based on the percentage of cells whose functions can be used after placement and routing of a set of benchmark circuits.

   Identify at least two critical failings of this methodology and comment on how it could be improved.

4. You have been approached by General Roman Pica, President of the island republic of Sans Serif (check a map of the Indian Ocean if you don't remember your geography), who has asked you to develop a spy satellite. You do not have access to ASIC technology, and because of functionality and board area requirements must use a commercial FPGA for critical circuits. You are likely to be assassinated if the system fails during its 10-year design lifespan. Which FPGA technology would you choose and why?

5. It has been suggested that a device consisting of a RISC microprocessor core surrounded by an FPGA would be very well-suited to embedded processor applications, such as laser printer controllers. The FPGA would provide a very flexible interface between the microprocessor and the print engine or other logic. Does this idea make sense? What should the interface be between the processor core and the FPGA? Are there any important disadvantages (device pin-out limitations?)

6. An obvious extension of FPGA architecture is to include analog functions within the pad ring to reduce chip count in mixed signal applications. Suggest suitable analog primitives for inclusion and outline methods of interfacing them to the digital core or the device. Is it possible to design such a device with a general enough analog section to be worth marketing?

7. Outline a procedure for determining the configuration of an EP1810 (or

more recent structured PAL) with its security fuse blown. Assume you have access to a well-equipped laboratory and a large number of devices to test. Suitable approaches might include applying vectors to the device or trying to reconfigure parts of the configuration store to eliminate the inputs from some product terms while mapping the effects of others. Would some opaque paint, a microscope, a steady hand, and a UV lamp come in handy?

8. Antifuse technology offers an advantage over fuse-based technology in channeled gate array architectures because only those devices corresponding to wires required by the user's circuit need to be programmed. Do antifuses offer the same benefits in PAL-type devices? Suggest reasons why there are no commercial antifuse-based PALs.

9. The Actel ACT1 module has three 2:1 multiplexers and a 2-input OR gate, with a total of nine inputs and one output. There are 547 modules in the A1020A part, which has 69 user input/output pins. How many should there be if Rent's formula applies, assuming an exponent of 0.5?

10. How would you provide a synchronizer circuit for an asynchronous input to a Xilinx XC3000 design?

11. Even a synchronizer may fail from time to time, if an input signal changes during its set-up and hold "window." Suggest a way of reducing the problem, even if it can't be totally eliminated.

12. Suggest three separate advantages of in-circuit reprogrammable FPGAs over fuse-programmable FPGAs.

13. Sketch the circuit for a 6-transistor static RAM cell. Assuming a minimum-size transistor has channel width and length of 2 micron and 1 micron, respectively, mark the width and length values for each transistor that is likely to give reliable operation.

14. The Actel ACT1 FPGA uses the circuit shown in Fig. 3–6. How would you implement the function $Y = A + B + C$?

BIBLIOGRAPHY

[Actel90]   Actel Corporation, *ACT Family Field Programmable Gate Array Data Book*, Actel Corporation, Sunnyvale, Calif., 1990.

[Algo91]   Algotronix Ltd., *Configurable Array Logic User Manual*, Algotronix Ltd., Edinburgh, UK, 1991.

[Altera87]   Altera Corporation, *ALTERA Data Book 1987*, Altera Corporation, Santa Clara, Calif., 1987.

[Baker90]   Baker, S., "Designers Want More from Next Generation of FPGAs," *Electronic Engineering Times*, pp. 45–46, 48, 53, September 17, 1990.

[Brown92]   Brown, S. D., Francis, R. J., Rose, J., Vranesic, Z. G., *Field-Programmable Gate Arrays*, Kluwer, 1992.

[Bursky91]   Bursky, D., *In-System Programmable Logic Keeps Delays Short*, Lattice Semiconductor Corporation, Hillsboro, 1991.

[Bursky92]   Bursky, D., "FPGA Advances Cut Delays, Add Flexibility," *Electronic Design*, pp. 35–43, October 1, 1992.

[Bursky92]   Bursky, D., "RAM-Based Logic Arrays Up Density, Cut Delays," *Electronic Design*, pp. 45–49, October 1, 1992.

[Byte87]   *BYTE*, Theme Issue On Programmable Hardware, January 1987.

[Carter86]   Carter, W., et al., "A User Programmable Reconfigurable Gate Array," paper presented at the IEEE 1986 Custom Integrated Circuits Conference.

[Chen82]   Chen, X., Hurst, S. L., "A Comparison of Universal-Logic-Module Realizations and Their Application in the Synthesis of Combinatorial and Sequential Logic Networks," *IEEE Transactions on Computers*, Vol. 31, No. 2, pp. 140–147, February 1982.

[Ebeling91]   Ebeling, C., Borriello, G., Hauck, S. A., Song, D., Walkup, E. A., "TRIPTYCH: A New FPGA Architecture," in *FPGAs*, pp. 75–90, (Moore, W., Luk, W., eds.) Abingdon EE & CS Books, Abingdon, England, 1991.

[El-Ayat88]   El-Ayat, K., et al., "A CMOS Electrically Configurable Gate Array," paper presented at the International Solid State Circuits Conference, San Francisco, Calif., 1988.

[Felton91]   Felton, B., Hastie, N., "Configuration Data Verification and the Integrity Checking of SRAM based FPGA's," *Proc. Oxford 1991 International Workshop on Field Programmable Logic and Applications Published as FPGA's*, (Moore, W., Luk, W. eds), Abingdon EE & CS Books, Abingdon, England, 1991.

[Glass85]   Glasser, L. A., Dobberpuhl, D. W., *The Design and Analysis of VLSI Circuits*, Addison-Wesley, 1985.

[Goering90]   Goering, R., "A Quiet Takeover in FPGA Synthesis," *Electronic Engineering Times*, p. 53, September 17, 1990.

[Gray89]   Gray, J. P., Kean, T. A., "Configurable Hardware: A New Paradigm for Computation," *Proc. Decennial Caltech Conference on VLSI*, Pasadena, Calif., March 1989.

[Guo92]   Guo, R., Nguyen, H., Srinivasan, A., Verheyen, H., Cai, H., Law, S., Mohsen, A., "A 1024 Pin Universal Interconnect Array With Routing Architecture," *Proc. IEEE 1992 Custom Integrated Circuits Conference*, pp. 4.5.1–4.5.4, 1992.

[Kean89]   Kean, T., *Configurable Logic: A Dynamically Programmable Cellular Architecture and its VLSI Implementation*, Ph.D. Thesis CST-62-89, University of Edinburgh, Dept. Computer Science, 1989.

[Mann77]   Manning, F. B., "An Approach to Highly Integrated Computer-Maintained Cellular Arrays," *IEEE Transactions on Computers*, Vol. C-26, No. 6, pp. 536–552, June 1977.

[Marple92]   Marple, D., "An MPGA-like FPGA," *IEEE Design & Test of Computers*, pp. 51–60, December 1992.

[Minn64]   Minnick, R. C., "Cutpoint Cellular Logic," *IEEE Transactions on Electronic Computers*, Vol. EC-13, pp. 685–698, December 1964.

[Minn67]   Minnick, R. C., "A Survey of Microcellular Research," *Journal of the ACM*, Vol. 14, No. 2, pp. 203–241, April 1967.

[MMI84]   Monolithic Memories Inc. *Programmable Logic Handbook*, Monolithic Memories Inc., Santa Clara, Calif., 1984.

[Mohsen88]   Mohsen, A., "Desktop-Configurable Channeled Gate Arrays," *VLSI Systems Design*, pp. 24–33, August 1988.

[Mohsen93]   Mohsen, A., "Programmable Interconnects Speed System Verification," in *Circuits and Devices*, pp. 37–42, IEEE Press, May 1993.

[Osann88]   Osann, B., Gamal, A. E., "Compare ASIC Capacities with Gate Array Benchmarks," *Electronic Design*, October 13, 1988.

[Pash89]   Pashley, R. D., Lai, S. K., "Flash Memories: The Best of Two Worlds," *IEEE Spectrum*, December 1989.

[Pless91]   GEC Plessey Semiconductors, *ERA60100 Electrically Reconfigurable Array Data Sheet*, GEC/Plessey, 1991.

[Prep93]   Programmable Electronics Performance Corporation, *PLD Benchmark Suite 1, Version 1.2*, 1993.

[QL91]   QuickLogic, *pASIC 1 Family, Very High Speed CMOS FPGA's Preliminary Data.*, QuickLogic Inc., Santa Clara, Calif., 1991.

[Rose92]   Rose, J., Tseng, B., Brown, S., "Using Architectural and CAD Interactions to Improve FPGA Routing Architectures," *Proc. First International ACM/SIGDA Workshop on FPGA's*, Berkeley, Calif., 1992.

[Savage76]   Savage, J. E., *The Complexity of Computing*, Wiley, 1976.

[Shoup70]   Shoup, R. G., *Programmable Cellular Logic Arrays*. Ph.D. Thesis, Computer Science Dept., Carnegie-Mellon University, March 1970.

[Trim94]   Trimberger, S. M., "Field-Programmable Gate Array Technology," Kluwer, 1994.

[Wahl67]   Wahlstrom, S. E., "Programmable Logic Arrays," *Electronics*, Vol. 40, No. 25, pp. 90–95, December 11, 1967.

[Walkup92]   Walkup, E., Huack, S., Borriello, G., Ebeling, C., "Routing Directed Placement for the TRIPTYCH FPGA," *Proc. First International ACM/SIGDA Workshop on FPGA's*, Berkeley, Calif., 1992.

[Wein91]   Weinmann, U., Kunzmann, A., Strohmeier, U., "Evaluation of FPGA Architectures," *Proc. Oxford 1991 International Workshop on Field Programmable Logic and Applications*, Published as *FPGA's*, (Moore, W., Luk, W. eds), Abingdon EE & CS Books, Abingdon, England, 1991.

[Weste93]   Weste, N., Eshraghian, K., *Principles of CMOS VLSI Design*, 2nd ed. Addison-Wesley, 1993.

[Xilinx92]   Xilinx Inc., *The Programmable Gate Array Data Book*, Xilinx Inc., San Jose, Calif., 1992.

CHAPTER 4

DESIGN PROCESS FLOWS AND SOFTWARE TOOLS

The purpose of this chapter is to:

- Describe the functionality of design tools, both generic and those appropriate to a field-programmable gate-array (FPGA)
- Describe some typical examples, from start to finish, of design process flows, using manufacturer-supplied cases. For simplicity only single-chip designs will be used at this stage. We include schematic-based, behavioral- and floorplan-based examples.

4.1 THE SOFTWARE TOOLBOX

Designing is a very exciting part of engineering. Leaving aside formal definitions, it is the phase of engineering where creativity and problem solving play the most important part. These activities allow explorations of design options by trial and error, engineering judgment, "guesstimation," analysis, measurement, simulation, breadboarding, and so forth. There is normally an overall strategy, however, to guide the transition from specification to implementation, as discussed in Chapter 1. What the engineer must do is flesh out a complete behavioral, structural, and physical description so that a design can be built and tested. With these often onerous tasks and informal procedures, we can expect tools to "get in the way" of designing. The purpose of this chapter is to be informative about the applicability of tools for FPGA design and suggest fairly loose design process flows. The treatment is based on taking a simple design example, the 7-segment display driver, through a behavioral and structural design process. This example is conceptually simple, but it is a nontrivial 4-input, 7-output function. It is also a standard transistor–transistor logic (TTL) catalog part, the TTL7446. This serves to emphasize alternatives in design process flows as well as highlighting the relevance, or irrelevance, of specific tools.

This treatment is in distinction to some more conventional approaches, mostly as found in manufacturers' literature, which often portray the design process as a sequential walk through a small number of design steps, yielding a perfect result every time.

Another source of confusion is the plethora of tools available today. This is because the electronic CAD industry has matured over the last 10 years into a number of sustainable businesses (see Chapter 7). The design bottlenecks of the mid-1970s have been eliminated by structured design techniques embodied in new tools and often the products of start-up companies. Today such companies are mature and concentrating on marketing their products. The noise level is rising, and it is important to be able to identify the functionality of a tool to assess its relevance to FPGA design. Table 4–1 enumerates tool types against design description and level of design abstraction.

As a starting point, let us examine the primary activities in designing. These may be termed design capture, design validation, and physical design. Figure 4–1 shows possible flows between activities as well as tools that can assist in the processes within activities. Note that the starting point for designing is the exis-

TABLE 4-1. Design Tool Space

Level of Design Abstraction	Tools for Design of		
	Structure	Behavior	Physical Layout
System, algorithm	HDL, schematic	HDL, functional simulator, synthesizer	Floor planner, partitioner, fitter
Processors, memories	HDL, schematic	HDL, functional simulator, synthesizer	Block generator
Registers, ALU	Schematic, HDL	HDL, logic simulator, synthesizer	Logic compiler, place and route
Logic	Schematic, HDL	Logic simulator, switch simulator, timing estimator, synthesizer	Place and route, block generator
Circuit	Schematic	Circuit simulator	Layout package

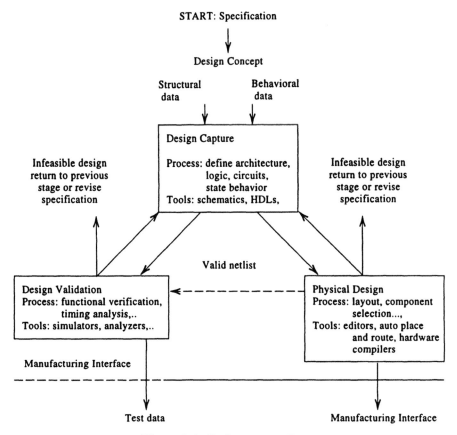

Figure 4-1. Design process flows.

tence of a specification and that the end point is the production of manufacturing data. Transitions in the flow are driven by design refinement, yielding acceptable or infeasible designs. Transitions to revise the specification are allowed.

Now in the case of FPGAs and our example, to get into the flow we need a specification. The specification of a 7-segment display driver is intuitively obvious, given a labeling scheme for the segments (see Figure 4-2) and no performance or electrical requirements. It could be, "drive the segments of the display to show the decimal digits 0–9 from their 4-bit binary representation as input." Well, how do tools in a contemporary toolbox help, given this simple specification? The following sections illustrate process steps.

4.1.1 Design Capture

All design capture tools provide functions for capturing design intent. They may capture structural intent, behavioral intent, or both. They may be graphi-

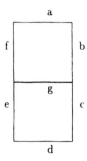

Figure 4–2. Labeling of 7-segment display.

cally based, for example, schematics, or language based, for example, hardware description language (HDL).

Behavioral Tools   Behavioral tools address the question "what do I want this circuit to do?" Since the behavior of a circuit is a mapping between a set of input states and a set of output states, dependent on internal state (for sequential circuits), then representations, such as truth tables, logic equations, and state descriptions, are particularly useful. Truth tables are a perfectly simple and universal behavioral description. The initial truth table for the display decoder is shown in Table 4–2. With the availability of programmable array logic (PALs),

TABLE 4–2. Truth Table for Display Driver

Input	a	b	c	d	e	f	g
0000	1	1	1	1	1	1	0
0001	0	1	1	0	0	0	0
0010	1	1	0	1	1	0	1
0011	1	1	1	1	0	0	1
0100	0	1	1	0	0	1	1
0101	1	0	1	1	0	1	1
0110	1	0	1	1	1	1	1
0111	1	1	1	0	0	0	0
1000	1	1	1	1	1	1	1
1001	1	1	1	1	0	1	1
1010	X	X	X	X	X	X	X
1011	X	X	X	X	X	X	X
1100	X	X	X	X	X	X	X
1101	X	X	X	X	X	X	X
1110	X	X	X	X	X	X	X
1111	X	X	X	X	X	X	X

several commercial behavioral HDL notations have emerged as de facto standards: ABEL, CUPL, PALASM. The PALASM2 form of the same design is shown in Figure 4–3. For the established PAL families there is even a standard file format for specifying fuse maps. In some cases these can be interpreted as truth tables, but they are really a physical description of features of a chip.

Synthesis   If behavioral tools only provided methods of describing circuit functions, then they would be at least useful in refining specifications, assuming the behavioral description could be animated. To take a first step to a real manufacturable entity, however, a set of elements with defined behaviors must be

```
TITLE   7SEG.PDS
AUTHOR     BART REYNOLDS AND THOMAS WAUGH
COMPANY XILINX
DATE    APRIL 8TH 1988
CHIP    7SEG PAL10H8
;Input Pins    1   2   3   4   5   6   7   8   9   10
               NC  NC  D0  D1  D2  D3  NC  NC  NC  NC
;Output Pins   11  12  13  14  15  16  17  18  19  20
               NC  NC  G   F   E   D   C   B   A   NC
;
;Input combinations
;
STRING ZERO        '/D3* /D2* /D1* /D0'
STRING ONE         '/D3* /D2* /D1*  D0'
STRING TWO         '/D3* /D2*  D1* /D0'
STRING THREE       '/D3* /D2*  D1*  D0'
STRING FOUR        '/D3*  D2* /D1* /D0'
STRING FIVE        '/D3*  D2* /D1*  D0'
STRING SIX         '/D3*  D2*  D1* /D0'
STRING SEVEN       '/D3*  D2*  D1*  D0'
STRING EIGHT       ' D3* /D2* /D1* /D0'
STRING NINE        ' D3* /D2* /D1*  D0'
STRING TEN         ' D3* /D2*  D1* /D0'
STRING ELEVEN      ' D3* /D2*  D1*  D0'
STRING TWELVE      ' D3*  D2* /D1* /D0'
STRING THIRTEEN    ' D3*  D2* /D1*  D0'
STRING FOURTEEN    ' D3*  D2*  D1* /D0'
STRING FIFTEEN     ' D3*  D2*  D1*  D0'
EQUATIONS
A = ZERO+TWO+THREE+FIVE+SIX+SEVEN
    +EIGHT+NINE+TEN+TWELVE+FOURTEEN
    +FIFTEEN
B = ZERO+ONE+TWO+THREE+FOUR+SEVEN
    +EIGHT+NINE+TEN+THIRTEEN
C = ZERO+ONE+THREE+FOUR+FIVE+SIX
    +SEVEN+EIGHT+NINE+TEN+ELEVEN+THIRTEEN
D = ZERO+TWO+THREE+FIVE+SIX
    +EIGHT+ELEVEN+TWELVE+THIRTEEN+FOURTEEN
E = ZERO+TWO+SIX+EIGHT+TEN+
    ELEVEN+TWELVE+THIRTEEN+FOURTEEN+FIFTEEN
F = ZERO+FOUR+FIVE+SIX+EIGHT+NINE
    +TEN+ELEVEN+TWELVE+FOURTEEN+FIFTEEN
G = TWO+THREE+FOUR+FIVE+SIX+EIGHT+NINE
    +TEN+ELEVEN+THIRTEEN+FOURTEEN+FIFTEEN
```

Figure 4-3. PALASM2 HDL for display driver. Figure courtesy of Xilinx Inc. ©Xilinx, Inc. 1989. All rights reserved.

hooked up to make a circuit. Now if the behavioral semantics of these elements are well understood, for example, in the case of logic gates, 2-level logic blocks like PLAs, then it is possible to transform a behavioral description into a structural composition of known parts. This is called *synthesis*. Trivial examples would include interpreting a logic diagram as a behavioral *and* structural design; mapping a set of logic equations into a PLA; decomposing an HDL into a set of register-transfer-level interconnected elements. *Optimization* is associated with synthesis and is applied to the automatic manipulation of logic equations to yield an optimal, in some sense, logic-level design. Today optimization and synthesis products are available from a range of companies.

Structural Tools   Structural tools address capturing the design statement, "I think this interconnection of units will exhibit the required behavior." This is the more traditional design metaphor, and it assumes the engineer is using knowledge of the behavior of units, experience, judgment, and so forth, in making a plausible design statement. Historically, this metaphor has always been supported by schematic tools. In the case of the display driver, a schematic is shown in Figure 4–4. This nonobvious design is structured across three levels of logic. The top level drawing uses a left-to-right signal flow convention.

Hardware Description Languages   In recent times HDLs like VHDL [Mazor93] and Verilog have emerged as alternative textual tools for design capture. Their present existence is based on work over a long period of time to discover how to exploit the power of programming notations in hardware design. In designs with repeated structures or conditional structures, there are obvious advantages in using HDL descriptions, assuming HDL compilers exist that can sensibly instantiate the design to a low-level netlist form.

This type of HDL, compared to the purely behavioral type, can be used for structural design and/or behavioral design. The most common use is as a structural design tool to allow more rapid generation of netlist data, that is, descriptions of interconnections of gate level elements. Figure 4–5 shows a VHDL description of the schematics.

4.1.2   Tools for Design Validation

Validation tools address the question "what will this (structural) design do and how fast will it do it?" A broad spectrum of simulator products, from circuit-level simulators, which solve the underlying differential equations by numerical methods, to *ad hoc* functional simulators in a high-level programming language, can be used. However, with the emergence of component families at medium-scale integration (MSI), large-scale integration (LSI), and very-large-scale integration (VLSI) levels, logic level simulators have become the key design validation tools. Since FPGAs by and large deliver gate level functions, logic level simulators are particularly relevant.

Logic simulators are good at answering the "what" question, at a cost in

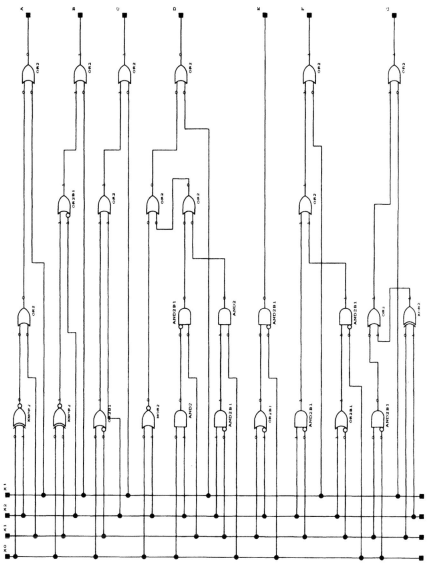

Figure 4-4. Display driver schematic.

STRUCTURE	BEHAVIOR
entity displaydriver is	entity displaydriver is
interface	generic list
port(x0 ,x1,.......:in boolean;	GENERIC(delay TIME: = 10ns)
a,b,c,d,e,f,g:out boolean);	port list
end displaydriver	PORT(signal x0:in boolean: ='0';
architecture STRUCTURAL of displaydriver is	...........:
body	.......x3:in boolean: ='0'
internal signals:	signal a: out boolean: ='0'
signal s1, s2,......	....
component declarations	....
component XNOR2	....
port (Q:outboolean;	....
A,B:outboolean);	g: out boolean: ='0');
end component;	END displaydriver
.	VARIABLE one, two, three,....
.	ARCHITECTURE behavior OF displaydriver IS
.	BEGIN
structural composition	a<=
XNOR2;port map(	b<=
.	c<=
.	d<=
.	e<=
.	f<=
end STRUCTURAL;	g<=
	END behavior

Figure 4-5. VHDL for display driver.

computer time. The "how fast" question has been addressed by simulation tools in which time delays are computed more accurately, such as by using *RC* circuit models in switch level simulators. These have proved essential tools in getting full custom VLSI designs to operate correctly the first time they are fabricated. Now with FPGAs the computation of wire path delays can be complicated because the paths are active in the sense that routing uses transistor switches and multiplexors. It is infeasible to compute the behavior of FPGAs at switch level. Delays through FPGA cells can, however, be modeled by a finite set of constants and path-delay computations built into timing estimators. Since the performance of a circuit is usually determined by a single critical path, estimator tools can replace timing analysis.

Our example is a purely combinational circuit, and the design can be validated by applying the ten legal input vectors and observing that the output vectors are consistent with Table 4–2.

FPGA technology raises some interesting questions on the relevance of validation tools. Simulation tools have only gained users in recent times due to rising complexity in systems design and difficulties in designing application-specific integrated circuits (ASICs). Before simulation, systems were built on breadboards with standard components and a rapid wiring technology (wrapping, Multiwire, etc). But FPGAs can be used as instantaneous breadboards and synthesis programs create valid designs algorithmically. The FPGA technology push is already creating more interest in design methodologies. One can predict that areas like design debugging will come under review now that equivalents to software debugging techniques are available in hardware.

4.1.3 Tools for Physical Design

Physical tools address the question "how do I make this (structural) design fit physical reality while meeting performance requirements?" All electronics technologies deliver finite spatial resources for building functions and communications (wires). Resources are especially tight with FPGAs, as the convenience of programmability is bought at the cost of chip area for control store.

Conceptually the simplest tool, and one that provides the essential handle on reality, is the *graphical editor.* For FPGAs it is most likely to be a *symbolic editor* since it is desirable to abstract away the underlying details of the silicon. The figures in this book mostly show symbolic artwork of two FPGA families.

The physical design process can be greatly assisted by automating the generation of random and regular logic. *Block generators* for regular structures such as read-only memories and programmable logic arrays are normally part of a software supplier's package. Generators can also be custom built by engineers using ordinary programming languages. For random logic, *placement-and-routing* routines can be used to build both random logic blocks and to assemble blocks at higher levels.

The total spatial demand of a design includes a component for function units and a component for wires. It is important to know early on if the spatial demand of a design can be met by the spatial capacity of a particular FPGA. *Estimator* and *fitter* programs assist in this task by computing function and wire demand for a particular design for comparison with members of a standard part family.

The result of running standard physical design software on the display driver example is shown later in Figure 4-13. It shows a logic cell array (LCA) implementation and two configurable array logic (CAL) implementations: one using a ROM generator and synthesis program and the other handcrafted logic. It exposes the eternal verity that humans can outperform algorithms, in this case by a factor of 2, provided the design is tractable and there is sufficient (human) design time.

It is likely the small example we have been using is only part of a bigger design. In fact it was taken from a VLSI class exercise in which the design specification is as given in Section 4.4. In this case a key physical design activity is *floor planning*, in which the gross disposition of units in the design and a wiring strategy for the design are defined. *Editors, generators, and place-and-route* programs can all assist the floor planning phase.

Precooked designs are also a useful source of tested designs with proven layouts. These are usually found in supplier- or user-distributed libraries [Newk83].

4.2 THE FPGA DESIGN DICHOTOMY

One of the interesting properties of FPGAs is that they merge what up until now have been two diverging families of electronic products: programmable logic devices, notably PALs, and ASICs, notably gate arrays and cell-based ICs. Each strand imposed a different implementation style on the engineer, each came with its preferred design process flow, and each came with its preferred toolset. The following sections set out to show explicitly how FPGAs can be designed either from an ASIC or PLD perspective.

Parenthetically, it is too simple to suggest that only two design methodologies and toolsets are important. In reality methodologies should be designed and toolsets chosen to match the end FPGA application. For example, one could classify the chief applications areas of programmable logic as: ASIC, ASIC emulation, and algorithm implementation/coprocessing, in which case the following observations would be relevant to method and toolset.

ASIC

Simple ASIC: A PAL design methodology that places emphasis on tools for capturing a behavioral description, optimizing logic equations and fitting the design to a member of a standard part catalog.

Complex ASIC: ASIC design places emphasis on both high-functionality tools for tasks like synthesis and automatic place-and-route, and low-level tools for complete design control and low-level optimization. More details are contained in the following sections.

ASIC Prototyping: The assumption here is that the real implementation is probably a gate array or cell-base IC (CBIC). So emphasis is in transforming a schematic to a netlist in the most painless way possible. Automatic tools for physical design are key. There is a desire for technology independence, but the preservation of gate-level equivalent circuits may be a better design goal.

Algorithm Implementation: Algorithm implementations usually exhibit some "natural" structure: cellular automata, systolic circuits, self-timed micropipelines, pipelined coprocessors, dedicated datapaths, and so forth.

Emphasis is on the very efficient design of a basic unit using low-level tools like symbolic editors and structure compilers.

4.3 DESIGN PROCESS FLOW: THE PROGRAMMABLE LOGIC DEVICE ROUTE

A typical programmable logic device (PLD) design process flow is shown in Figure 4–6. The starting *specification* might be informal and hand drafted in anything from an HDL to a collection of Boolean equations. *Design capture* moves the design into the CAD environment and requires the engineer to restate the creation for machine consumption. This might be preparing a file in a preferred notation or marking entries in a table. *Synthesis and optimization* uses algorithms to manipulate the logic design to improve it by exploiting don't care states to minimize the number of gates used. *Function verification* may be a unit-delay simulator to generate circuit outputs, or may amount to a manual inspection of truth table data. *Device fitting* matches logic/gate demand and input/output (I/O) demand to part family members. Finally, *physical design* produces manufacturing data, a binary stream, for programming specific devices. This must be achieved by generating a layout of the required circuit in the chosen FPGA cell and wire scheme. It may amount to running a simple logic block generator or it may be placing and routing random logic using manual and automatic software tools.

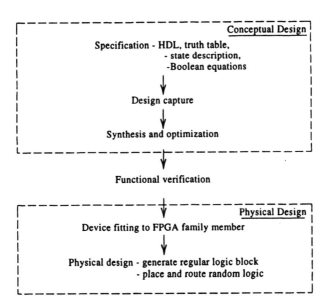

Figure 4-6. PLD design process flow.

4.3.1   Conceptual Design of Display Driver

In the case of a CAL design the specification is given in Table 4–2. The minimization of this table using ESPRESSO [Brayton84] is shown in Table 4–3. Now this is a standard sum-of-products form that we can expect to implement within an array of cells that allows a two-level logic structure to be built.

In the case of the LCA implementation, because there is no "natural" form for implementing a two-level logic structure, designs must be created as fully instantiated (flat) netlists. For the display driver design specified in the PALASM2 of Figure 4–3, a netlist must be optimized by proprietary tools to accommodate implementation in configurable logic blocks (CLBs) and the result merged with a top-level schematic to create the complete design.

4.3.2   Design Verification of Display Driver

In the case of the CAL design, since the logic was synthesized there is no formal verification step other than informal inspection of the truth tables.

In the case of the LCA design, the flat netlist of logic primitives can be exercised with a logic simulator. The result of this for a *test pattern* of the ten digits is shown in Figure 4–7. Readers can manually construct the digits from the output to confirm the correct functions are being computed.

4.3.3   Physical Design of Display Driver

In the case of the LCA implementation, the result of applying placement and routing algorithms to the merged netlist is shown in Figure 4-23.

In the case of the CAL implementation, physical design can be automatic, as in the synthesized ROM logic block of Figure 4–21, or physical design can be place and route (manual or automatic) from a suitable gate-level netlist. Using

TABLE 4–3. Minimized Segment Truth Table

Input	a	b	c	d	e	f	g
X0X0	0	0	0	0	1	0	0
X00X	0	1	1	0	0	0	0
X000	1	0	0	1	0	1	0
XX11	1	1	1	0	0	0	0
X100	0	1	1	0	0	1	1
X101	1	0	1	1	0	1	1
X01X	1	1	0	1	0	0	1
X110	1	0	1	1	1	1	1
1XXX	1	0	0	1	0	1	1

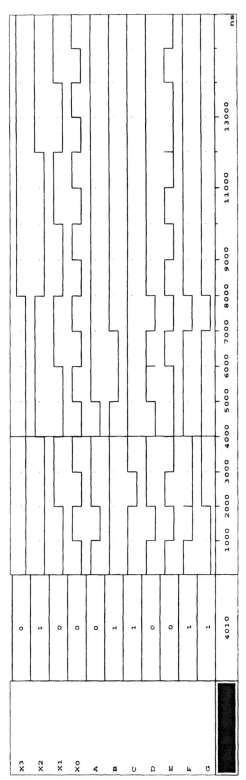

Figure 4-7. Result of simulating display driver.

115

the gate-level schematic of Figure 4–4 yields the manual design shown in Figure 4–22. The synthesized ROM is further described in Section 4.5.1. It is interesting to compare the quality of the logic synthesis with that of a manual implementation generated with software design tools. The configurable logic ROM implementation requires an 11 (4 inputs plus 7 outputs)-by-8 (product terms) array of cells compared with an 11-by-4 array when implemented by hand. The following points are worth noting:

1. *Flexibility.* The greatest advantage of the human-generated implementation is the way the layout of the logic unit has been optimized to fit in with the chip pin-out requirements and the counter design. Although there is a structure to the layout (note that input variables are routed horizontally across the array and outputs are collected using vertical wires), it is specific to this particular example.

2. *Variable Ordering.* In the automatically-generated array the order of the input variables in the cascade of gates is fixed. Only the function performed by gates in the cascade can be changed. The human implementation achieves a much better factorization of the logic equations by changing the order of variables in the gate cascades and using trees rather than simple cascades of gates. This can only be achieved by having a special routing plan for each function implemented.

3. *Design Time.* Although the automatic implementation is much less efficient, it only took about 10 minutes. The human-generated implementation took several days.

4. *Design Size.* This example approaches the limit of the size of circuit which may be designed efficiently by a person, and at this level of complexity, human design may surpass automatic design. But for the most part circuit optimization can be left to algorithmic methods.

4.4 DESIGN PROCESS FLOW: THE APPLICATION-SPECIFIC INTEGRATED CIRCUIT ROUTE

There are many sources of ASIC design process flows. VLSI design methodologies [Mead80], [Weste93] and ASIC manufacturers [Naish88] are good sources. The former place greater emphasis on layout issues, such as wiring management, to achieve optimal physical designs, while the latter largely rely on structural design to manage the whole process flow. A generic model for ASIC process flow is shown in Figure 4–8. Both the Gajski–Kuhn and more traditional forms are shown. This indicates the refinement of a *specification* to a *structural design* before entering design validation and physical design processes. In reality the behavioral and structural descriptions are built by stepwise refinement of the design. A typical ASIC design process flow, represented by paths in the Gajski–Kuhn diagram, shows the three design descriptions being built and

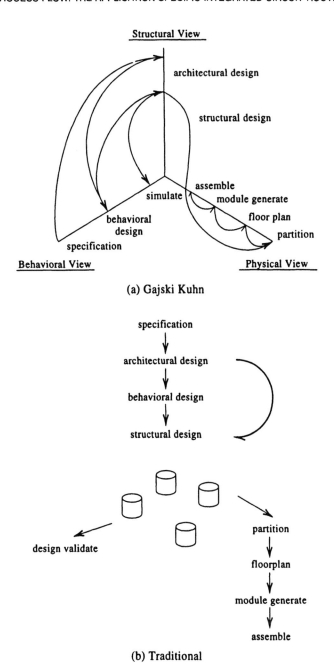

(a) Gajski Kuhn

(b) Traditional

Figure 4-8. ASIC design process flow.

the grain of the design unit decreasing. Thus a starting behavioral *specification* posits a *structural* design. This could be a composition of interconnected function units. This, in turn, could be stepwise refined by expanding to a structural design of simple elements, a gate-level netlist, or synthesizing a two-level logic block.

To illustrate the flow let us return to the display driver example. In fact, the 7-segment display driver was part of a larger timer design exercise for a VLSI course. It had the specification: Design a simple stopwatch to count in tenths of a second to one minute and display the current time on three 7-segment displays (tenths, seconds, and tens of seconds). The watch is controlled by three signals: INIT clears the watch and puts it in the "stop" state, SS start/stop is a high-going edge to start the watch from the stop state (a high-going edge in the start state puts the watch in the stop state), CLOCK, a 10-Hz signal.

4.4.1   Conceptual Design of Stopwatch

The 7-segment decoders provide a good example of "random" combinational logic, while the counters provide a good example of classic sequential logic. This design uses three separate units for the three displays although the design complexity and area could be reduced by implementing it as a single-state machine with multiplexed displays (since the large 7-segment decoder logic would not need to be duplicated). This is necessary to comply with the design specification given.

The Counter   The counter is built from four toggle flip-flops (Figure 4–9). The basic 4-bit ripple counter is converted to a decade counter by a gate that sets the clear line when the counter gets to ten. The output of this gate is also used as the clock for the succeeding counter. The counter can also be cleared by the user's INIT signal. Providing the clear capability is the only real problem

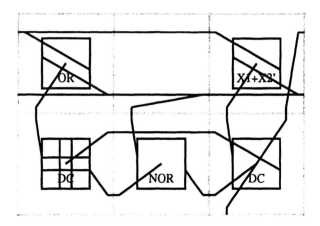

Figure 4-9. Toggle flip-flop design.

in the design of the toggle flip-flop (the basic D latches have only clock and D inputs). The clear is provided by extra logic gates that force 0s onto the D inputs and 1s onto the clock inputs. A basic master–slave flip-flop can be built with only two D latch cells, whereas this clearable implementation requires six cells. The layout is shown in Figure 4–10.

The Decoder   The decoder takes advantage of the ability to produce any function of two Boolean variables within one cell and uses three levels of logic rather than the two-level logic normally used to implement such functions. Its schematic description is given in Figure 4–4 and physical design in Figure 4–22 later.

The Control Logic   The controller function (at the bottom left of Figure 4–11) is implemented using a toggle flip-flop. The design is the same as those within the counters. The toggle flip-flop is clocked by the start-stop input and its output determines whether the counter should be stopped or run freely. The initialize signal clears the control flip-flop and stops the counter. The counters are stopped by ANDing the 10-Hz clock with the output of the control flipflop:

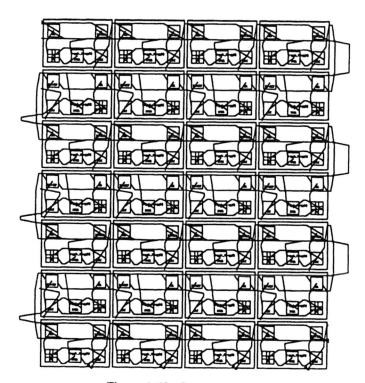

Figure 4–10. Counter design.

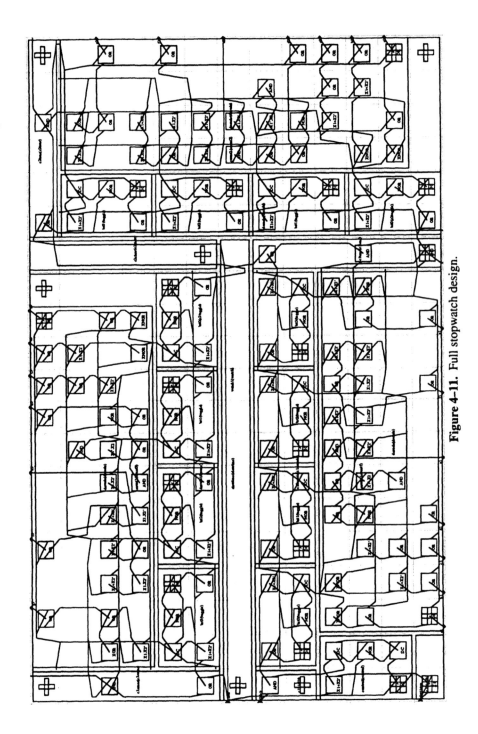

Figure 4–11. Full stopwatch design.

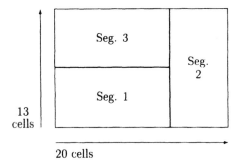

Figure 4-12. Stopwatch floorplan.

thus when the output of the control flipflop is 0, the counters clock inputs are held low, and when it is 1 the counters receive the 10-Hz clock input.

4.4.2 Design Verification of Stopwatch

See Problem 3.

4.4.3 Physical Design of Stopwatch

The floorplan of the full watch circuit is given below as Figure 4-12 and the layout in Figure 4-11. The floorplan is based on using three sides of the design to make connections to each of the displays accessible and the fourth side to get the control signals into the chip. Note that the floorplan requires simple transformations, rotations, and mirroring of the basic unit.

4.5 LIBRARIES AND DESIGN IDIOMS

In a sense design is idiomatic. Engineers can express designs in modes particular to a set of components at a specific level of design abstraction, for example, register transfer elements, or components particular to an implementation style for example, small-scale integration (SSI), MSI, and LSI TTL [TTL88]. If one adopts a bottom-up view of the world, then large designs are viewed as made up from aggregations of elementary components, usually gates. Since electronic logic by and large evolved from TTL elements, designs are perceived as compositions of TTL primitives. History has created a data base of collective design experience. This data base may be mined to create new designs from old experience, provided a set of primitive components exists in the new implementation style. This view has led the ASIC vendors to reproduce TTL libraries for customers' use in designing (see Table 4-4). Alternatively, if one adopts a top-down view of the world, large designs are composed from generic

TABLE 4-4. Fragment of an ASIC Library

Class	Element	Conventional Example (TTL)	Parameterizations
Combinational	NAND	00, 01, 10, 11, 12, 20, 22, 30	Number of inputs
functions	NOR	02, 27	Number of inputs
	NOT	04	Number of inputs
	XOR	86	Number of inputs
Storage	D flip-flop	74, 175	
functions	Latch	75	
	JK flip-flop	76	
	Shift register	91, 99, 164, 178	Length
	Register	173	Length
	Register file	170, 172	Breadth, depth
	ROM		Breadth, depth
	RAM		Breadth, depth
Information	Selector	150, 154	Size operands
switches	Multiplexer	298	Size operands
Data	Adder	84	Size operands
operator	Counter	160, 168	Length
	ALU		Size operands
	Decoder	46	

high-level elements, such as counters, ALUs, and register files, whose specific features are defined in the design refinement process. This view of designing has led the ASIC suppliers to provide parameterized register-transfer (RT) and processor-memory switch (PMS) level component libraries, Table 4-4.

These hard and soft libraries are equally valid ways of collecting design experience and making it available to practicing engineers in tried and tested forms. Hard libraries try to maintain historical certainty in the encapsulation and functions of their elements. In a sense, they are fossilized design fragments that may limit the optimality of complete designs. Soft libraries can provide "made to measure" components for optimal designs at the expense of variations in performance for particular instantiations.

4.5.1 Parameterized Libraries

It is often very useful to think of library components as elements "sized" to a set of parameters: an n input gate, an n word by m bit stack, and so forth. In building a circuit the parameters are replaced by integer constants to suit the application. A simple way of satisfying this requirement would be to fill a library with all useful instantiations of a parameterized module and select a particular one by indexing from the parameter. This approach allows for more precise characterization of library elements at the expense of more storage. An alternative approach is to use the parameters in a program to *generate* the precise instance required. Two examples of this approach are described in the following subsections.

Parameterized Modules   The requirement is to build a count "up-to-n" circuit. A generic counter and comparator, and constant generator, could be used to fit the requirement. The alternative approach would be to compose a counter from stages, each of which could test for a 0 or 1 depending on the position of these binary digits in the constant. By adding comparator gates, see Figure 4–13, to a basic toggle register we have the elements for building a count up-to-n circuit. The power of a programming language can be harnessed to assemble such a part. We need to build a vector of counter stages, each of which is conditionally defined. The iteration and conditional selection features of a programming language are well-suited to this task, provided there is a library of routines for describing and instantiating cells. The fragment of C code shown in Figure 4–14 shows this for assembling the "onestage" and "zerostage" of Figure 4–13. With $upto = 5$, the count-to-five circuit of Figure 4–15 would be generated.

Block Generators: The Configurable Logic ROM Generator   With cellular FPGAs there is likely to be a simple way of implementing a two-level structure. In the case of CAL it is a configurable logic ROM. We will describe how it works by first discussing a simpler but less efficient scheme.

Simplified Version   This version consists of an n-bit decoder, an "AND" plane, producing 2^{n-1} minterms feeding a special "OR" plane which uses two gate functions. As shown in Figure 4–16, the Algotronix CAL cell has four inputs, one per side. Any two can be selected as X1, X2 for the evaluation of an arbitrary Boolean function. The simplified CAL-ROM layout is shown in Figure 4–17. If the row is selected, the cell function depends on whether we require 0 or 1 output for this particular bit. On the other hand, if the row is not selected, we simply pass through the input received from the cell below, to take care of the case where the selected row is below. If the selected row is above, the output of this cell is of no consequence. Figure 4–18 gives the CAL cell configurations.

Compact Version   The height of the array can be cut in half, and the decoder width reduced by one cell. The last input variable is introduced at the bottom of each OR-plane column, as shown in Figure 4–19, and each cell in the OR-plane computes a function of this variable and one of the minterms. If the row is selected, the input from below must be A0. If the row is not selected, it may either be below or above the selected row. In either case, it simply passes on the input received from below—either A0 or the output of the selected row. The cell function chosen depends on the value desired for A0 = 0 and A0 = 1, as

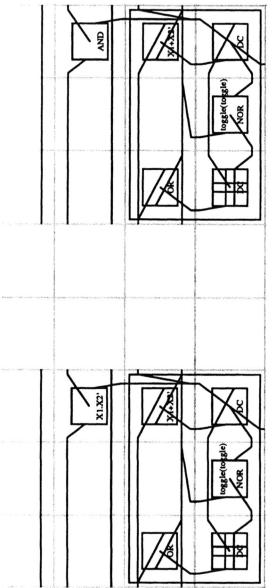

Figure 4-13. Stages for count-to-*n* circuit.

```
new_cell(FIXED,''U3'',0,1,c);

n=0;

x=1;y=0;

for (i=upto;i!=1;i=(i>>1}}
    {
        sprintf(str,''CNT%d'',n);
        if (i&1)
            {
                new_instance(''onestage_sch'',str,FIXED,x,y,TR_NULL);
            }
        else
            {
                new_instance(''zerstage_sch'',str,FIXED,x,y,TR_NULL);
            }
        n=n+1;
        x=x+3;
    }
```

Figure 4-14. CAL operation.

shown in Table 4-5 and Figure 4-20. The program *lisa* automatically generates this arrangement for a multiple-output function given an arbitrary truth table.

Figure 4–21 shows the resulting layout of the CAL cell array, in which the 4 inputs appear at the lower left hand edge, q3, q2, q1, q0 and the outputs a, b, ... , g at the upper edge. Figure 4–22 is a manually-composed alternative, with the inputs at the left and outputs at the right. Figure 4–23 is a layout for a Xilinx XC3020 design using the logic schematic given in Figure 4–4 as input.

Silicon Compilation   The examples in this section of parameterized modules and generated blocks have shown physical synthesis from high level descriptions. The term "silicon compilation" [Gray79], has been applied to this process. In the case of the counter modules, the start point was a number of schematics for count cells, and a C program was designed to compose the cells to form the function. Because the start point for this process was a structural description, the C program and (software) library functions represent a *structure compiler*.

In the case of ROM block generator, the start point was a truth table, so the process was *behavior compilation* and the synthesis software represents a *behavior compiler*.

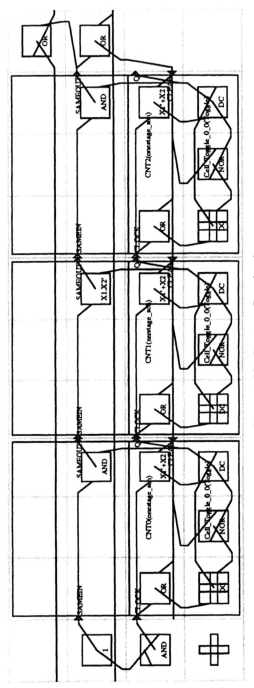

Figure 4-15. Count-to-five circuit.

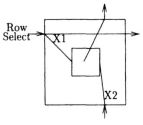

From cell below

Figure 4-16. CAL cell. Note: the output is a function of the West (×1) and South (×2) inputs.

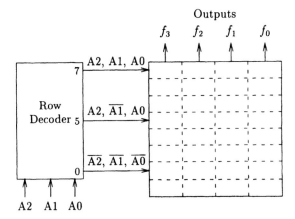

Figure 4-17. Simplified CAL–ROM layout.

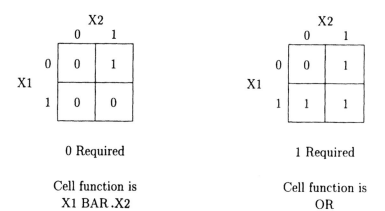

0 Required

1 Required

Cell function is
X1 BAR .X2

Cell function is
OR

Figure 4-18. CAL cell configuration.

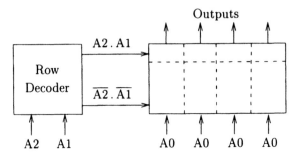

Figure 4–19. Compact CAL–ROM layout.

TABLE 4–5. ROM Truth Table

Product (X_1)	Input (X_2)	Output (F)
0	0	0
0	1	1
1	0	$f(x_0,\ldots,x_{n-1},0)$
1	1	$f(x_0,\ldots,x_{n-1},1)$

		X2			X2			X2			X2	
		0	1		0	1		0	1		0	1
Row Selected	0	0	1		0	1		0	1		0	1
X1												
Row Selected	1	0	0		1	0		0	1		1	1

$$X1BAR.X2 \qquad X1 \oplus X2 \qquad X2 \qquad X1 + X2$$

f(A2,A1,0)	= 0	= 1	= 0	= 1
f(A2,A1,1)	= 0	= 0	= 1	= 1

Figure 4–20. CAL cell options.

Both examples show the power of silicon compilation techniques in generating substantial design fragments quickly and with guaranteed structural integrity.

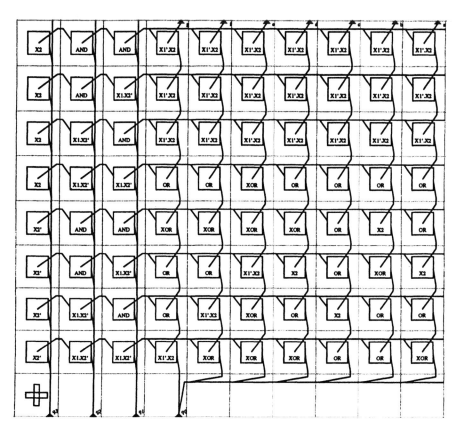

Figure 4–21. Physical designs for the display driver: ROM-based CAL design.

4.6 PLACEMENT, ROUTING, AND WIREABILITY

An eternal requirement in CAD tool provision is for automatic place and route, preferably with 100% guaranteed success and with a short run time. Unfortunately, placement and routing takes place within the context of a real design and physical reality imposed by one or more FPGAs, the implementation medium. Any design contains a demand for wires with its point-to-point connections

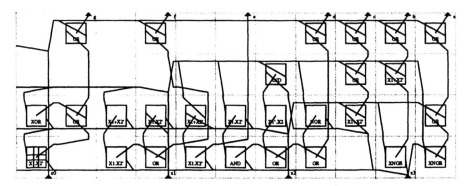

Figure 4–22. Physical designs for the display driver: manual CAL design.

and bus structures. Since the FPGA contains a finite number of wires, all FPGA architectures have a defined wiring capacity. When there are gross discrepancies between the wiring demand of a particular design and the wiring capacity of the target FPGA, it is likely to be difficult to discover an implementation by any method including advanced placement and routing algorithms. It is worth trying to understand the relationship between wiring capacity and demand so that better engineering decisions can be made about the suitability of a particular FPGA for a particular design.

4.6.1 Rent's Rule and Package Pin-outs

Rent's rule was originally "discovered" from examining packages of logic modules [Russo71]. It attempts to answer the question, "How many connections (n) are required to a structure holding a number of components (N) each of which has a number of connections (m)?" (see Figure 4–24). The relationship can be stated as $n \approx m * N^{(1-p)}$, where p is Rent's coefficient (≈ 0.5). It has an intuitive explanation if one imagines a square array of components on a board. Cutting the board in half, creating two edge connectors, would expose $m\sqrt{N}$ wires. The rule can be applied as a "sanity check" on components that deliver random logic, like FPGAs, which are made of N logic cells with m pins contained in packages of n pins. To make the most use of an FPGA while implementing random logic, the ratio of user I/O package pins to connections to the logic cell should be according to Rent. This exercise is left to the reader to be applied to the commercial offerings at any point.

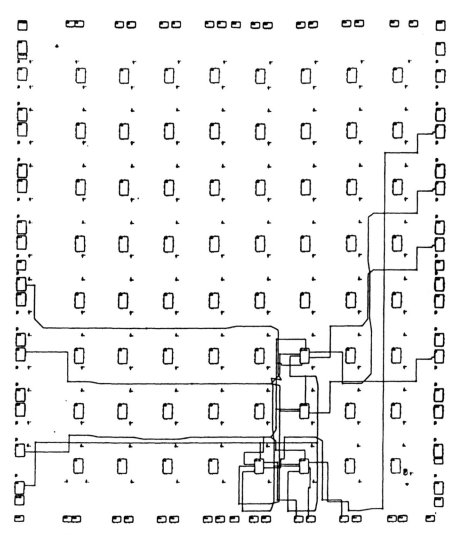

Figure 4-23. Physical designs for the display driver: LCA design.

4.6.2   Rent's Rule and Wireability

Heller et al. [Heller78] were the first to attempt an analysis of wiring demand, in this case for logic designs in the context of gate array "images." They addressed questions such as: What characterizes useful gate array architectures? How big should wiring channels be? What is the average interconnection length of wires? What is the distribution and number of interconnections?

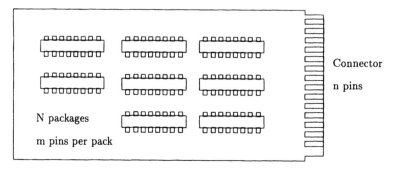

Figure 4-24. Two levels of physical hierarchy.

Simple one- and two-dimensional models (see Figure 4–25) can be used. This shows three terminal logic elements communicating with a wiring channel of fixed capacity (the capacity in the two-dimensional case is the sum of the horizontal and vertical wiring channels). By using Rent's rule to compute average wire length and making an assumption on the distribution of wires, it is possible to estimate a channel capacity that will allow the interconnection of a given number of logic elements. This is shown in Figure 4–26. It shows that even for relatively low gate counts, the ideal channel capacity is high, but as the gate count grows logarithmically, the channel capacity grows linearly. The analysis also covers variation for m terminal logic elements. The result indicates that to help the wireability of a design, the FPGA architecture, or structures built from it in the case of channelless arrays, should support channel capacities corresponding to gate count as in Figure 4–26.

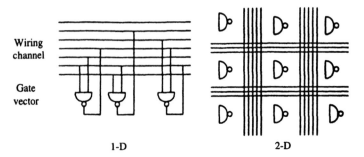

Figure 4-25. Idealized wiring models.

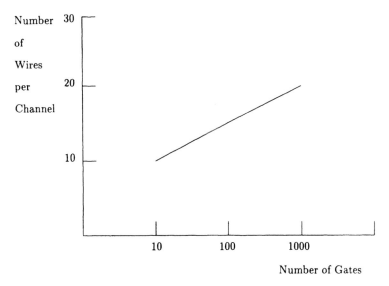

Figure 4-26. Variation in wire demand with gate count.

4.6.3 Partitioning Designs within and across Chips

Partitioning is important in three areas:

- Partitioning the resources within a single FPGA to support multiple designs

- Partitioning a design into subsystems for placement onto regions of an FPGA
- Partitioning a very large design across more than a single FPGA part

An example of the first case is shown in Figure 4–27. In this case, each of the subsystems is self-contained and can be designed in isolation. There are at least two important design decisions: can the subsystems be fitted onto the chip? and does the pin-out make sense at the board level? It is likely that there is more than one choice of implementation of each subsystem, and that in the *parcel packing* problem, in laying out the chip, the modules may have alternative shapes. This degree of freedom can be important in making feasible designs. The second question can only be answered in the context of the board design and involves matching the wire demand of the chip pin-out to the wire capacity of the board (defined from the copper dimension design rules and number of interconnect layers).

In the second case the need for partitioning comes from a requirement to divide a large design into subunits for implementation, the traditional divide and conquer approach to engineering problems.

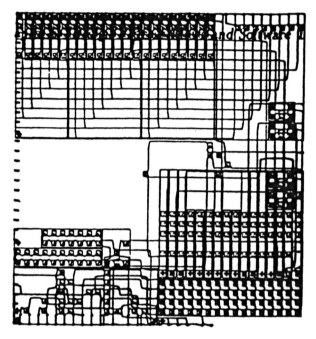

Figure 4-27. Multiple designs on a chip.

PROBLEMS

1. Find a simulator and simulate the display driver design from the logic.

2. Verify Table 4-2 as a correct behavioral description.

3. Verify the same logic block by developing expressions for the outputs evaluating these expressions for the ten binary constant inputs.

4. Simulate the whole design of the stopwatch.

5. Comment on the overpinning or underpinning of some commercial FPGA parts.

6. Describe a wiring strategy for building random logic within a cellular FPGA consistent with wireability rules.

BIBLIOGRAPHY

[Arnold91]   Arnold, W., "VHDL makes bid for FPGA designs," *EDN*, August 8, 1991.

[Brayton84]   Brayton, R. K., Hachtel, G. D., McMullen, C. T., Sangiovanni-Vincentelli, A., *Logic Minimization Algorithms for VLSI Synthesis*, Kluwer, 1984.

[Bursky92]   Bursky, D., "Module Library Seeks Consistency in FPGA Design," *Electronic Design*, pp. 31–33, October 1, 1992.

[Egan91]   Egan, B. T., "Device-independent Layout Toolset for FPGAs," *Computer Design*, p. 117, December 1991.

[Francis91]   Francis, R., Rose, J., Vranesic, Z., "Chortle-crf: Fast Technology Mapping for Lookup Table-Based FPGAs," *Proc. 28th ACM/IEEE Design Automation Conference*, Association for Computing Machinery, pp. 221–233, 1991.

[Gajski88]   Gajski, D. D., *Silicon Compilation*, Addison-Wesley, 1988.

[Gray79]   Gray, J. P., "Introduction to Silicon Compilation," *Proc. 16th Design Automation Conference*, pp. 305–306, June 1979.

[Heller78]   Heller, W. R., Michail, W. F., Donath, W. E., "Prediction of Wiring Space Requirements for LSI," *Journal of Design Automation and Fault Tolerant Computing*, Vol. 2, No. 2, pp. 47–144, 1978.

[Mazor93]   Mazor, S., *A Guide to VHDL*, 2nd ed., Kluwer, 1993.

[Mead80]   Mead, C. A., Conway, L., *Introduction to VLSI Design*, Addison-Wesley, 1980.

[Naish88]   Naish, P., Bishop, P., *Designing ASICs*, Wiley, 1988.

[Newk83]   Newkirk and Mathews, *The VLSI Designer's Library*, Addison-Wesley, 1983.

[Russo71]   Landman, B. S., Russo, R. L., "On a Pin Versus Block Relationship for Partitions of Logic Graphs," *IEEE Transactions on Computers*, Vol. C-20, p. 1469, 1971.

[Small91]   Small, C. H., "FPGA Design Methods," *EDN*, pp. 114–122, August 5, 1991.

[TTL88]   *The TTL Logic Data Book*, Texas Instruments, 1988.

[Weber90]   Weber, S., "Here's a Synthesizer that Supports VHDL," *Electronics*, April 1990.

[Weste93]   Weste, N., Eshragian, K., *Principles of CMOS VLSI Design*, Addison-Wesley, 1993.

CHAPTER 5

CASE STUDIES

The purpose of this chapter is to:

- Illustrate the stages in transforming a problem definition into a working solution

- Provide illustrations of typical design tools

- Show the usefulness of hierarchy

We have deliberately chosen elementary examples, which for the most part only use a small portion of a field-programmable gate array (FPGA) chip, apart from the final example of the videostore controller. The problems have been carried out with Xilinx and Algotronix FPGAs, using CAD tools obtained from these companies and ViewLogic Inc. Since CAD software is regularly improved, and command sequences change, any detailed information on particular CAD tools would probably be out of date by the time this book is published. We recommend that you obtain the latest editions of data books, user guides, and so forth, from the companies or their local distributors. At the end of the chapter there are suggestions for projects you might like to try for yourself.

The Xilinx examples have been developed for a generally available demonstration board, which is shown in Figure 5-1. It has eight switches for input, eight individual light-emitting diode (LED) displays for output, and a 7-segment numerical LED display. Some of the examples have been devised to fit this restricted set of circumstances.

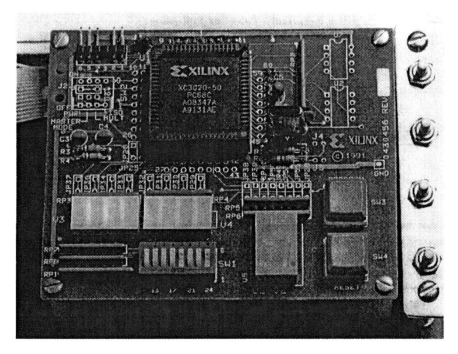

Figure 5-1. Xilinx demonstration board. Photograph courtesy of Xilinx, Inc. © Xilinx, Inc. 1991. All rights reserved. (Photograph by P. Crockett)

5.1 COMBINATIONAL CIRCUITS

5.1.1 Parallel Adder Cell

The simplest form of parallel adder is a *ripple adder*, which consists of a cascade of 1-bit full adder cells. Each cell has inputs A, B along with carry input C. It produces outputs SUM and CARRY, determined by the Boolean equations for a full adder, corresponding to the truth table shown in Table 5-1.

$$SUM = A.\overline{B}.\overline{C} + \overline{A}.B.\overline{C} + \overline{A}.\overline{B}.C + A.B.C$$

$$CARRY = A.B + A.C + B.C$$

Xilinx Implementation   The equations may be entered directly as the F and G outputs of a Xilinx 3000 series Configurable Logic Block (CLB), since each output can be an arbitrary function of up to four variables chosen from a total of five inputs. Since the functions are implemented by look-up tables, there is no advantage in manipulating the equations further. For such a simple case it is easy to enter the details directly on the CLB array with the editor *XACT*. Figure 5-2 shows the block concerned, while Figure 5-3 shows the routing to

TABLE 5-1. Truth Table for Full Adder

C	A	B	SUM	CARRY
0	0	0	0	0
0	0	1	1	0
0	1	0	1	0
0	1	1	0	1
1	0	0	1	0
1	0	1	0	1
1	1	0	0	1
1	1	1	1	1

input and output pads. The routing was determined by *XACT* after each net had been given as a list of pins. The configuration of each input or output block can also be specified with *XACT*, in this case direct inputs and outputs. The design details were saved to a file to be used as input in generating a configuration bit-stream file for downloading to the chip itself.

Alternatively, a schematic diagram for the adder may be entered as a logic circuit, as shown in Figure 5–4, which was prepared with the editor *ViewDraw*. This was used to generate a netlist, that is, a file specifying the logic elements used and how they are interconnected. The netlist can be used for functional simulation with a simulator such as *ViewSim*, as shown in Figure 5–5. Since the design has not at this stage been mapped to an actual FPGA, this is only a functional simulation, and there is no useful timing information. Translation to an actual Xilinx configuration will be deferred until we have a more substantial example.

Algotronix Implementation   Since the configurable array logic (CAL) block functions have two inputs, the equations need to be reexpressed:

$$SUM = (A \oplus B) \oplus C$$

$$CARRY = (A.B) + ((A + B).C)$$

The 1-bit adder can be laid out in a block of 3×3 CAL cells as shown in Figure 5–6. The graphical editor *clare* was used for this purpose, and allows the user to specify the function of each cell and routing to and through it. The lower left cell holds the datum for the block. Note that the cell is arranged so it can be cascaded vertically, with the least-significant bit at the bottom.

5.1.2   Parallel Adder

We can assemble a ripple-carry adder by simply cascading the full adder. We use a 4-bit example.

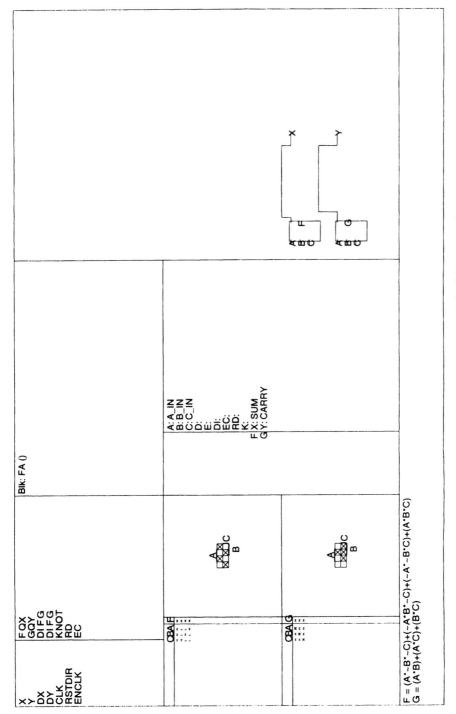

Figure 5-2. Configurable Logic Block for full adder cell.

139

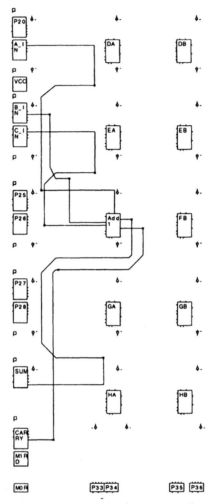

Figure 5-3. CLB array for full adder cell (*XACT*).

Xilinx Implementation Figure 5-7 shows a schematic prepared with the schematic capture program *ViewDraw*. There are four instances of the full adder cell referred to in Section 5.1.1. To use it with the demonstration board, we need a top-level schematic, which is shown in Figure 5-8. This shows the specific input and output pads, which are connected to the dual-in-line switches and LEDs, respectively. Again, the design may be simulated at this stage, that is, at a functional level, and Figure 5-9 shows results of applying a set of input vectors VA, VB resulting in the output vector VSUM. The process of converting the design into an FPGA implementation requires the following steps:

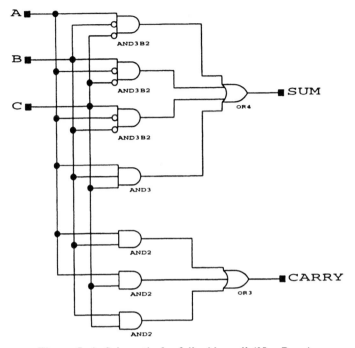

Figure 5-4. Schematic for full adder cell (*ViewDraw*).

- Derive a netlist from the schematic editor. This specifies the circuit in logic detail, still in terms of idealized elements.

- Map the logic circuit to the particular technology of the Xilinx 3000 series CLBs, and input/output blocks (IOBs). This is a complex process, since each CLB can generate two output signals, and the aim is to reduce the total number of CLBs required. At the same time, some simplifications can be made, for example, redundant logic can be removed.

- Placement, which starts from a random assignment of CLBs to positions in the logic array. For this design, the IOB positions are predetermined by the demonstration board. The initial placement is evaluated in terms of estimated wire length, based on the connection points of each net. The placement is improved with an iterative process known as *simulated annealing*, which moves CLBs to reduce the estimated wire length.

- Routing. Each net is connected according to the netlist, and uses the variety of available routing resources: direct connections from a CLB to its immediate neighbor, connections via switch-matrices, and long horizontal or vertical connections. This process results in a file containing details of the placement and routing.

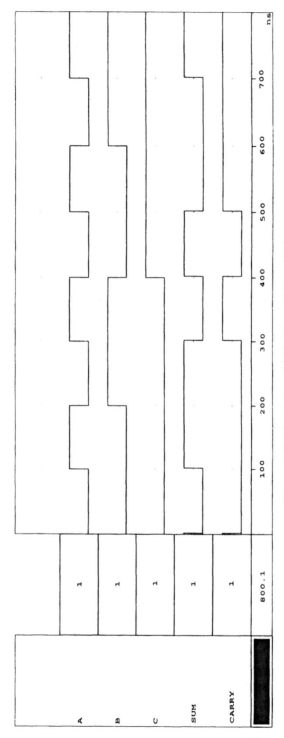

Figure 5-5. Simulation of full adder cell (*ViewSim*).

142

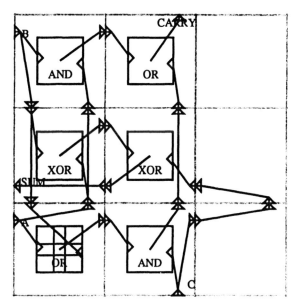

Figure 5-6. Configurable array logic for full adder.

- Bit-stream generation. The bit stream specifies the "program" for the FPGA, that is, the memory bits which control the function and internal connections of each CLB, the settings of all interconnect switches, and the mode of operation of each IOB.

The bit stream can be downloaded to the demonstration board, and the design checked with switches and lights. Later we will discuss a more systematic way of testing using random patterns.

Algotronix Implementation   The graphical editor *clare* was used to create four instances, as shown in Figure 5–10. Note that the cells cascade by abutment. The design was placed on the Algotronix CHS2×4 board described in Chapter 6, and was positioned in the northwest corner so that signals could be applied and monitored easily.

5.2 SEQUENTIAL CIRCUITS

5.2.1 Decade Counter

This design was implemented for a Xilinx 3020 FPGA with the aid of the *View-Draw* schematic entry program, the *ViewSim* simulator, and Xilinx software for CLB mapping, placement, routing, and so on. The design illustrates alternative

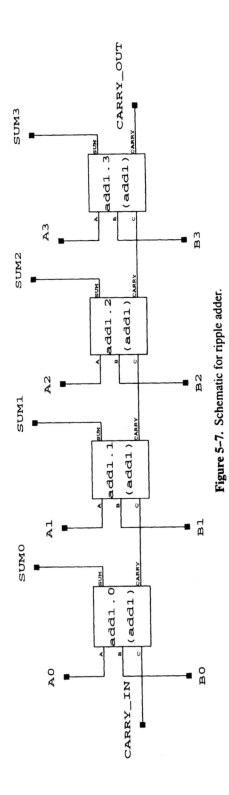

Figure 5-7. Schematic for ripple adder.

144

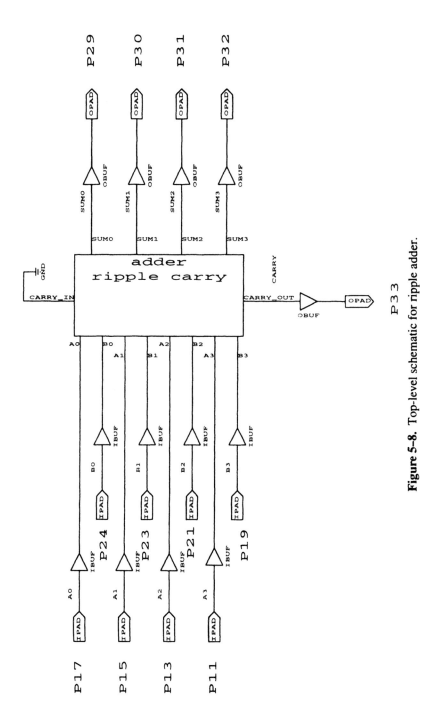

Figure 5–8. Top-level schematic for ripple adder.

145

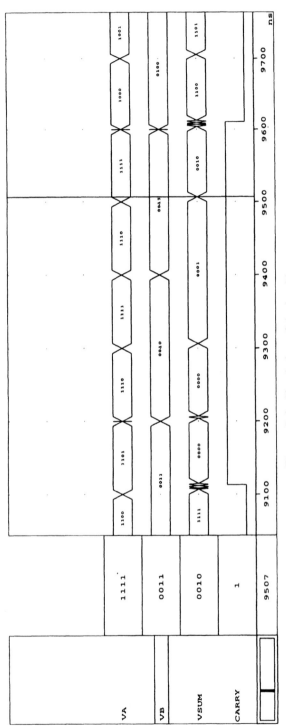

Figure 5-9. Simulation of ripple adder.

146

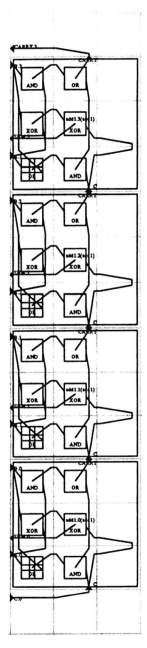

Figure 5-10. CAL layout for ripple adder.

ways of creating a decade counter:

- Using a macro element for a synchronous decade counter functionally equivalent to the 74160 TTL component
- As a collection of gates and flip-flops
- By direct entry to CLBs

Figure 5–11 shows the top-level schematic. The demonstration board has an *RC* controlled oscillator based on a single configurable logic block. The GOSC macro, shown in the lower left of the figure, produces a clock that runs at approximately 100 Hz when connected to external *R* and *C* components through pins 12 and 14. Another pin is connected to a dual in-line package switch that determines if counting takes place, or otherwise holds the counters clear, depending on the signal COUNT_EN. The oscillator is connected to the global clock GCLOCK, which in turn increments the least-significant decade counter. Figure 5–12 shows the schematic diagram for the 74160 synchronous counter. Figure 5–13 shows an encoded state machine design. The next state (N) variables are determined from the present state (P) variables. Figure 5–14 shows the state machine for the decade counter. Figures 5–15 and 5–16 show the basis for the design, which takes advantage of unassigned states that will of course never be entered, that is, decimal 10–15, and assigns 0 or 1 depending on the resulting simplification in the Boolean equations. For example, in deriving the least-significant bit N_0 of the next state, the box corresponding to present state $\overline{P}_0\overline{P}_1P_2P_3$, that is, "12" (decimal) is assigned to 1 to allow the whole column to be taken, and later combined with the right-hand column as $\overline{P}_0$. The fifth D flip-flop is used to delay the carry-out following state "9" until the next count pulse arrives. Figure 5–17 shows how the CLBs may be set up directly by the user, that is, assigning their mode and Boolean equations to be implemented. Note that the three alternative methods are shown for illustrative purposes, and that in practice the 74160 macro method would be preferred by most users.

The schematic information was used to generate a netlist for use by Xilinx software, which first mapped the logic to CLBs, and then determined a good placement on the 8 × 8 CLB array. The routing was completed automatically, and the CLB array layout is shown in Figure 5–18. The *RC* oscillator CLB is at site BA in the upper left. Note that after buffering by the clock buffer it drives two vertical clock lines in the first two columns. Some connections between adjacent CLBs are made by direct connection, which is fast, while others pass through the much slower switch matrices, revealed by the sloping routing. Each decade uses four CLBs. Figure 5–19 shows the settings of a particular CLB at location FE—this corresponds to the two least-significant flip-flops at the left-hand side. Interestingly, the mapping process has swapped the roles of the two outputs, presumably to reduce interconnection delay, as can be seen by comparing the figures. The configuration detail shows that both of the edge-triggered D flip-flops are clocked on a rising clock edge (K), provided the

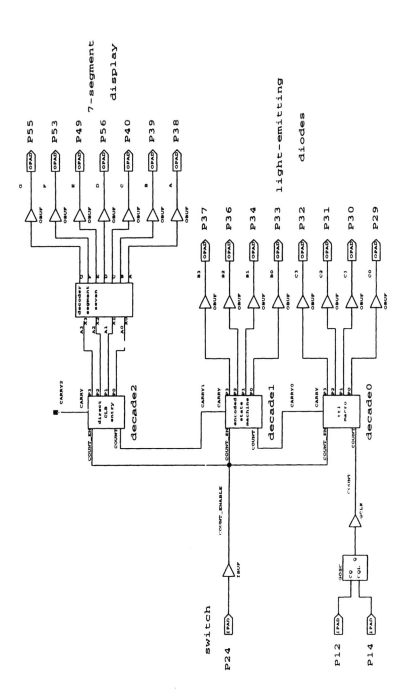

Figure 5-11. Top-level schematic for 3-decade counter.

149

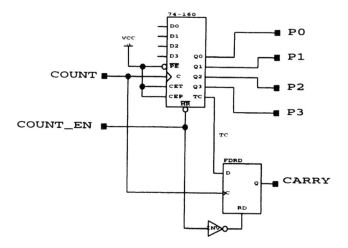

Figure 5–12. Macro cell for 74160 decade counter.

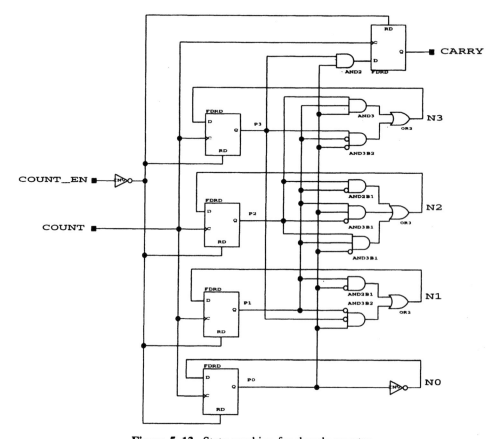

Figure 5–13. State machine for decade counter.

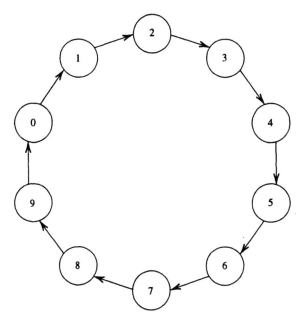

Figure 5-14. State sequence for decade counter.

clock is enabled (EC). The reset-direct (RD) signal is used to hold the counters clear.

5.3 PSEUDORANDOM NUMBER GENERATION

Random numbers can be very useful in simulation and testing digital circuits. Here we will use these numbers in testing the parallel adder described earlier. The term *pseudorandom* is used because the process is in fact completely predictable. The linear feedback shift register (LFSR) method is a particularly simple one, which can generate a sequence of length $2^n - 1$ for a register n bits long, provided it has the correct feedback connections. Figure 5–20 shows a 4-bit LFSR that can generate a sequence of length 15, not including the all-1s state, which is a *lock-up state*—once entered, the register will stay in this state indefinitely. Table 5–2 shows the feedback connections to produce a maximal length sequence for various register lengths.

5.4 RANDOM TESTING

For large systems, random testing is often a practical alternative to exhaustive, or case-by-case testing, and may be built into integrated circuits and systems.

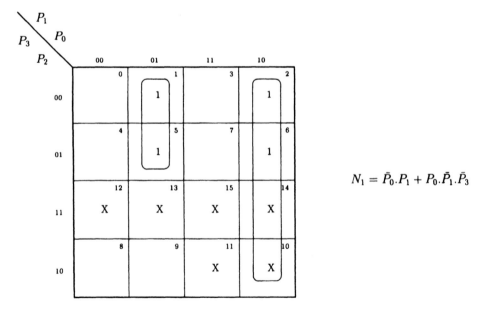

Figure 5–15. Equations for state machine: state encoding for decade counter, less-significant bits.

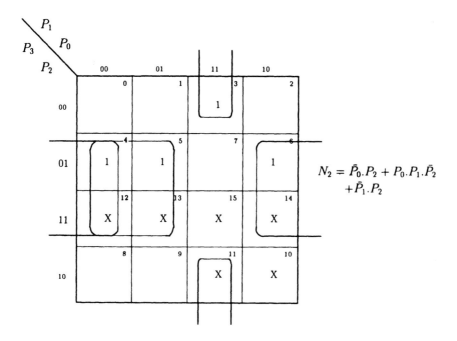

$$N_2 = \bar{P}_0.P_2 + P_0.P_1.\bar{P}_2$$
$$+\bar{P}_1.P_2$$

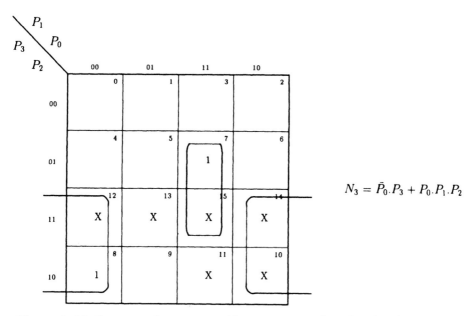

$$N_3 = \bar{P}_0.P_3 + P_0.P_1.P_2$$

Figure 5-16. Equations for state machine: state encoding for decade counter more-significant bits.

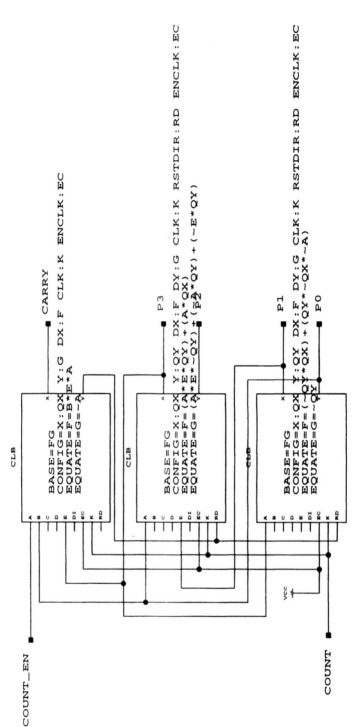

Figure 5–17. CLB entries for decade counter.

154

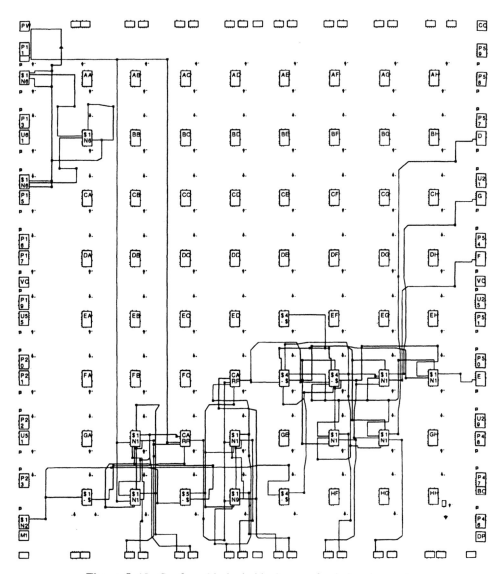

Figure 5-18. Configurable logic block array for 3-decade counter.

Input patterns may be readily generated with the LFSR method just described. *Signature analysis* is a technique for compressing the resulting output patterns into a short word whose final value indicates success or failure. While compression inevitably could allow some circuit failures to produce an identical signature, the risk is usually small.

We will take the 4-bit ripple adder described in Figure 5-4. Figure 5-21

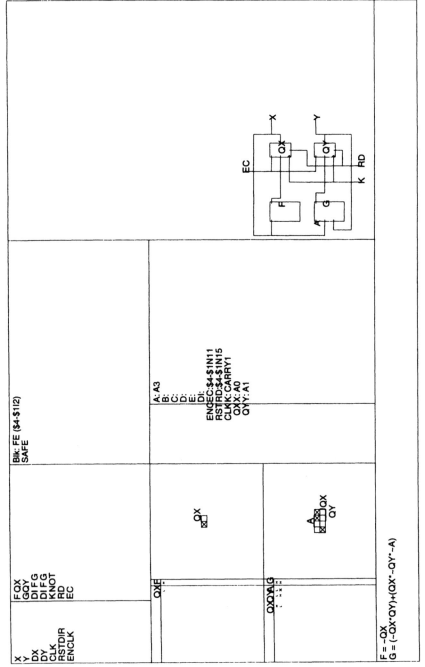

Figure 5-19. CLB configuration.

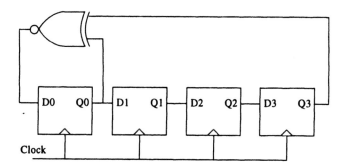

Figure 5-20. Linear feedback shift register.

shows the top-level schematic. Since there are eight input bits, along with carry-in, we will use a 9-bit pseudorandom number generator. To compress the four sum bits and the carry-out into 4 bits to be displayed on the demonstration board LEDs, we use a 4-bit signature analyzer.

5.4.1 Signature Analyzer

The signature analyzer is an adaptation of the LFSR. At every clock cycle, a set of outputs from the ripple adder is loaded in parallel to an LFSR, with the feedback connections given earlier. These are XORed with the previous register contents as shown in Figure 5-22.

TABLE 5-2. LFSR Connections for Pseudo-random Sequence Generation

Register Length	Feedback Connections
2	0, 1
3	0, 2
4	0, 3
5	1, 4
6	0, 5
7	2, 6
8	1, 2, 3, 7
9	3, 8

Adapted from J. Mavor, M. Jack, and P. Denyer, *Introduction to MOS LSI Design*, Addison-Wesley, 1983, p. 118. © 1983, Addison-Wesley Publishing Co. Inc., reproduced with permission.
Note: For a register length of 8, form the input by two EXCLUSIVE-OR gates feeding a third.

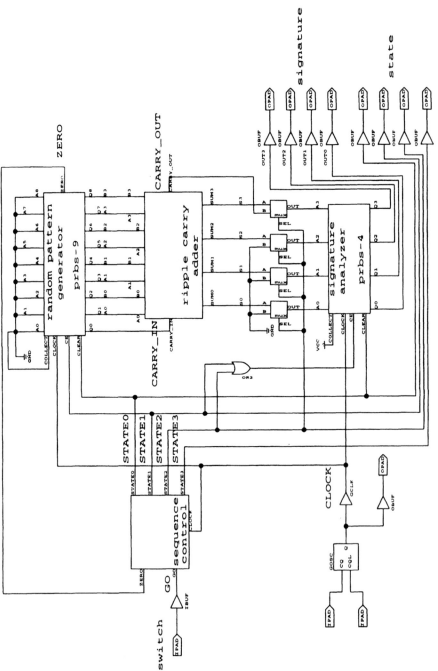

Figure 5-21. Top-level schematic of a parallel adder.

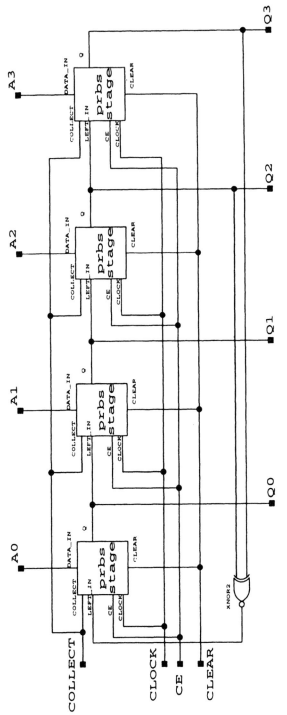

Figure 5-22. Signature analyzer.

159

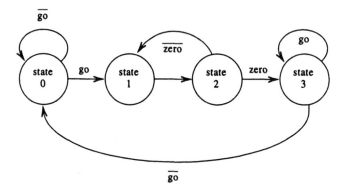

Figure 5-23. State diagram.

5.4.2 State Machine

As discussed in Chapter 2, state machines can be implemented in different ways. Encoded state machines may minimize the storage required, but at the expense of decoding logic, reducing speed. Here we use the one-hot method, that is, one bit per state. The four states are as follows:

1. Initial state: wait for switch to be pressed
2. Accumulate signature from four output bits in signature analyzer
3. Accumulate carry-out bit in signature analyzer
4. Display 4-bit signature on LEDs

Figure 5-23 shows the state diagram and Figure 5-24 shows the schematic. Note that State0 has inverting logic on both input and output, so that it automatically goes high when the FPGA is powered-up. Also, the State3 output is used to reset states 1 and 2 in the unlikely event of a logic state error, for example, if either bit was simultaneously asserted with State3.

5.5 SYSTOLIC SORTER*

This example is included to suggest that FPGAs may provide novel ways of solving well-known problems. Sorting is required in many computer applications, particularly commercial ones. Here we look at a high-speed sorter, but one confined to miniscule amounts of data. It is described as *systolic* because it uses a repetitive block structure, and has a regular data flow. In general, each item to be sorted consists of a number of fields, of which one is selected as

---

*Advanced topic to be omitted on first reading.

Section 5.5 was contributed by Christopher Kappler.

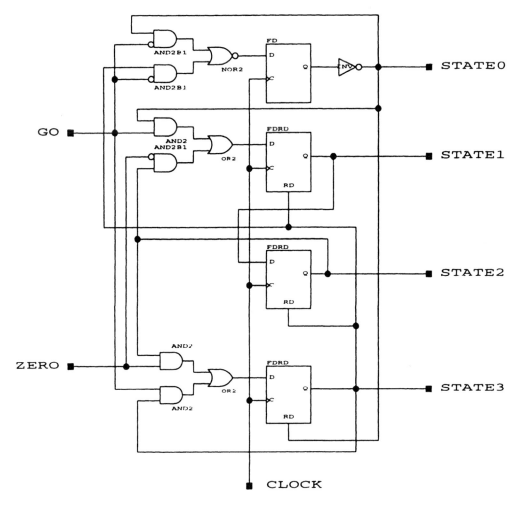

Figure 5-24. Schematic for state machine.

a *key*, on which to sort. For simplicity we regard the key as a nonnegative integer, and assume that we wish to sort items in ascending order of their keys. For simplicity, we concentrate on sorting the keys.

Knuth [Knuth73] distinguishes some basic sorting methods:

Sort by insertion: Find the correct place to insert an item in an already-ordered list

Sort by exchange: Consider pairs of keys, and swap them if out of order

Sort by enumeration: Find the smallest (or largest) key and remove the item to a new list. Repeat until the original list is empty.

The scheme described here is a combination of the first two methods. We assume that the items to be sorted arrive individually, so it makes sense to keep previous arrivals in order—we choose ascending. Borrowing a technique from full-custom VLSI design, we make up blocks of cells, and arrange for simple connections of data and control signals. The overall floorplan is shown in Figure 5–25. Each key is stored in a vertical column of one-bit blocks, with the least-significant bit at the top, and the most-significant bit adjacent to the control block at the bottom. New keys arrive at the left-hand side, and will "ripple" to the right, as they are compared with stored keys until they fall into the correct column. Each control block, of which there is one per key, simply uses the result of the arithmetic comparison made above:

```
if the stored key (S) is smaller than the one to its left (L),
    key L is passed to the cell on the right, i.e. bypassing S
otherwise, L must be stored in place of S, and S passed to the
    right
```

Figure 5–26 shows the data flow for the comparator cell, as implemented in

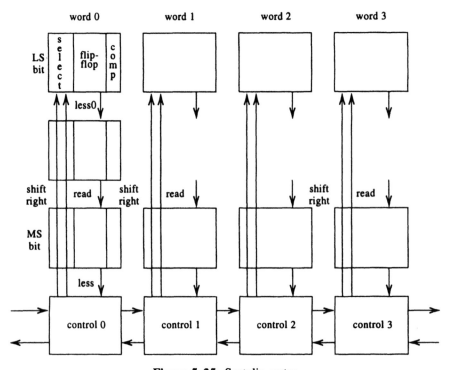

Figure 5-25. Systolic sorter.

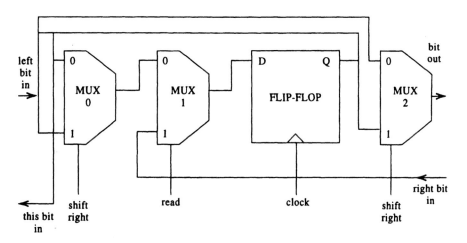

Figure 5-26. Sorter comparator cell—data flow.

Algotronix CAL logic. When all the keys have been submitted, the sorted list is returned by a series of left shifts, that is, so the smallest key emerges first.

In every column an arithmetic comparison is made, commencing with the less–significant bit at the top of the key. Each bit stage generates a signal "less," which indicates that, based on the series of bits so far, the stored key is less than the one to its left. This result may change as the more significant bits are considered. The comparator logic is illustrated in Figure 5–27, and is described as follows:

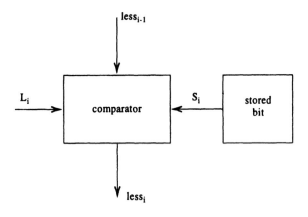

$$less_i = less_{i-1} (L_i \equiv S_i) + L_i \bar{S}_i$$

Figure 5-27. Sorter comparator cell. Comparison logic.

```
if the left-item bit and the stored bit are equivalent, pass
    on the "less" result from the ls comparator above.
otherwise, if the left-item bit is a 1, set "less" to 1 or if a
    0, then set "less" to 0.
```

It is implemented in the 1-bit comparator shown in Figure 5–28.

The control block is shown in Figure 5–29. Before sorting starts, the CLRb signal sets all the D flip-flops to 1, and as keys appear, 0s are propagated through the control blocks. When the set of keys to be sorted has been entered, the results are retrieved in an ascending order by issuing a set of "read" instructions, which shift the contents of the control and key blocks left. Figure 5–30 shows an overall view of the sorter.

5.6 MULTIPLIERS

Multiplier designs are a simple way of studying different varieties of digital logic designs. It is possible to develop different multiplier examples to study the varieties of design approaches and implement these designs using FPGAs. In the following sections Xilinx 3000 implementations are assumed, but the approaches vary from fully automated to handcrafted with corresponding gains in performance.

5.6.1 Parallel Multipliers

The simplest of the multiplier designs is a parallel-combinational logic multiplier. This multiplier produces a result by adding the partial products of equal binary weight with the carries of the lower binary weight. The design consists simply of AND, OR, XOR, and inverter gates at the top-level schematic.

Schematic Entry   Figure 5–31 is an example of a 4- × 4-bit combinational logic multiplier. The design was created using ViewLogic *WorkView*. Using CAD tools, a logic design can be entered directly as a top-level schematic, manually connecting gates together. To obtain more information about creating a schematic design, refer to the current Xilinx and/or Viewlogic *WorkView* manuals.

Functional Simulation   It is always a good idea to check the design functionality before actually continuing with the creation of the layout file. The software used to create the schematic design provided support for a functional simulation of the schematic circuit. Refer to Figure 5–32.

Section 5.6 was contributed by Roberto Melo.

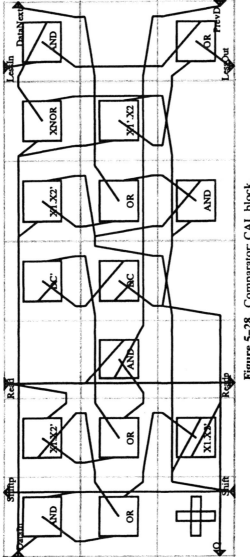

Figure 5–28. Comparator: CAL block.

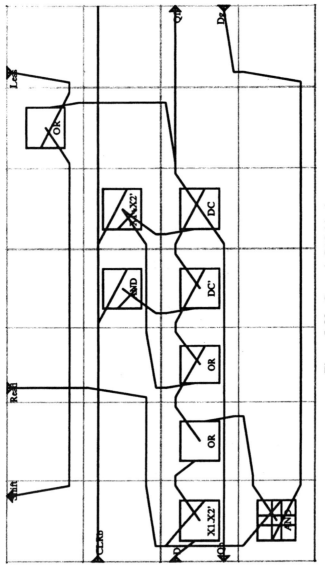

Figure 5-29. Control: CAL block.

166

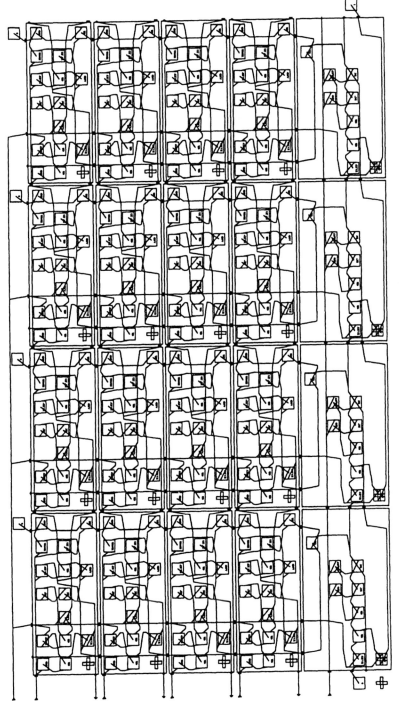

Figure 5–30. Overall layout of sorter.

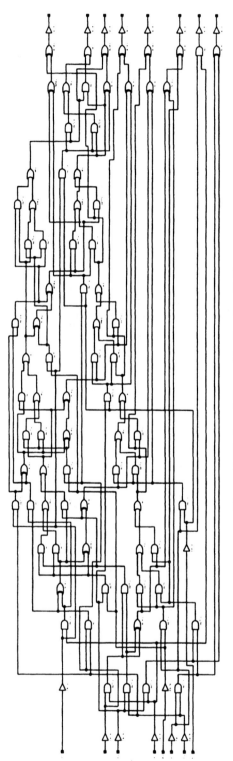

Figure 5-31. 4 × 4-bit combinational multiplier.

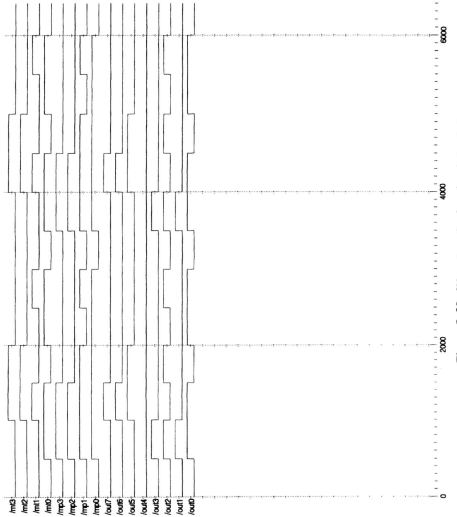

Figure 5–32. Waveform for functional simulation.

169

File-conversion Process   In order to be able to create a Xilinx layout for the parallel multiplier, it is necessary to follow a series of steps to convert the file to the correct format. The file-conversion process consists of the following steps:

1. Generate a "wirelist" (net) file from the schematic level file
2. Generate a netlist file from the wirelist file
3. Generate a layout file using the automatic router

Speed   Most of the technology used today requires the use of high-speed circuits. The speed performance of the Xilinx design will be affected by several factors: choice of part being used, the arrangement of the programmed logic within the circuit, and the efficiency of the layout itself.

XACT Design Entry   It is possible to enter a design directly by using *XACT* (the Xilinx design editor). This can be done by configuring the blocks directly, using logic expressions instead of entering a schematic. Figure 5–33 gives an example of the multiplier as entered using *XACT*.

5.6.2   Serial Multiplier with Parallel Addition

Another example of a multiplier circuit is a serial multiplier. The main difference between the parallel logic multiplier and the serial multiplier is the introduction of memory and timing in the design.

Schematic Entry   Figure 5–34 is a schematic for a serial parallel multiplier created using ViewLogic *WorkView*.

The serial multiplier can be processed as before to generate the Xilinx layout file. Figure 5–35 shows the serial multiplier layout configuration for a 3000 family Xilinx chip.

5.7   A PARALLEL CONTROLLER DESIGN*

An outline of the design and implementation of a video framestore design is presented that used the Petri net method described in Chapter 2, and is implemented on a Xilinx LCA.

The function of the framestore is to receive or transmit digital video data from a memory in a raster scan format. Region of interest (ROI) is supported, allowing the reception and transmission of frames of any size. Video data arrive on a 16-bit-wide bus every 100 ns. A frame synchronization signal defines

---

*Advanced topic to be omitted on first reading.

Section 5.7 was contributed by Erik. L. Dagless and Jonathan M. Saul.

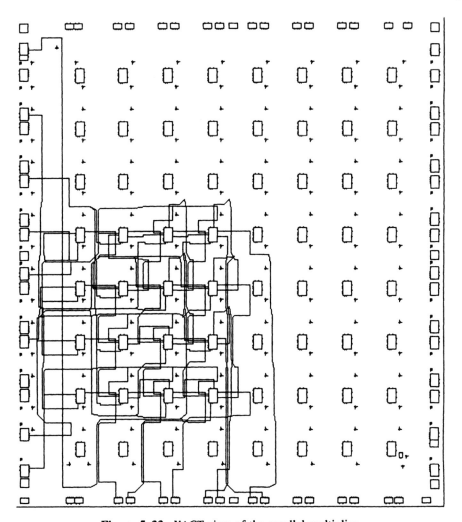

Figure 5-33. *XACT* view of the parallel multiplier.

the start of a field of data of 260 lines by 760 pixels. Each line starts with a horizontal synchronization signal. The video controller has to deposit the data in a video framestore in the correct order (interleaving two fields to create a full frame) and to manage accesses to the memory. A second independent video channel operates at the same time, but it must access a different block of memory. A transputer is able to access both memory blocks while video operations are being performed. At the end of a frame, the video channels may be required to switch memory banks, and this must be handled by the controller.

The controller has a number of registers containing its operating parameters, such as horizontal start and end count, vertical start and end count, and start

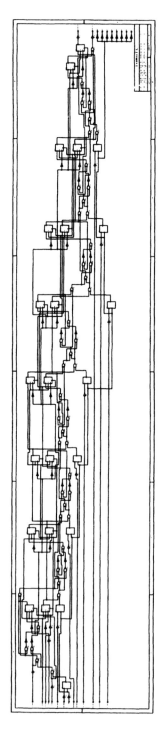

Figure 5–34. Schematic for the serial multiplier.

172

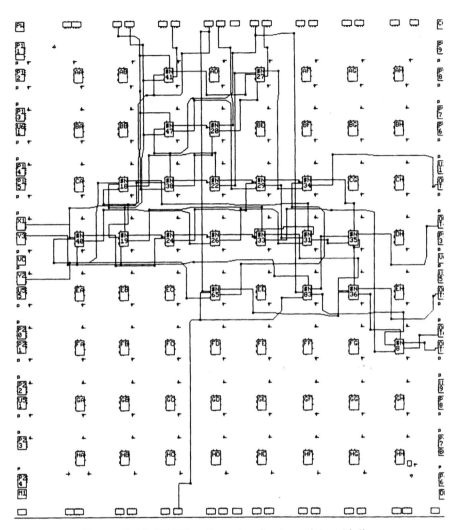

Figure 5-35. *XACT* configuration for the serial multiplier.

address in memory. Figure 5-36 shows the datapath structure of the controller design. It contains all the datapaths and a large Petri net controller and has been implemented in a Xilinx 3090 FPGA.

5.7.1 Operation of Part of the Petri Net Controller

The controller Petri net uses inhibiting and enabling arcs and is made up of many small linked Petri nets. To illustrate both the Petri net technique and its use in hardware design, a small fragment of the controller is described. Figure

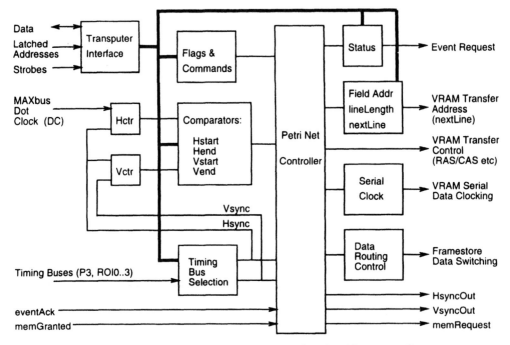

Figure 5-36. Simplified block diagram of the MAXbus controller.

5-37 shows the parts of the controller associated with generating the horizontal synchronous output signal, 'HsyncOut', and with determining the position of active pixels within a line. Consider that the circuit is initially idle, and is to be operated as a timing master, with 'HsyncOut' connected back to the controller's 'Hsync' input. Although 'Hsync' is not directly used in this part of the circuit, its assertion will cause the external pixel counter, 'Hctr' in Figure 5-36, to be reset and thereafter to count toward the register values 'Hstart' and 'Hend', so that the Petri net inputs 'HctrAtHstart' and 'HctrAtHend' are asserted at the appropriate times.

An image transfer is initiated when an "arming" transition fires in another part of the net, causing a token to arrive in P3. This token is removed on the next clock cycle, so that the arming signal is only one cycle wide. The arming signal enables transition T4, so that on the next clock cycle T4 fires, removing the token in P4 and thereby releasing the "done" output to indicate that the controller is running. The arming signal also enables transition T1 so that on the next clock cycle the token in P2 moves to place P1, asserting 'HsyncOut'. Having no other associated conditions, transition T2 will immediately fire on the following clock cycle, returning the token to P2. 'HsyncOut' is thus one cycle wide.

As mentioned earlier, the generation of the 'HsyncOut' signal causes the

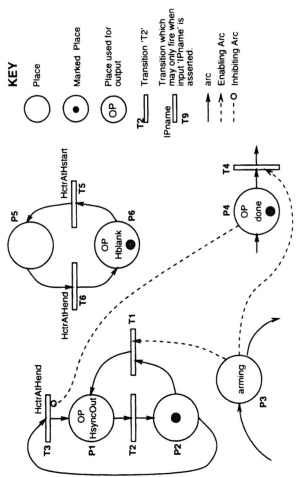

Figure 5-37. A small part of the controller.

175

pixel counter to be cleared, and to count toward 'Hstart' and 'Hend'. When 'Hctr' reaches 'Hstart', 'HctrAtHstart' is asserted, T5 fires, and 'Hblank' becomes inactive. External circuitry (the serial clock in Figure 5–36) uses this signal, together with a 'Vblank' signal generated elsewhere, to decide whether to clock active data. Later, 'HctrAtEnd' is asserted and T6 fires, reenabling 'Hblank'. The assertion of 'HctrAtHend' also has the effect of firing transition T3, thereby generating a further 'Hsync' output from place P1, to indicate the start of a new line. The process continues until a token arrives at P4 indicating that the sequence is done and this inhibits T3 from firing.

5.7.2 Characteristics of the Design Technique

It can be seen that the small 'Hblank' circuit lies in a separate Petri net running in parallel with the rest of the circuit. The introduction of parallelism in this conventional way is over and above the parallelism that can be expressed within a Petri net. Parallelism is used in the circuit both to have more than one task running at a time and simply to express the design more easily. In the case of the 'Hblank' circuit, this convenience allows the implementation to be a natural expression of the definition of horizontal blanking, taking place from the end of one line to the start of the next.

5.7.3 Implementation on XC3090

The design was entered in schematic form to the ViewLogic CAD system. Four designs have been produced: an 8-bit design and a 16-bit design, each with and without ROI capability. These have all been simulated using nominal delays for the logic cell array (LCA) circuit components.

The full 16-bit design uses 83% of the 320 CLBs and 86% of the 144 IOBs available. This design could not be routed automatically on the tools available at the time (1991). An early effort to cut down the design to 68% CLB usage also proved to be unroutable using automatic tools. For comparison, an inoperable version with 50% CLB usage was routed automatically. With smaller array parts, automatic routing was successful at 80% CLB usage. However, it was clear that the place-and-route strategies in the software could not cope satisfactorily with the larger arrays.

These problems were overcome using informal tools from Xilinx for routing a functional block at a time. This system allows the designer to carry out floor planning, leaving space for routing channels, which the automatic tools cannot do. The automatic router is then run on the small blocks, where it manages to achieve a higher packing density. Each iteration adds one functional block to the work already routed; earlier routing is copied into the current iteration using the place-and-route program's (APR) guide option. Manual intervention, using the *XACT* LCA editor program, is needed to tidy up the design at each stage. The newer design tools from the manufacturer more adequately deal with these problems, as will be seen shortly.

As a result of this experience the following hints are offered for future users:

- Supplement long lines by routing out on one side of the chip and back in the other side.
- Bring signals used in a number of places into the chip using multiple pins.
- Minimize three state buffer usage as they reduce access to nearby CLBs.
- Minimize use of the RD and CKEN pins on CLBs, as these cannot be swapped to other locations in the way that, say, X and Y can, to make routing easier. The exception is when driving a number of these pins from the same long line.
- When using outer long lines to drive, the three state input to IOBs indicate this to the router with a small piece of manual prerouting.

Two further problems were encountered. The first arises when routing a block that has a pin that is to be connected to another block that has yet to be routed. The pin can become buried with no access path to it. To overcome this a dummy circuit is added, using *XACT*, connecting to such pins, thereby forcing a route to be found before the current iteration can be declared complete.

The second problem arises when copying routing information from a previous iteration. During the routing process CLB pins are swapped about to make routing easier. When copying routing information from the previous iteration, the router attempts to repeat the pin swaps already decided on. However, it occasionally fails, believing the pin swaps to be illegal (which they sometimes are until other pin swaps have been done first). This is tiresome, especially when it involves the loss of routing done manually. When the problem is observed, the solution is to return to the circuit diagram and lock the correct pin designations in place.

During the time of preparing this book, there have been substantial improvements in computer-aided design support. Following the successful completion of the original design at Bristol University in 1991, the design files were made available to Direct Insight Ltd. (U.K.). In 1993 the design was completed using NeoCAD software for Xilinx FPGAs, and with the aid of a 50 MHz PC486 computer. The standard placement-and-routing package was run with 100 cost tables. No timing constraints were specified, and so the system ran without timing optimization. After 108 hours, it had tried 64 cost tables, and one of these resulted in a fully-routed chip, taking 1 hour and 25 minutes. Twenty-eight had less than 10 nets unrouted, and human intervention could probably have quickly resulted in other fully-routed options. The fully-routed version was run through five cost-based clean-ups and five delay-based clean-ups, taking a further 18 minutes. The design achieved a 6.3 MHz clock rate. Following further routing iterations over 24 hours, the clock rate had increased to 7 MHz. This is comparable with the existing design, which operates reliably at 6.75 MHz. A layout for the final NeoCAD design is shown in Figure 5–38.

In 1994 the current production release of Xilinx software XACT 5.0.0 was

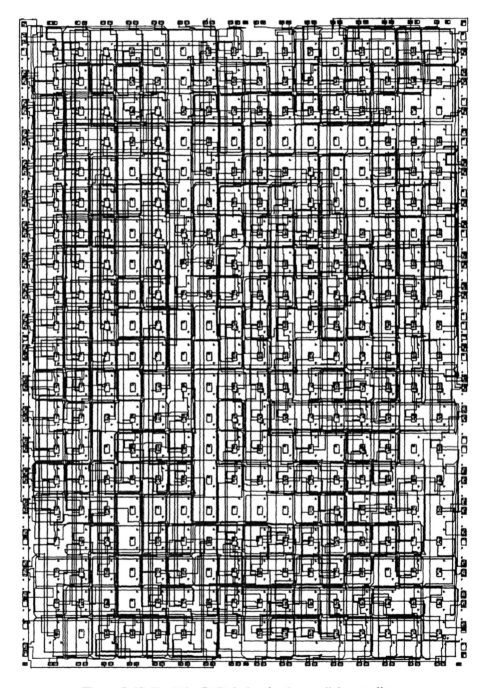

Figure 5-38 Final NeoCAD design for the parallel controller.

run with XACT-Performance enabled, so that the resulting circuit would run at its highest speed. After 82 hours on Sun Microsystems SPARC 10 workstations, the system had generated 11 full-routed designs out of 16 attempts. The first fully-routed result was available after 1 hour and 49 minutes. The varied results were produced by selecting different placement parameters, including the placement "seed" and "placer effort." The clock rates for fully-routed chips varied from 5.4 MHz to 6.9 MHz. Six of the 11 fully-routed designs performed at 6.0 MHz or faster. The best two results gave speeds of 6.8 and 6.9 MHz, which compare favorably with the existing design (6.75 MHz). A layout for the fastest Xilinx design is shown in Figure 5-39.

5.7.4 Conclusions

The full 16-bit version of the controller was eventually routed. While in 1991 this took over four months of continuous effort, more recent CAD software allows rapid completion of quite complex designs to specified performance criteria. An 8-layer printed-circuit board has been designed and manufactured, and there are now more than 25 copies of the design in routine use.

SUGGESTIONS FOR PROJECTS

1. Faster adder circuits based on carry-lookahead logic [Wakerly90]. Note that the Xilinx 4000 series incorporates carry-lookahead logic in its CLBs.

2. Arithmetic-logic unit. (see [Wakerly90]).

3. Design an elementary processor. (see [Segee91]).

4. Adapt the sorter design for another FPGA family.

5. Boundary Scan. Boundary Scan testing has recently become standard, and considerably simplifies testing both chips and their printed circuit board environment. See [Maunder90] for details.

6. Dynamic memory controller. Dynamic memory requires periodic refresh to avoid loss of contents. For example, the Intel 4116 16K DRAM is organized as 128 rows and 128 columns. Each row can be read and rewritten in a single cycle, and each must be visited every 2 ms.

7. Asynchronous serial data transmission and reception. The RS232 standard defines start and stop bits for the 8-bit characters. Using a clock running at 4 times the nominal baud rate, it is possible to sample the incoming bits correctly. The transmitter design is simpler than the receiver.

8. Manchester-coded data transmission. Manchester coding carries both data and timing information on the same channel, and the edge transitions in each bit time allow a receiver to adjust its clock by speeding up or slowing

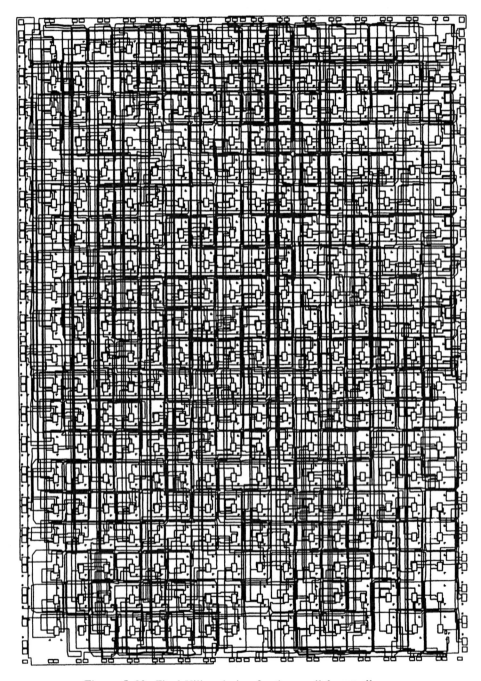

Figure 5–39. Final Xilinx design for the parallel controller.

down from the nominal bit rate. The receiver design calls for a phase-locked loop, which can automatically adjust the sampling rate.

PROBLEMS

1. Develop a CAL design for a 4-bit parallel adder based on the well-known propagate/generate scheme, that is, for the ith stage

$$P_i = A_i \oplus B_i$$
$$G_i = A_i.B_i$$

Assume that A_i and B_i are presented along the lower edge of each 1-bit block, with the carry coming in from the left-hand side. The sum should appear along the top edge, and the carry out along the right edge. If the evaluation of a cell function takes 8 ns, plus 2 ns for output, and cross-cell routing takes 2 ns, how long will the 4-bit carry take?

2. Show how the Xilinx XC3000 CLB can provide a 1-bit adder–subtractor cell for a parallel adder. The cell will have inputs A, B, and Carry/Borrow, along with a control input that is high for add and low for subtract. Write the equations for the combinational logic. Assign CLB inputs and outputs that would make sense for fast operation of a parallel adder–subtractor, that is, using direct interconnect, and state the preferred orientation, that is, horizontal or vertical.

3. A 4×4 combinational multiplier has been discussed. How would you adapt the design to turn it into a pipelined version, that is, one that could simultaneously handle a number of multiplicands (Ys) for a constant multiplier (X), with a new multiplicand entering and an 8-bit product leaving each clock cycle? Can the block organization be improved to minimize the delay per stage, that is, to eliminate waiting for carry propagation? Give an approximate estimate for the multiplication rate that might be achieved, and the time each multiplication spends in the pipeline. Assume an XC3020-70 speed part, and that every net has a delay of 2 ns.

4. The Xilinx FPGA software goes to some length to remove redundant logic, prior to technology mapping. What problems does this cause for detailed simulation, and how are they corrected?

BIBLIOGRAPHY

[Barrie92] Barrie, P., Cockshott, P., Milne, G. J., Shaw, P., "Design and Verification of a Highly Concurrent Machine," *Microprocessors and Microsystems*, Vol. 16, No. 3, pp. 115–123, 1992.

[Bitton84] Bitton, D., DeWitt, D. J., Hsiao, D. K., Menon, J., "A Taxonomy of Parallel Sorting," *Computing Surveys*, Vol. 16, No. 3, pp. 287–318, 1984.

[Conner92] Conner, D., "Taking the First Steps," *EDN*, pp. 98–112, April 9, 1992.

[Hatam86] Hatamian, M., Cash, G. L., "A 70-MHz 8-bit × 8-bit Parallel Pipelined Multiplier in 2.5-μm CMOS," *IEEE Journal of Solid-State Circuits*, Vol. SC-21, No. 4, pp. 505–513, August 1986.

[Hillen90] Hillen, K. K., Fawcett, B., "Build Reconfigurable Peripheral Controllers," *Electronic Design*, pp. 69–78, March 8, 1990.

[Knapp90] Knapp, S. K., "Accelerate FPGA Macros with One-hot Approach," *Electronic Design*, September 13, 1990.

[Knuth73] Knuth, D. E., *The Art of Computer Programming*, Addison-Wesley, 1973.

[Maunder90] Maunder, C. M., Tulloss, R. E., *The Test Access Port and Boundary Scan Architecture*, IEEE Computer Society Press, 1990.

[Maunder92] Maunder, C. M., Tulloss, R. E., "Testability on TAP," *IEEE Spectrum*, pp. 34–37, February 1992.

[Mavor82] Mavor, J., Jack, M., Denyer, P., *Introduction to MOS LSI Design*, Addison-Wesley, 1982.

[Perkins91] Perkins, D. M., Burton, P. C. M., "A Digital Design Laboratory Using CAE Tools and Programmable Gate Arrays," *1991 ASEE Annual Conference Proceedings*, pp. 767–771, 1991.

[Russell89] Russell, G., Sayers, I. L., *Advanced Simulation and Test Methodologies for VLSI Design*, Van Nostrand Reinhold, 1989.

[Schlag91] Schlag, M., Chan, P. K., Kong, J., "Empirical Evaluation of Multilevel Logic Minimization Tools for a Field-Programmable Gate Array Technology," *FPGAs*, Moore W., Luk M., Eds., Abingdon EE & CS Books, pp. 201–213, 1991.

[Segee91] Segee, B., Field, J., *Microprogramming and Computer Architecture*, Wiley, 1991.

[Wakerly90] Wakerly, J. F., *Digital Design Principles and Practice*, Prentice-Hall, 2nd ed., 1994.

CHAPTER 6

COMPUTATIONAL APPLICATIONS

This chapter is intended to illustrate the use of field-programmable gate arrays (FPGAs) in computational applications. The following topics are covered:

- The state of the art in FPGA computers
- The Algotronix CHS2×4 Custom Computer
- Example applications:
  1. Data Encryption Standard
  2. Self-timed first-in first-out buffer
  3. Self-timed genetic string distance evaluation
  4. Cellular automaton
  5. Place-and-route acceleration
  6. Motion estimation

6.1 THE STATE OF THE ART

As we saw in Chapter 3, the use of FPGA devices as computing structures is motivated by the perceived performance and price performance advantages of hardware customized for a particular application, over more general-purpose computing structures. In particular we can identify the following key advantages:

1. There is no overhead associated with fetching and decoding instructions.
2. Bus structures can be tailored to the operation: for example, an operation that had five input operands and one output could have five input buses

and one output bus, allowing it to complete in a single cycle. On a conventional architecture, assuming all operands were in memory, at least six cycles of the shared data bus would be required.

3. Arithmetic units can be provided for nonstandard operations.

4. Operation units need be no longer than required. For example, if we are operating on 8-bit data, we would use an 8-bit adder; this adder could be four times smaller and faster than a 32-bit adder in a conventional machine.

5. Because tailored operation units are smaller we can have more of them, thus allowing a more parallel solution to increase performance.

6. When the computer is intended to process a stream of high bandwidth input data, the peripheral interface itself can be implemented on the programmable device. In these applications the speed at which the host can transfer data from the peripheral to the special-purpose computer through its bus would not be a bottleneck.

The main disadvantage of configurable hardware as a computing medium is the difficulty of hardware design compared to software design. Configurable computing structures are therefore, most suited to relatively simple operations that must be repeated many times, and are usually proposed as accelerators within conventional computers.

At the present time, there are several commercially available configurable hardware computers targeted at application-specific integrated-circuit (ASIC) emulation, for example [D'Amour89]. More general-purpose configurable hardware computers are becoming available. At the time of writing there are three fully developed systems:

1. The Paris Research Laboratory of Digital Equipment Corporation has developed supercomputer class configurable hardware add-on boxes for DEC workstations [Bertin89]. These systems can be configured with multiple boards each of which contains 25 Xilinx chips (XC3020's or XC3090's) and fast RAM memory. Benchmark results for this system configured to solve ten real-world applications are presented in [Bertin92].

2. SPLASH [Gokh91] is a two-board add-on to a SUN workstation containing 32 Xilinx 3090 programmable gate arrays and 32 memory chips closely associated with the Xilinx chips. The architecture is optimized for a particular problem—pattern matching DNA sequences—and in this application routinely achieves speed-ups of 10 to 1 over a single processor Cray 2.

3. The Algotronix CHS2×4 custom computer was developed as a demonstration system for the CAL1024 chip and is an add-on board for PC/AT class computers. It is a relatively low-cost system and is currently in use in more than 30 universities and research laboratories, mainly in Europe.

In this chapter we use the CHS2×4 as a concrete example of a configurable hardware computer and describe several applications for it that illustrate some typical techniques.

6.2 ARCHITECTURE OF THE CHS2×4

The architecture of Algotronix's configurable array logic (CAL) technology [Algo91] is particularly suited to the building of arrays of chips to form a single computing surface [Gray89]. The CHS2×4 and its associated software have been designed and built to explore this aspect of FPGA usage.

The CHS2×4 contains up to 9 CAL1024 chips and 2M bytes of static RAM. Two boards can be connected together to form a system with a 4 × 4 array of CAL chips for computation and up to 4M bytes of static RAM. The CHS2×4 board is supported by the configurable logic software (CLS) software suite, including a graphical editor and an on-line debugger, and a library of interface routines that can be called from the user's C programs.

6.2.1 Hardware Architecture

Architecturally the CHS2×4 system consists of three hardware subsystems (see Figure 6–1). These are:

1. PC interface and control subsystem.
2. computation subsystem.
3. memory subsystem.

The bus architecture, Figure 6–2 allows the memory subsystem and CAL configuration memory of the computation subsystem to be read and written from the host processor. Configuration memory and the memory subsystem share an

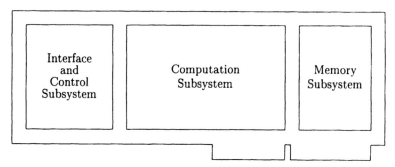

Figure 6–1. CHS2×4 board. Figure courtesy of Xilinx, Inc. © Xilinx, Inc. 1991. All rights reserved.

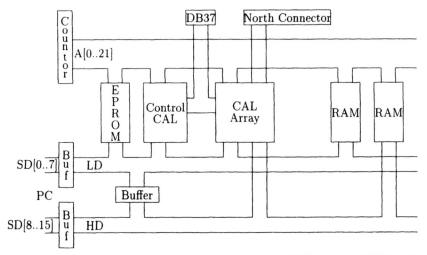

Figure 6-2. CHS2×4 block diagram. Figure courtesy of Xilinx, Inc. © Xilinx, Inc. 1991. All rights reserved.

address space local to the board. In addition, the computation array may execute memory operations, using the counter as an address register, synchronized to the host clock.

The four main busses on the CHS2×4 board interconnecting the major subsystems shown on these figures are:

1. *Address Bus* (A[0..21]). This bus is used to address the CAL control store, the static RAM data memory and the EPROM that contains the power-up configuration for the control CAL.
2. *Low Data Bus* (LD[0..7]). This is the main data bus on the board and connects the PC data bus, the CAL control store, the data memory, and the initial configuration EPROM.
3. *High Data Bus* (HD[0..7]). This bus is used in conjunction with LD[0..7] to allow 16-bit transfers between the PC, the data memory, and the computation array inputs and outputs. In addition, the computation array can simultaneously read 8 bits from the memory and write 8 bits to the memory using LD and HD together.
4. *Control Bus* (Mode[0..2]). The mode bits of the control bus determine the use to which the data busses will be put, as detailed in Table 6–1.

The PC interface-and-control subsystem has the task of handling communications with the host PC/AT and controlling transfers on the internal busses of the CHS2×4. For maximum flexibility this subsystem is based around a CAL1024 chip whose configuration is loaded from an EPROM when the PC/AT is reset or powered up.

TABLE 6-1. Bus Usage Modes

Mode	Operation
0	Reload control CAL
1	Write counter
2	8-bit Write on LD[0..7], 8-bit Read on HD[0..7]
3	16-bit Write
4	16-bit Read
5	8-bit Write
6	8-bit Read
7	No operation

The CHS2×4 is accessed through 16 locations in the PC/AT's input/output (I/O) space using a protocol implemented by the control CAL. The bottom four bits of the address bus during a board access are used to determine the operation to be performed, which is completed during the same I/O cycle. This technique is faster than using an I/O cycle to transfer an instruction to the board, followed by a second cycle to transfer the associated data.

The computation subsystem of the CHS2×4 board consists of a 2 × 4 array of CAL1024 chips and appropriate address decoding for their control store, which provides random access to cells within the array for defining logic circuits and sensing function unit outputs. Access to the periphery of the array is available via the system busses and a number of connectors. At the north boundary the four CALs are fully pinned out to a 128-way header connector. This connector may be used to connect to a neighboring CHS2×4 board, allowing a large system containing a 4 × 4 array of CAL chips to be built. The west boundary of $CAL_{0,1}$ is fully pinned to a 37-pin DIN connector, which appears on the back panel edge of the PC/AT board. This connector may be used to directly connect external devices to the board. This bus is also connected to the west boundary of the control CAL to provide communication between the computation array and the control subsystem—this could be used, for example, to indicate the termination of an algorithm running on the computation array. In addition, at the east boundary, the high data (HD) and low data (LD) busses connect to every fourth boundary cell. At the west boundary of $CAL_{0,0}$ both the HD and LD busses are connected to boundary cells. These connections support transfers to and from the on-board memory.

The memory subsystem provides the computation array with high bandwidth access to a large local data memory, thus supporting systolic and pipelined computations where data are streamed through the CAL array. It contains four 32-pin sockets for static RAMs and associated address decoding. These sockets can be filled with 128K × 8 SRAM chips, 128K × 8 SRAM hybrids or 512K × 8 SRAM hybrids. If all four sockets are filled with 512K hybrids, a 2M-byte memory is provided.

The software support for the CAL architecture and the CHS2×4 custom computer consists of a computer-aided engineering (CAE) environment and an applications environment. This is shown diagrammatically in Figure 6–3.

The CLS CAE environment contains components for both automated and manual CAL configuration. It consists of the following programs

- *clare* The configurable logic array editor (*clare*) is a graphical tool for manipulating cellular designs. The user builds a design as a hierarchy of blocks, each of which may contain individual configurable cells and instances of other blocks. Point-to-point routing within blocks may be interactive or automatic via a maze router. The editor supports physical design, in a symbolic form, by allowing the user to allocate cells. At the same time, structural design is supported by allowing the user to display nets and manage interblock and intracell wiring. Designs are saved in a text file, the *.cfg* file, that is read by other programs to produce the bit patterns to personalize a CAL chip or CHS2×4 board.

- *laura* and *libcal* *laura* is the equivalent of a block generator in ASIC chip design. The purpose of *laura* is to provide a programming interface that designers can use to produce and manipulate *.cfg* files. *laura* is intended to complement *clare* by facilitating parameterization of layouts. Basic library elements may be generated manually and then manipulated algorithmically. This is particularly useful in producing highly regular systolic designs. *libcal* provides routines for reading and writing the Algotronix data file formats and defines the main data structures used by Algotronix programs.

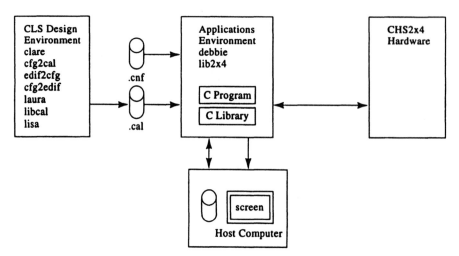

Figure 6–3. Software architecture. Figure courtesy of Xilinx, Inc. © Xilinx, Inc. 1991. All rights reserved.

- *lisa*   The *lisa* program generates CAL configuration *.cfg* files suitable for placement and routing with the *clare* graphical editor automatically from truth tables.

- *edif2cfg*   The *edif2cfg* program automatically generates CAL configuration *.cfg* files suitable for placement and routing with *clare,* automatically from Electronic Design Interchange Format (EDIF) netlists, which in turn can be created by the OrCAD or ViewLogic schematics packages.

- *cfg2edif*   The *cfg2edif* program extracts netlist and timing information from placed-and-routed CAL designs.

- *cfg2cal*   The *cfg2cal* program generates binary programming information for a given CAL board from a *.cfg* file, output by the *clare* graphics editor or another tool. *cfg2cal* can also generate hex files for use by EPROM programmers to allow CALs to be used in stand-alone applications.

The CAL architecture offers the designer unique facilities for monitoring and changing the internal state of an FPGA in real time. The *debbie* program provides an interactive debugging environment for users of the CHS2×4 board. *debbie* provides windows to monitor the state of internal cells on the CAL array and the values in the memory and counter register on the CHS2×4 board. The values produced by individual cells are displayed as either a red (for logic 1) or blue (for logic 0) band above the corresponding gate. Cell functions and routing are determined by decoding the array control gate. Cell output logic values are determined by reading back the cell output bit of the control store and not by simulation of the user's design.

The CHS2×4 board is controlled via an applications program running on the PC/AT, which takes charge of disk access and displaying results as well as computations not suited for implementation on CALs. Thus, the support software for the CHS2×4 board takes the form of a library of C routines *lib2×4*, which can be called from an applications program written by the user.

As well as allowing access to the local memory for transfer of data and results, these routines provide for access to the CAL's control store. This permits dynamic reconfiguration of individual resources, such as routing multiplexers and function units, as well as monitoring cell outputs. It is also possible to programmatically clear any latch in the circuit implemented on CALs. The software tracks the mapping of gate component names in the user's schematic to cell coordinates, allowing reference to gates by name in the user's control program. This feature means the user programs that access the CAL control store need not be changed when the design placement changes. It is also possible to reconfigure the control CAL using the C library to provide new ways of accessing the board within a given application.

6.3   DES ENCRYPTION

In 1977 the United States National Bureau of Standards (NBS) promulgated a new standard for encryption of unclassified data [NBS77] based on a proposal by IBM, the Design Encryption Standard (DES). Since then, this algorithm has become the *de facto* standard for data encryption worldwide. The algorithm is very suitable for implementation in hardware and several commercial products are available. In this section, we first outline the DES algorithm and secondly develop an implementation. DES provides an excellent example of an algorithm that can be speeded up greatly by bit-level hardware implementation. In this section, we develop a CAL implementation of DES: a more detailed presentation of this work appeared in [Kean89].

DES is a substitution cipher on 64-bit binary vectors based on a 56-bit key. The strength of DES lies in the complexity of the substitution. Two good introductions to DES are [Tanenb81], and for a more in-depth analysis [Konh85].

6.3.1   The DES Process

The DES algorithm is illustrated in Figure 6–4. All the f-boxes are identical, and it is obvious that a major design decision is whether to have one reusable f-box, or 16 separate ones to allow pipelining. We will consider the major components in the block diagram individually. We will try to give an idea of the size of the wiring channels (unfortunately channel density cannot be quoted because it depends on the ordering and spacing of the ports, which is implementation-dependent) and we will give the number of product terms in a minimized PLA implementation (determine using ESPRESSO) for the logic blocks.

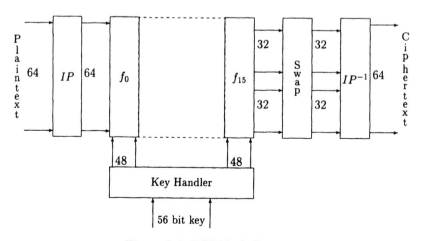

Figure 6–4. DES block diagram.

Permutations IP and IP^-1   The first step in the DES algorithm is to apply an initial permutation IP to the plaintext. The permutation is applied in reverse IP^{-1} as the final step. These permutations involve simple wire swapping and could be implemented using the channel router, but the resulting channel would be wide. The permutations are highly structured and more cost effective implementations than straightforward wire swapping can be found.

Design of the f-Box   The heart of the DES process is the f-box, which performs the function $\pi:(L, R) \rightarrow (R, L \oplus T(R))$, where L and R represent the left and right 32 bits of the 64-bit input. The transformation T is composed of an expansion (bit copying) to 48 bits modulo 2 addition with a key, substitution (in which each group of 6 bits is taken as representing a binary number, which is then substituted for another 4-bit binary number using a lookup table, bringing the size back to 32 bits) and a 32-bit permutation (wire swapping).

The major components in the DES f-box are illustrated in Figure 6–5. The important point to note is that the width of any hardware implementation is fixed by the number of bits to be operated on. We must concentrate on reducing the length of the unit. We will now consider the components of the f-box in order, left to right.

1. Expansion. This step involves expanding groups of four bits in the data to six bits by copying the outer two bits as shown in Table 6–2. This step fixes the height of the implementation as at least 48 cells.

2. XOR with key. This is the critical operation in the whole cipher since this

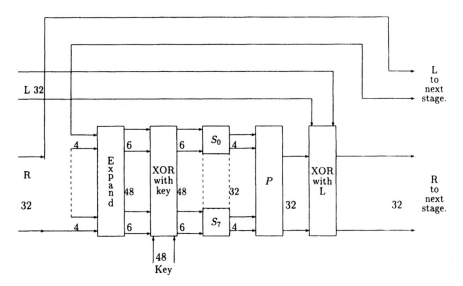

Figure 6–5. DES f-box block diagram.

TABLE 6-2. DES Expansion

Before	After
x_0, x_1, x_2, x_3	$x_{31}, x_0, x_1, x_2, x_3, x_4$
x_4, x_5, x_6, x_7	$x_3, x_4, x_5, x_6, x_7, x_8$
x_8, x_9, x_{10}, x_{11}	$x_7, x_8, x_9, x_{10}, x_{11}, x_{12}$
$x_{12}, x_{13}, x_{14}, x_{15}$	$x_{11}, x_{12}, x_{13}, x_{14}, x_{15}, x_{16}$
$x_{16}, x_{17}, x_{18}, x_{19}$	$x_{15}, x_{16}, x_{17}, x_{18}, x_{19}, x_{20}$
$x_{20}, x_{21}, x_{22}, x_{23}$	$x_{19}, x_{20}, x_{21}, x_{22}, x_{23}, x_{24}$
$x_{24}, x_{25}, x_{26}, x_{27}$	$x_{23}, x_{24}, x_{25}, x_{26}, x_{27}, x_{28}$
$x_{28}, x_{29}, x_{30}, x_{31}$	$x_{27}, x_{28}, x_{29}, x_{30}, x_{31}, x_0$

is the only point where the output ciphertext is modified by the key. A different 48-bit key derived from the user-supplied 56-bit key is used in each f-box.

3. S-Box. The S-box or substitution box has 4 outputs and takes 6 inputs, 4 "data" and 2 "control." The control inputs select one of four 1-to-1 substitution functions over 4-bit binary integers. There are eight separate S-boxes, each of which uses different functions. These units are most naturally implemented as blocks of combinational logic. Running the functions through ESPRESSO produced very little minimization; all 8 S-boxes required more than 50 product terms. This is presumably because the cryptographic properties of DES require an irregular function, whereas logic minimization relies on finding regularities.

4. P-Box. The P-Box or permutation box does a simple wire-swapping operation on its inputs. The layout can be realized with a channel-router, given a reasonable area.

5. XOR and Swap. The swap is necessary because without it only the right half of the plaintext would interact with the key. This would imply that 32 bits of the ciphertext would be identical to 32 bits in the plaintext (which 32 bits in ciphertext and plaintext would depend on the initial and final permutations). The XOR is also crucial to the complexity of the cipher because without it there would be two groups of 32 bits in the ciphertext, each of which depended only on a group of 32 bits in the plaintext. Instead of being a 64-bit, 16-stage cipher, it would be two separate 32-bit, 8-stage ciphers and hence much easier to crack.

Final Swap   The final swap has the effect of canceling out the swap in the final f-box. This cancellation is done to keep the cipher symmetrical so that decryption can be done by reencrypting with the same key; thus only one DES unit is required (not two, one for encryption and one for decryption).

Design of the Key Handler   This logic controls the key that is applied to

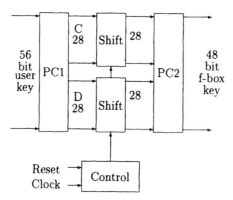

Figure 6–6. DES key handler.

the f-box at each stage of the DES operation. This logic is determined by the key-schedule. The design of the key-handling unit is shown in Figure 6–6. We describe the major components in turn.

1. PC1. The PC1 unit applies an initial permutation to the bits of the key. This unit is 56 bits wide. It can be implemented using a channel router, but the channel is fairly wide and better implementations based on the structure of the permutation are possible.

2. Shifters. After the initial permutation the key is broken up into two 28-bit segments C and D which do not come into contact with each other again. At each stage in the cipher the C and D keys are shifted circularly a number of times, determined by the controller according to the key schedule.

3. PC2. The PC2 unit takes the C and D input keys and does a selection and permutation operation on them, selecting 48 bits from the 56-bit key. The top 24 bits of the result all come from C and the bottom 24 bits all come from D, so it is possible to view PC2 as being two separate 28 to 24 bit units. The resulting 48-bit number is used as the key in the f-box. Again this unit can be implemented using a channel router, and in this case the channel is reasonably small.

4. Controller. The controller generates either one or two clock pulses for the shift registers at each stage of the cipher according to whether one or two key shifts are specified in the key schedule.

6.3.2 Implementation of DES

Floorplan   When we consider the amount of logic required to implement an f-box, it becomes obvious that we cannot hope to have 16 of them in a rea-

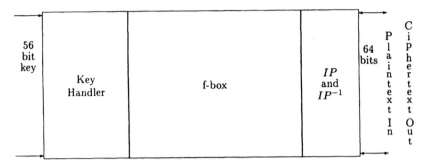

Figure 6–7. DES floorplan.

sonable sized array. Instead, we must use the same box for every stage of the cipher. We wish to avoid bringing the key in from the bottom because at least 48 cells will be required to input a 48-bit vector: if it is brought in from the side, then no extra cost is incurred because the unit must be at least 48 cells high anyway. We also note that IP and IP^{-1} can be implemented in the same wiring area. This suggests the floorplan shown in Figure 6–7.

Layout of f-Box When we examine Figure 6–5 it appears that large wiring areas will be required for the L and R 32-bit words. It is also apparent that all the signals go from left to right: this would imply a large waste of cell resources since the basic cell can route right to left as well. After a little thought, it becomes clear that a much better layout of the f-box is possible (Figure 6–8). By using registers at the right-hand side we have avoided wasting large areas transporting L and R through the unit. By interleaving L and R we have made it extremely easy to XOR adjacent bits and swap over prior to the next stage. We are making use of the cell's ability to route R right to left to bring it to the left-hand side for the initial expansion and XOR with the key. We now consider the design of the major f-box components in turn.

1. S-Box. We start with the S-box because it is the most complex component and will constrain the rest of the design. In order to make use of the logic synthesizer described in Chapter 4, we have to adopt an AND plane/OR plane type layout for this unit with six input signals and four output signals. This means that the design will be nine or ten cells wide, depending on the logic synthesis method used. We can see from the floorplan that as well as performing the logic function, the S-box unit must route four bits of the R vector right to left: this is easily done using the right-to-left connections in the OR-plane. All the S-boxes will be expanded to be the same width as the one with the largest number of product terms.

   The S-boxes were implemented using the CAL ROM generator and required 32 product terms. Although the logic block is only nine cells

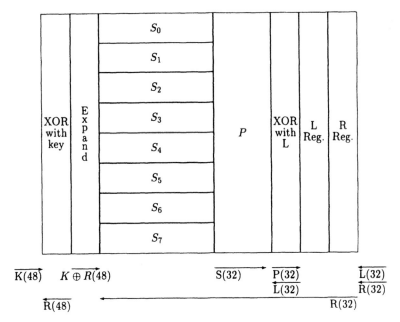

Figure 6–8. F-box floorplan.

wide, we choose to use an extra line of cells between each S-box unit, making its effective width 10 cells and fixing the height of the f-box at 80 cells. There are two advantages to this: first, by increasing the height of the wiring channels we simplify the routing problem, allowing a solution using fewer tracks; second, the extra width simplifies the design of the other f-box components.

The S-box outputs are generated in the order in which they appear on the opposite side of the P-box wiring channel rather than the "numerical" order of the standard. This reduces the number of tracks required to implement the P-box. Note that the right-to-left connection of R shown on the diagram is accomplished by overlaying a routing symbol on the automatically generated S-box design: this is possible because the right-to-left connections are not used by the ROM.

2. Expansion and Key XOR. It turns out to be easier at the cellular level to implement both these functions within the same subunit. Note that there are in fact three slightly different designs for the first, last, and intermediate expansion units because there is a (x_0, x_{31}) wraparound connection. The 80-cell path for this wraparound connection is the limiting factor for pipelining this design. All but the first two columns of cells in the expansion unit are overlaid on the S-box, so its effective width is only two cells: note the extra routing to bring the last bit of $K \oplus R$ to all the OR plane columns of the ROM.

3. P-Box. The P-box is a large wiring channel that runs the whole length of the f-box. As well as implementing the wire swapping, it also realigns the ports ready for the next stage. The R vector can travel across the top of the wiring channel very easily since no right-to-left connections will be used: there is no need to inform the channel router about these signals.

4. L/R Registers XOR and Swap. The L and R registers are implemented as master–slave flip-flops to allow a new value to be loaded while keeping the previous value stable. The registers are broken down into 4-bit units which occupy 10 cells (pitch matched to an S-box). Within these units the bits are interleaved: swapping is implemented simply by a transfer between adjacent registers.

The layout of the whole unit is given in Figure 6–9. Note how the individual components fit together and that the signal flow scheme allows a very high utilization of cell resources.

Layout of Key Handler   The layout of the key handler can follow the block diagram exactly. We will consider the implementation of the major subcomponents in turn.

1. PC-1. This routing converts eight 8-bit bytes into a 56-bit number by throwing away the most significant bit of each byte and doing some simple scrambling of the remaining bits. It is questionable whether it is worth the overhead of hardware implementation, since it will only be used when the key is changed, and this is a relatively rare event. Fortunately, the permutation is structured in such a way that it can be implemented using shift registers rather than a large wiring channel [Hoorn84]. The shift register technique is explained in more detail for the *IP* channel discussed later: its application to this channel is slightly less straightforward.

2. Shifters. These are implemented as clocked master–slave registers with a feedback path. The shifters are pitch matched to the controller in width and to the wiring channels in height. The number of clock pulses determines the number of shifts. The layout is given in Figure 6–10.

3. Controller. This unit can be implemented simply as a finite state machine using the logic synthesizer. It must generate either one or two clock pulses for the shifters on each f-box cycle: to do this it is clocked twice at the start of each f-box cycle and cycles around a 32-state sequence. The reset signal clears the state machine ready for the first cycle and is routed to the shift registers to load the next key through PC-1. When reset is low the registers are configured as two 28-bit circular shifters. In this case Papakonstantinou's algorithm [Kean89] provides a slightly better solution that the ROM generator. A small amount of manual routing is necessary for the feedback terms: the generator could easily be extended to do this automatically. Note that the layout (Figure 6–11) could be optimized by

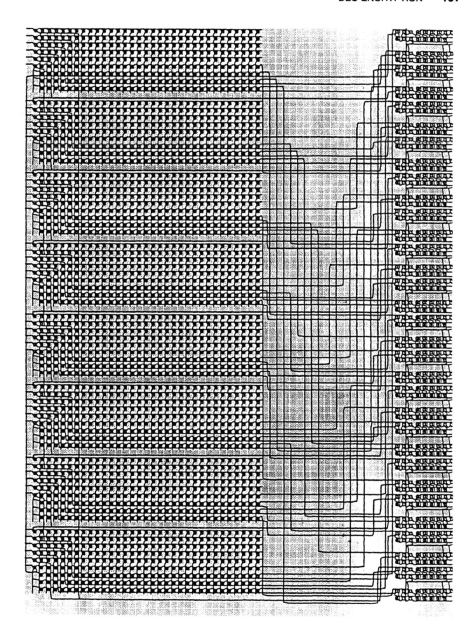

Figure 6-9. F-box layout.

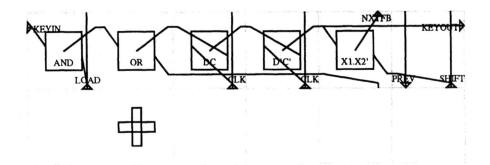

Figure 6–10. Shifter layout.

using unused multiplexers within the logic array to provide the feedback connections.

4. PC-2. This unit is implemented using the channel router: it performs a permutation and selection operation on the shifted 56-bit key to generate a 48-bit key for the f-box. Since only 48 bits are used some of the ports on the left of this wiring channel are unconnected.

The layout of the whole unit is given in Figure 6–12.

IP and IP^{-1}   The initial permutation is given in Table 6–3. A straightforward implementation of this large wiring area would require at least 37 cells. The size of this requirement has to do with both the permutation itself and the fact that we are implementing both *IP* and *IP^{-1}* in the same channel. This means that there are 64 input and 64 output ports on both sides of an 80-cell channel heavily constraining the channel routing (there are very few "free" columns that the router could use to reorder nets). This channel is a problem for silicon implementations of DES as well, and we can borrow a technique from [Hoorn84], [Hoorn88] to implement it in a reasonable width. The technique relies on regularities in the *IP* permutation and replaces the large channel with a small one and some shift registers: it has the side effect of reducing the data rate, but this is not a problem since the speed of the implementation is constrained by the f-box circuits, which are used sixteen times for every input through *IP*. The design is shown in Figure 6–13 and the layout in Figure 6–14.

6.3.3 Pipelining

The design of DES encryptor just described would be unnecessarily slow because of the accumulated delays through the f-box. It was decided, there-

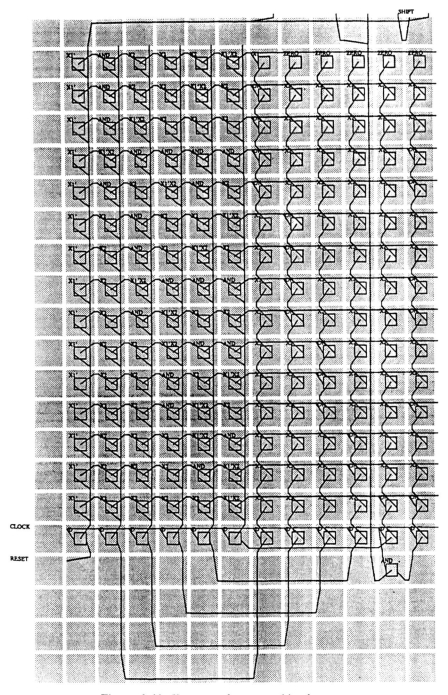

Figure 6-11. Key control state-machine layout.

Figure 6-12. Key control unit layout.

TABLE 6-3. DES Initial Permutation *IP*

L							
57	49	41	33	25	17	9	1
59	51	43	35	27	19	11	3
61	53	45	37	29	21	13	5
63	55	47	39	31	23	15	7
R							
56	48	40	32	24	16	8	0
58	50	42	34	26	18	10	2
60	52	44	36	28	20	12	4
62	54	46	38	30	22	14	6

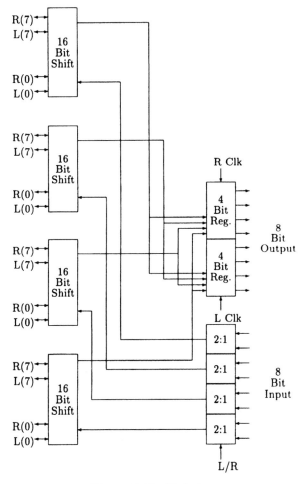

Figure 6-13. *IP* design.

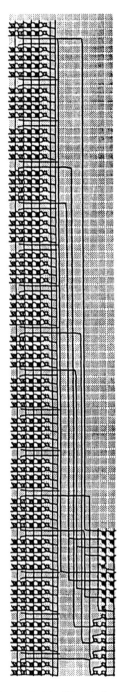

Figure 6–14. *IP* unit layout.

fore, to separate the f-box into four pipelined stages to increase throughput. Note that the delays within the key controller and the *IP* unit are relatively unimportant because the computation within the f-box is much more complex and is repeated sixteen times for every data input, and keys are changed relatively infrequently. Any reasonable design of these units will be able to keep the f-box supplied with data and keys.

It was decided to aim for a throughput of 500,000 encryptions per second with a constant key. To achieve this rate, one 64-bit ciphertext word must be calculated every 2 μs. Since the f-box unit is used sixteen times for each ciphering operation, partially ciphered data must leave the f-box every 125 ns. Table 6–4 shows the approximate delays through the major f-box components (we take routing delay through one cell as 2.7 ns and calculation and output routing delay as 10 ns—these figures are for 256-cell CAL chips designed in 1987, the CAL 1024 devices are faster). We can see that some of these components must be broken up into several pipeline stages to meet the performance objective. The last column of the table shows the number of stages required. Within the CL-ROM we choose to place pipeline registers between the AND and OR planes as well as horizontally across the array. This decouples the AND plane calculation time, which is quite high since there are six inputs. With pipelining between the planes as well as three stages across the array (two with 11 product terms and one with 10) we have a stage delay of $(m - 1)r + 11c = 3 \times 2.7 + 11 \times 10 = 118.1$ ns. The ability to pipeline these large combinational logic units is a partial compensation for the loss in speed caused by using large numbers of 2-input gates rather than a single high fan-in gate. Pipelining within wiring channels is easy to provide using the function units of the cells within the channel.

With the suggested pipelining, the only stage that is close to the 125-ns limit is in the KEYXOR unit—if this proved to be a problem, a slightly more complex routing arrangement could split the 80-cell top-to-bottom wraparound connection among several of the right-to-left routing stages—extra pipeline stages would not be required. The total pipeline length is 10 stages. Extra registers must be provided at the right side of the f-box unit to store the 'L' vectors corresponding to the ten 'R' vectors at the various pipeline stages within the f-box. The pipeline registers themselves are fairly small, requiring only two cells for

TABLE 6–4. Delay through Major f-Box Stages

Unit	Direction	Route	Compute	Time (ns)	Stages
PBOX	R to L	20	0	54	1
SBOX	R to L	32	0	86.4	1
KEYXOR		85	1	239.5	2
SBOX	L to R	4	37	380.8	4
PBOX	L to R	65	0	156	2

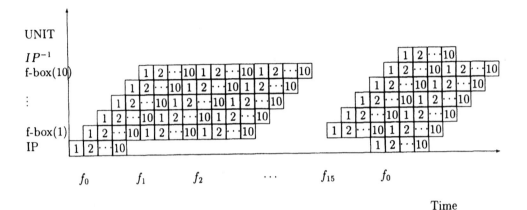

UNIT

IP^{-1}

f-box(10)

⋮

f-box(1)

IP

$f_0 \qquad f_1 \qquad f_2 \qquad \cdots \qquad f_{15} \qquad f_0$

Time

Figure 6–15. Pipelining scheme.

each master–slave register. They are clocked using the G1 and G2 global signals since propagation delay on the pipeline clock is an important consideration.

The time-line for the pipelining scheme is given as Figure 6–15. The delay through the f-box is $16 * (10 * 125 \text{ ns}) = 20 \ \mu s$. It seems natural to pipeline the input and output phases through IP, with this giving a total delay through the encryptor of 60 μs. In applications where large amounts of data have to be encrypted the throughput is of paramount importance, so this is a reasonable design. We could, however, reduce the delay to around 25 μs by removing the extra IP pipelining at a small cost in throughput.

6.3.4 Performance

The performance of DES implementations can be measured in two ways: the number of encryptions per second with the same key and different data, and the number of encryptions per second with a different key and the same data. The second metric corresponds to 'key-trial' in an attempt to break the cipher, the first to normal use of the cipher. The present design is optimized for normal use, so we will concentrate on this problem. Table 6–5 shows figures for some DES implementations: the figures for SUN workstations are using the UNIX *crypt* function in the C library. This implementation is not particularly efficient and it is likely that the times could be significantly improved by recoding in assembly language and taking advantage of space–time trade-offs by using large data arrays to compute S-box functions. The time for a single encryption is given, as well as the number of encryptions per second to show the effect of pipelining. The transputer array figure is a notional one assuming 1000 transputers and that each transputer has a good DES program, allowing encryption ten times faster than a SUN 3/260: it is intended to illustrate the limitations of conventional parallel computers in this application. The time for the custom

TABLE 6-5. DES Encryptor Comparison

Implementation	Encryption Time	Encryptions/Second
CAL	60 μs	500,000
Custom chip	2 μs	500,000
SUN 3/50	0.5 sec	2
SUN 3/260	0.22 sec	5
Transputer array	0.02 sec	50,000

chip is taken from [Hoorn88]. This claimed to be the fastest DES chip available with a throughput of 32M bits/sec (or 500,000 64 bit words/sec). Note that this chip has extra control logic to handle the more complex modes of DES defined in [NBS80] and also provides several registers for secure storage of keys on the chip. The CAL design makes use of several optimizations developed by the group that designed this chip. Although the CAL appears to be as fast, it should be pointed out that 3-μm processing technology was used in the custom chip, which would be expected to be slower than the 2-μm technology on the CAL, and the CAL figures are based on circuit simulations rather than measurements on fabricated chips.

The CAL implementation of DES (including pipeline registers) requires an array of cells 88 cells high by 90 cells wide (27 for the key controller, 60 for the f-box, and 13 for *IP*). This could be provided using a 6-by-6 array of 16 × 16 CAL chips or a 3-by-3 array of 32 × 32 CAL1024 chips. The entire DES encryptor would fit on a single printed circuit board even with low-density 16 × 16 chips.

6.4 SELF-TIMED FIRST-IN FIRST-OUT BUFFER

The principles of self-timed systems have been known for many years, but such systems are rarely implemented because of their complex hardware, despite the advantages of flexible data rates and the avoidance of metastability problems. The self-timed environment prototypes (STEPs) are a collection of primitives used for implementing self-timed systems. The example discussed here was proposed by Sutherland [Suther89]. Many computing applications use a first in, first out (FIFO) buffer, often implemented as a simple circular queue. This is a memory structure that will hold a sequence of data, and output it in the same order as entered. To build a circular-queue FIFO in a synchronous environment, one must use memory elements that are addressed by two counters acting as pointers. The "in" pointer indicates the address to be filled next, while the "out" pointer identifies the first location to be read. The state of the FIFO, full or

---

Section 6.4 contains contributions by Christopher Kappler and originally appeared in "FPGAs," (Moore, W., Luk, W.) Abington EE & CS Books, 1991.

empty, is calculated by subtracting "out" from "in". FIFO control is complicated by synchronization issues and may be unreliable if the FIFO filling and FIFO emptying processes are asynchronous. Sutherland's self-timed FIFO design is entirely different. The basic operation resembles flow through a pipeline. Data are written to one end and read out from the other. The state of each memory location is either full or empty. If a location is empty, it will pass data through. However, if it is full, it will maintain its own contents. If the first location is full, then the FIFO is full. If the last location is empty, then the FIFO is empty. The entire control circuitry consists of only one gate per location, and the resulting speed may be faster than most synchronous FIFOs.

6.4.1 STEP Elements

The self-timed environment is regulated by the handshaking of event signals. An "event" is defined here as a change of state in a control signal. A rising edge has the same significance as a falling edge and both are treated as equivalent events. An XOR gate provides an ideal merging function for events. If either input to an XOR gate undergoes an event, the XOR will cause an event on its output. A Muller-C (Figure 6–16) [Suther89] element provides a rendezvous function for events. There must be an event on each input to a Muller-C before it will cause an event to be output:

$$C := A.B + B.C + A.C$$

To understand the behavior of a Muller-C, imagine the following sequence: assume that A, B, and C are all at logic '0'. If there is an event on A, C stays at '0', but when B rises to meet A, C also rises to a logic "1". If B were to then have another event, C would remain at '1' until A experienced an event,

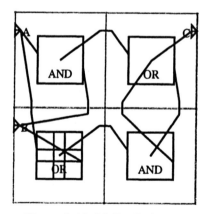

Figure 6–16. Muller C-element.

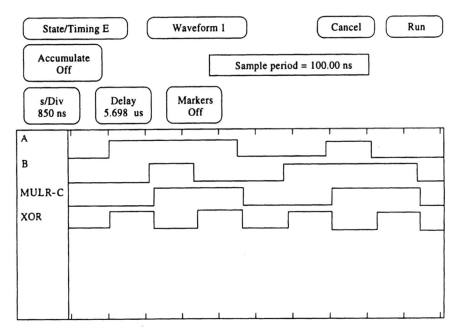

Figure 6–17. STEP waveforms.

to match B. Only then would C fall. The Muller-C waits for events on both inputs before it outputs an event. Figure 6–17 shows the behavior of an XOR as well as a Muller-C element, as recorded by a logic analyzer.

6.4.2 CAL Implementation

Figure 6–18 shows a variant of the Muller-C element referred to as *CnotM*, because it has one inverted input and an active-low clear. Figure 6–19 shows the corresponding circuit. It is important to remember that in the self-timed environment, memory elements (similar to D flip-flops) must be triggered by either the rising edge or the falling edge of the control signal. Figure 6–20 shows an event-triggered D-type element, while Figure 6–21 shows its circuit. It comprises two D latches in parallel. One is latched high and the other is latched low. The output always comes from the nontransparent latch.

6.4.3 Filling the Self-timed FIFO

Figure 6–22 shows just the control structure of a 4-stage micropipeline. The output of each Muller-C can be used to control one storage location. Notice that the right-hand input of each Muller-C element is inverted, signified by a bubble.

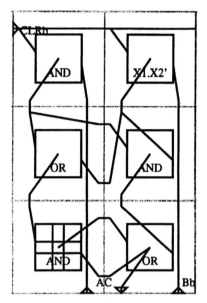

Figure 6-18. CnotM element.

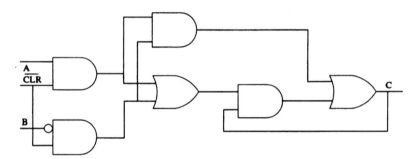

Figure 6-19. CAL CnotM circuit.

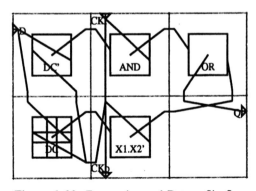

Figure 6-20. Event-triggered D-type flip-flop.

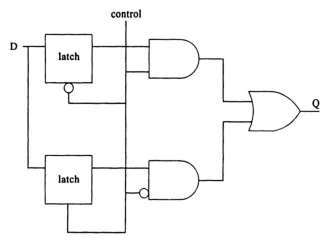

Figure 6–21. Event-triggered D-type circuit.

1. Entering Data. Assume that all logic levels in Figure 6–22 are initially zero, that is, for an empty FIFO. If Rin ("request in") is raised to a '1', while R2 is a '0', R1 will rise. Likewise, if R1 is a '1' and R3 is a '0', R2 will rise. R3 also rises, followed by R4. Now imagine that each R(n) signal is the control input to four dual-edge D-type flip-flops, that is, for a 4-bit-per-stage pipeline. Each time one of the control signals changes, the data are moved one position to the right. Eventually Rin may fall. If R2 is a '1' and Rin is a '0', then R1 will fall. R1 and R3 cause R2

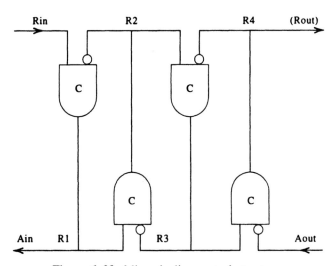

Figure 6–22. Micropipeline control structure.

to fall, then R2 and R4 cause R3 to fall. However, Aout ("Acknowledge Output") may not have been changed by the receiver. When R3 falls, R4 does not follow, because there has not been an acknowledge event on Aout. The FIFO now contains two distinct data values. Each stage of the FIFO receives a request signal and provides an acknowledge signal. When the next data value is passed down the FIFO, R3 is still waiting for an acknowledge from R4, so R3 will not flip. The data will only be piped as far as R2. Changing Rin a fourth time will flip R1 only.

2. A Full FIFO. One could now imagine that new data were placed on the input to the FIFO and Rin was toggled. No event would occur on R1. The "write request" would not be acknowledged. When Rin and R1 are not equivalent, the FIFO is full. The exception to this rule would be the short time that it takes R1 to flip under normal operating conditions but, even then, it would be destructive to toggle Rin when R1 has not even had the chance to change.

3. Reading from the FIFO. Each stage reacts to the previous stage by acknowledging that it has received the data. If stage 4 does not contain the data in stage 3, then stage 4 has never acknowledged stage 3. In the same way if we have read the output of the FIFO and would like it to display the second value entered, we simply toggle Aout. Refer to Figure 6–22 again, and recall the values of the control lines:

$$R1 = `0' \qquad R2 = `1' \qquad R3 = `0' \qquad R4 = `1'$$

If Aout were raised to '1', R4 would be driven to a '0'. The change in R4 would trigger R3 to a '1', and R2 would change to a '0'. If we toggle Aout again, the control values will shift right again, along with the data.

4. Empty Test. When R4 is equal to Aout, the FIFO is empty. The reading device should only read from the FIFO, when R4 (Rout) is not equal to Aout. If they are equal, then a "read request" has not occurred, and there are no data to read.

5. Functional Demonstration. Figure 6–23 is a test, performed in the sequence described earlier. It may be helpful to reread the beginning of this section while reviewing the figure.

Figure 6–24 shows CAL implementations of the four-stage control unit. Figure 6–25 shows the same construction with the event-triggered flip-flops inserted.

6.4.4 Designing in CAL

The design was tested on the CHS2×4 board described earlier in this chapter. At first the design was spread over the array of CAL chips, with no regard

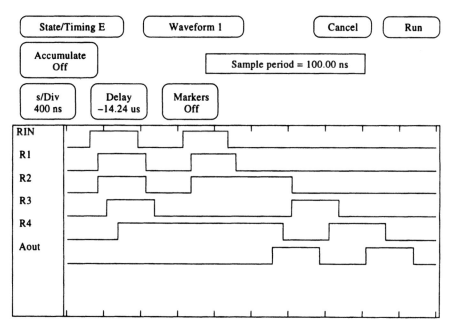

Figure 6-23. Filling the CAL FIFO.

to chip boundaries, but unreliable operation was traced to the fact that some Muller-C elements were split between chips, introducing an extra feedback loop delay of about 40 ns. The design was relaid to avoid splitting and the problem eliminated.

6.4.5 A Full-custom Self-timed FIFO

While the CAL configuration is eminently suitable for experiments with self-timed systems, it carries a lot of structural overhead, that is, configuration memory and multiplexer control. To place these complications in perspective, a custom chip was designed for the self-timed environment, and was fabricated by a 2-μ bulk CMOS n-well process. One structure on this chip is a 15-stage FIFO constructed with the self-timed design principles described earlier. It has been tested with the same measuring equipment used for the CAL implementation. Data can be passed through 12 stages of the FIFO in about 210 ns. Figure 6–26 shows the waveforms of R2, R5, R8, R11, and R14 in the STEP FIFO as it passes data forward. However, this speed is not maintained through the I/O pads. On-chip, the FIFO would appear to be able to handle switching speeds as high as 57 MHz, but with the pads included the maximum speed is 29 MHz. Data are preserved at these speeds.

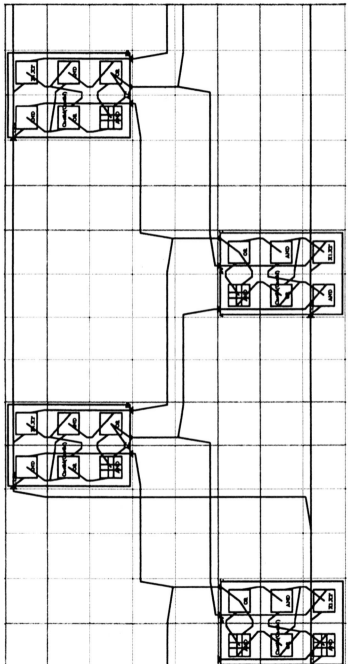

Figure 6–24. CAL micropipeline.

212

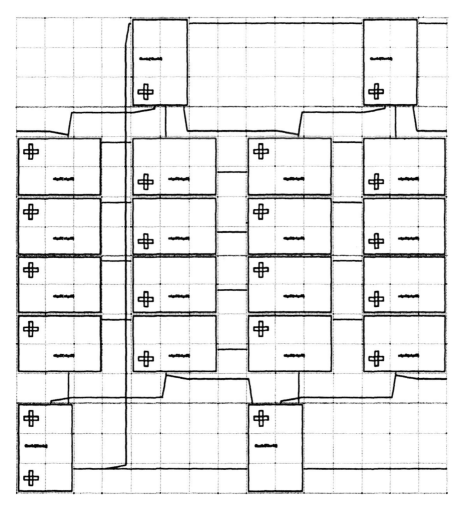

Figure 6-25. CAL FIFO.

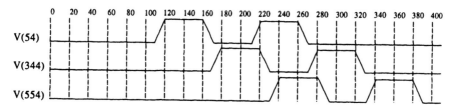

Figure 6-26. Full custom test.

6.4.6 Conclusions

The CAL design of a STEP FIFO runs at approximately 15 MHz, while the custom VLSI implementation runs at 29 MHz. It is surprising that the CAL configuration is not substantially slower. This indicates that in the future, most experiments could be done in CAL only, since it is nearly as fast as a custom chip.

6.5 SELF-TIMED GENETIC STRING DISTANCE EVALUATION

6.5.1 String Comparison

The *string comparison problem* is to find the minimal distance between two strings from a user-defined alphabet set, where the distance between two strings is defined as the cost of transforming one string into the other. Any string can be transformed into another with the aid of the operations insert, delete, and substitute. Distance is considered as the weighted sum of such operations. For example, one way to turn 'ATGC' into 'AATG', would start by substituting the second letter 'T' in 'ATGC' with 'A', substituting the letter 'G' in 'ATGC' with 'T', and substituting the fourth letter 'C' with 'G'. Alternatively, we could insert an 'A' before 'ATGC', and delete the fourth letter, 'C', in 'ATGC'. If we define the cost of both insertion and deletion operations as '1', and a substitution operation as '2', then the distance between 'AATG' and 'ATGC' is '6' using the first method, and '2' with the second. In the absence of any better alternative, the minimal distance between 'AATG' and 'ATGC' is '2'.

String comparison is a common and important operation in almost all information retrieval systems, such as text retrieval, dictionary searching, and biomorphic database retrieval. It is regarded as one of the Grand Challenge computing problems of this decade.

6.5.2 Genetic Sequence Comparison

The *genetic sequence comparison* problem is a special case of the *string comparison problem* applied in the field of molecular biology. Spectacular advances in medicine have come from the decoding of genetic material and the comparison of chains from different organisms. While there are only four characters in the genetic "alphabet," chains may be hundreds of thousands of characters in length. There is a growing data base of decoded genetic material, which is regularly searched for close matches for a newly determined chain. A chain of DNA consists of the four bases, adenine, cytosine, guanine, and thymine, which are abbreviated A, C, G, and T, and so the alphabet set for Genetic Sequence

---

Section 6.5 was contributed by Christopher J. Kappler, Kang Shen, John Oldfield, and Charles Stormon, and originally appeared in "More FPGAs," (Moore, W., Luk, W.) Abingdon EE & CS Books, 1994.

Comparison problem is (A, C, G, T). Given a chain of DNA as the source string, we need to compare it with any chain from a data base of known DNA and find the DNA structures with the minimal distances from the source DNA chain.

6.5.3 Dynamic Programming Algorithm

Given two genetic sequences, we want to find the minimal distance between them. Fortunately, this problem has an optimal substructure property, which allows us to use dynamic programming techniques. This property appears to have been discovered by Levenshtein [Kohon87]. Let $X = (x_1, x_2, x_3, \ldots, x_m)$ and $Y = (y_1, y_2, y_3, \ldots, y_n)$ be two input strings. Let $d_{i,j}$ be a minimal distance between $(x_1, x_2, \ldots, x_i)$ and $(y_1, y_2, y_3, \ldots, y_j)$. Then,

$$d_{0,0} = 0$$
$$d_{i,0} = d_{i-1,0} + \text{cost of a deletion operation}$$
$$d_{0,j} = d_{0,j-1} + \text{cost of an insertion operation}$$
$$d_{i,j} = \min \begin{cases} d_{i-1,j} + \text{cost of deleting } x_i \\ d_{i,j-1} + \text{cost of inserting } y_j \\ d_{i-1,j-1} + \text{cost of substituting } x_i \text{ with } y_j \end{cases}$$

(If $x_1 = y_j$, then the cost of substituting x_i with y_j is 0.)

If we store the distance values in a matrix, the optimal substructure determines that each value $d_{i,j}$ in the matrix depends only on the values of the anti-diagonal lines above and to the left. A dynamic programming algorithm based on the preceding optimal substructure property is then used to solve the string comparison problem. As an example, here is the distance matrix by applying the dynamic programming algorithm to the comparison of AATG with ATGC:

$$\text{source string: AATG}$$
$$\text{target string: ATGC}$$

			A	A	T	G
		0	1	2	3	4
A	1		0	1	2	3
T	2		1	2	1	2
G	3		2	3	2	1
C	4		3	4	3	2

The matrix contains the distances for substring comparisons as well as the final distance in the lowest right-hand element. In consequence, what appears to be a quadratic problem can in fact be solved with a linear array of processing elements.

6.5.4 Implementation Considerations

Many different implementations of this well-known dynamic programming algorithm have been developed. Lipton [Lipton85] presented a linear systolic array implementation using an nMOS prototype, later to be known as Princeton Nucleic Acid Comparator (P-NAC), to be used in searching genetic data bases for DNA strands. The source and the target strings are shifted into an array of processing elements (PEs) simultaneously from the left and the right, respectively. Each character is separated by a null element so that simultaneous left and right shifts may be performed without missing any character comparisons. This is referred to as the *bidirectional* algorithm. When two nonnull characters enter a PE from opposite directions, a comparison is performed. A clock is used to control the data flow, and all PEs can work in parallel. To compare two strings of length n in one pass requires $2n$ PEs. Subsequently, the algorithm was used with the SPLASH 1 and SPLASH 2 architectures, which consist of regular arrays of Xilinx 3000 and 4000 series FPGA chips, along with considerable amounts of RAM. These implementations gave higher performance as well as opportunities for exploring variations in the basic algorithm. Hoang [Hoang93] reported a SPLASH 2 implementation for the algorithm, which could search a data base at a rate of 12 million characters per second. Hoang also developed an interesting variant known as the *unidirectional* algorithm. This requires only half the number of PEs, that is, n. The source string is loaded at the outset by storing it in the array, starting from the leftmost PE. It allows multiple string comparisons by streaming target strings through the array one after another, with a control character separating each string.

It is clear that applying the algorithm to problems of serious interest in molecular biology will require literally hundreds of thousands of PEs, and it will be difficult to synchronize their operation with a conventional clocking scheme. Following earlier work with self-timed micropipelines, we decided to implement a small-scale version of the unidirectional algorithm on an array of Algotronix CAL1024 FPGA chips. The CAL architecture has a number of attractive properties for this application:

1. The fine-grain architecture is economic for self-timed primitives.

2. The chip I/O pad arrangements allow vertical and horizontal cascading without limit.

3. The array can be dynamically reconfigured in an incremental manner.

Some of these general features are illustrated in Figure 6–27, as implemented on an Algotronix CHS2×4 board which fits into a standard IBM PC or clone. Each chip can hold two PEs. There is a start-up stage where we load the source string and initialize the pipe of PEs. Since the organization is self-timed, there are no synchronization issues, even allowing for the delay in crossing chip boundaries, and the design runs at its maximum speed as well as being simple.

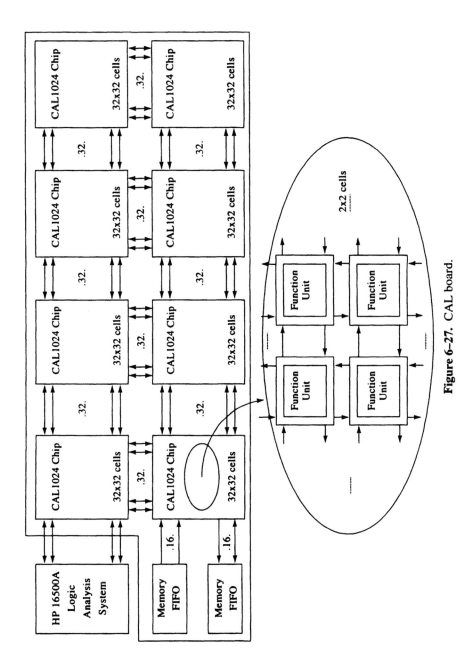

Figure 6–27. CAL board.

TABLE 6-6. DNA Benchmark Performance

Hardware	Specifics		CUPS
Splash 2	unidir; 16 boards		43,000M
Splash 2	bidir; 16 boards		34,000M
Splash 2	unidir; 1 board		3,000M
Splash 2	bidir; 1 board		2,100M
CAL	unidir; 384 PEs		873M
Splash 1	bidir; 746 PEs		370M
MP-1	8K PEs		32M
CM-2	16K PEs		5.9M
BSYS	100 PEs		2.9M
SPARC 10/30GX	gcc-O2		1.2M
P-NAC			1.1M
VAX 6620	VMS: CC		1.0M
SPARC 1	gcc -O2	0.87M	
486DX-50 PC	DOS; gcc -O2		0.67M

Adapted from Hoang, 1993.

6.5.5 Performance Evaluation

Hoang [Hoang93] used the number of cells (entries in the distance matrix) updated per second (CUPS) to measure the performance of an implementation, and we have simply added an entry to the published table (see Table 6–6). The generated delay for each PE in our implementation is 440 ns. If a pipe has N PEs, then the pipeline is capable of $2.273 \times N$ MCUPS with the Algotronix CAL. Note that the CAL implementation assumes 384 PEs.

6.5.6 The Self-timed Implementation*

The Algorithm   Imagine that in the pipeline shown later in this section, the target string $T_{j-2}, T_{j-1}, T_j, T_{j+1}$ is flowing through the array of processor stages. In the stages, source values $S_{i-1}, S_i, S_{i+1}, S_{i+2}$ are held, one per stage (see Figure 6–28).

Calculating the distance in stage $i, d_{i,j}$ then becomes a matter of simply choosing the minimum from $(d_{i-1,j}) + 1$, $(d_{i,j-1}) + 1$, or P. If T_j is equal to S_i, P has a conditional value of $(d_{i-1,j-1})$ or $(d_{i-1,j-1}) + 2$ otherwise. Once stage $i + 1$ accepts target value T_j, the distance value calculated in stage i is pushed onto a two-position stack. This allows memory of past $d_{i,j-n}$ distances for use in future distance calculations.

*The assistance of Dzung T. Hoang and Jeffrey M. Arnold is gratefully acknowledged. The work was supported by the New York State Center for Computer Applications and Software Engineering at Syracuse University.

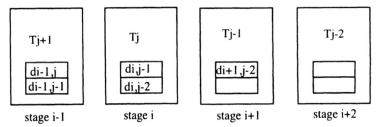

Figure 6–28. Pipeline of processor elements.

Why Self-timed? There are three potential advantages in making a self-timed implementation of an algorithm.

- Reduced power consumption
- Ease of design, which in this example, translates into infinite cascadability
- The ability for a circuit to run at its maximum speed, instead of assuming the worst-case speed, as for a synchronous alterative

Our implementation fully capitalizes on the first two advantages, but does not utilize the potential speed gain. In a clocked system, all stages experience a rising and falling of a clock signal. In self-timed pipelines like this one, one edge is used instead of two, and that single edge is only present in active stages. Idle stages experience no edge at all. The simplicity of design was the main motivation for this self-timed implementation. If it is attractive to the user of this genome distance calculator to have 25,000 chips placed end to end, then that user may do just that with no consideration of clock skew or synchronization problems. In order to make the components of the PE as simple and straightforward as possible, they are not internally self-timed. The worst-case time of the PE was accurately calculated (440 ns), and an equal delay is generated using propagation through buffers of a forward request signal. This design decision robs the design of its potential speed within chip, but still allows for delay variation at chip boundaries.

The Implementation The pipe is made of type-A elements and type B elements in an alternating fashion (see Figure 6–29). There is a type B element between each two type A elements, and therefore the first and last elements are type A elements. The type A elements are stacks with adders, and the type B elements find the minimum of three numbers.

The recursive part of the algorithm is implemented as follows. Suppose a type B element is in stage i with target character T_j passing the stage. When the type B element determines the minimum distance, corresponding to $d_{i,j}$, it takes its first input from the top of the stack of its left-hand type A element, with one added to it, that is, $d_{i-1,j}+1$. It takes another input from the top of the

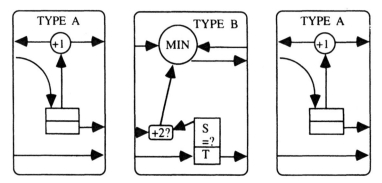

Figure 6-29. Type A and type B stages.

stack in its right-hand type A element, again with one added, that is, $d_{i,j-1} + 1$. The third input comes from the bottom stack of its left type A element, which holds the value $d_{i-1,j-1}$. Now the target character is compared with the source character. If they differ, 2 is added to the value, stored in the bottom stack of its left type A element. Otherwise the characters are the same, and the distance is passed onto the type B element unchanged. This element passes on the result to the next stage by placing it on the top of the stack in its right-hand type A element. From the top of the stack, 1 is added to the value, as stated in the algorithm.

Figure 6-30 shows a complete processing element as implemented in Algotronix CAL, with its subunits unexpanded, while Figure 6-31 is fully expanded. Figure 6-32 shows the minimum unit.

Control The pipeline is controlled with a standard micropipeline handshaking protocol as described in Sutherland's 1989 Turing award paper, "Micropipelines" [Suther89]. There is a fixed delay of 440 ns placed between the Muller-C output and the uninverted input of the next stage (see Figure 6-33).

There is one event that occurs between the control structure and the stacks that lie in the type A stages that is not standard protocol for a micropipeline. When the Muller-C elements are being forcefully cleared by a global clear signal, the stacks do not hold any events caused by this operation. Therefore, the pipeline can be filled with values and the stacks can be set according to the calculations that take place in the pipeline. Then the pipeline can suddenly be emptied, but retain the data values that were formed in the filling process. This is needed in the loading process.

Loading Source Values Originally, the pipe is empty. The source values are entered into the pipe from the left side with a standard *request–acknowledge* protocol. During this loading process, the initial distance of each source character is loaded in each stage.

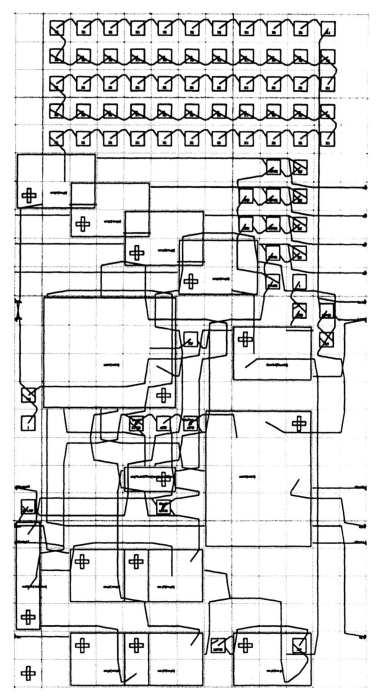

Figure 6-30. CAL layout of a single stage of the pipeline (hierarchical).

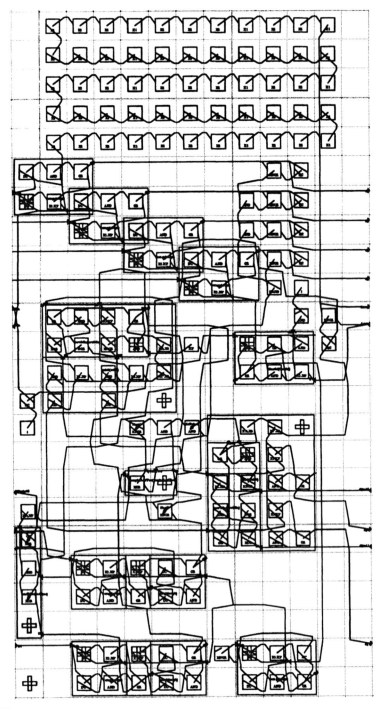

Figure 6-31. CAL layout of a single stage of the pipeline (fully expanded).

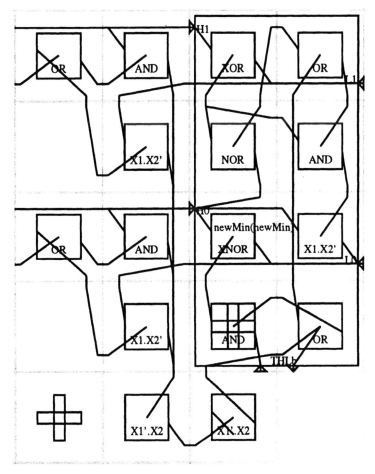

Figure 6-32. CAL block for minimum determination.

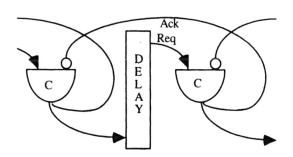

Figure 6-33. Self-timed signaling.

The Algotronix CAL architecture has two global lines, G1 and G2. In order to signal the pipeline that loading is in progress, G1 is set to 1 and held high throughout loading. While G1 is high, the MIN calculator in the type B stage shuts down, and simply passes the value that enters from the left side of the B cell. The top of each stack adds one to the distance value that it receives from the left. The user must set the proper initial distance value to be entered into the pipeline from the left stage. The formula for the initial distance is given later in this section.

If the source string has length s, and the pipe has n stages, then the number of empty stages is $e = n - s$. It is important that the leftmost source value stored in the pipeline has the distance value 1. In order to guarantee this, an initial distance must be entered in the left-hand side of the pipe that has a modulo 4 sum of 0 in the last empty stage. The formula $d_i = (4 - (e \bmod 4)) \bmod 4$ gives that distance. This input distance is the same for all source characters. The entire source string may then be entered using the request-acknowledge protocol (see Figure 6–34). Note that the modulo 4 scheme allows an arbitrary number of PEs to be cascaded, that is, it is totally scalable.

Once all source values are loaded, G1 is lowered, then G2 is lowered and raised again in order to forcefully clear the FIFO control lines. The data values of source and distance are maintained in the stages during this clear procedure.

Empty Stages   The pipeline may be longer than the source string. If this is the case, it is important for a stage to know that it is empty. Using a micro-pipeline, it is obvious that a stage is empty whenever Req is equal in value to Ack. This can be seen in Figure 6–33.

The global signal G1 is lowered at the end of the loading of the source value. When it is lowered, the source characters are latched in the stages. The empty signal for each stage is also latched, so any stage that is empty at the end of the loading process, is given a permanent Empty signal. These stages act as nonprocessing FIFO stages in the distance calculation.

Conclusion   The self-timed organization is attractive for problems of substantial size, and adapts to variations between individual chips as well as chip–chip boundary delays. It is scalable, and adaptable to alphabets of different

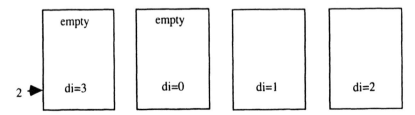

Figure 6–34. Initial loading of pipeline distances.

size. Thus it could be adapted to the protein sequence problem which requires a set of about 15 distinct characters. The CAL1024 chips used in this experiment were implemented in 1.5-μ CMOS technology, and would be faster as well as denser with current submicron fabrication technology. While any large-scale implementation would justify the design and fabrication of a full-custom chip, with both higher density and speed, FPGAs allow rapid prototyping of a detailed design as well as experiments, such as different weight factors. Distance evaluation is only one aspect of the overall requirement, and further work is needed in the recognition of multiple subsequences and other structural features in string comparison.

6.6   CELLULAR AUTOMATON

Recently, much attention has been focused on cellular automata simulations of physical problems: [Wolfram86] contains a collection of important cellular automata papers, and [Toffoli87] provides a much more approachable introduction to the topic based on one particular cellular computer, the CAM-6.

The goal of these models is to set up a "universe," based on a particular cellular automaton rule that mimics physical reality in some way, and observe its evolution. This is to be contrasted with the more traditional approach in [Prest84], where automata are used as data-processing devices to produce desired transformations in image processing. Of particular interest are the cellular automata models for fluid flow simulation: currently, a large fraction of the world's supercomputer time is consumed by this type of problem, and cellular automata models promise cheaper and more powerful computers for this application. Although there was initially a degree of skepticism about cellular automata models in the physics community, much work has been done in the last few years in validating the cellular models, and they have gained wide acceptance. Validation has been done both against experimental results and by showing mathematically that the cellular models approach known differential equations (e.g., the Navier-Stokes equation) for particular "regions" of interest.

In this section, we outline the design of a CAL-based machine for solving such problems. This work was originally presented in [Kean89].

6.6.1   The Model

The most commonly used cellular automaton rule for fluid flow simulation is called *hexagonal lattice gas* and simply specifies what happens when molecules collide on a hexagonal grid. All molecules are assumed to have the same mass and velocity: the density of the grid (i.e., the proportion of lattice sites that are populated at the start of the simulation) is proportional to the fluid's Reynold's number. An example rule is shown in Figure 6–35. In the "before" step all the arrows face toward the current site and in the "after" step all the arrows face away: thus the situations can be coded as six-bit numbers representing the

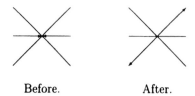

Before.   After.

Figure 6–35. Example lattice gas collision rule.

presence or absence of a particle traveling in a particular direction. Note that to model real fluids properly the rules must obey certain physical properties (e.g., conservation of momentum) and are symmetrical with respect to rotation and reflection.

To obtain interesting results we usually wish to place some object within the fluid. At those sites on the edge of the object a different set of rules will be used, for example, particles reflect back with angle of reflection equal to angle of incidence. It is inefficient to reconfigure the update unit when these sites are being computed, so the normal technique is to add an extra bit plane that contains 1s along the outline of the obstacles. We then use an automaton rule with 7 inputs and 6 outputs (since the obstacles do not move) specified as the normal 6-bit rule when the seventh plane is 0 and the reflection rule when it is 1.

The rule in Figure 6–35 does not use a true hexagonal grid, but has approximated the hexagon on a rectangular grid using 45° diagonals: this is an acceptable transformation in most cases and is necessary to match the structure of the RAM memory that will hold the model points. In some cases a more accurate approximation will be required; this approximation involves a slight increase in complexity and some unused store in the RAM.

Another point of interest is that the "after" stage in our example is not the only one that conserves momentum—particles could also leave on the other two diagonals. Rules that make random choices between different possibilities are also of interest and can offer increased accuracy. While it is inefficient to add randomization at each individual node update, other techniques, for example, using one possibility on "odd" lattice sites and the other on "even," or using one possibility on "odd" update cycles, can be used and are reasonably effective.

Although the basic computation is very simple, to get good results it must be repeated on an extremely large grid of points (2048×2048 is not uncommon) and perhaps 10,000 iterations must be run between samples. One such cycle would involve about 42×10^9 node updates. The need for parallel processing is obvious. After enough cycles have been run, the model is divided up into larger sectors with about 64 sites per sector. The average direction of the molecules within each sector is converted into an arrow, whose length represents the number of particles heading in the most common direction and a diagram such as Figure 6–36 is produced, clearly showing the structure of the flow. The site data can also be used to calculate numbers of

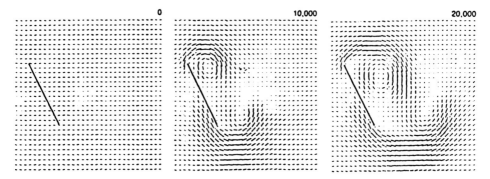

Figure 6–36. Example of output from lattice gas model.

interest, such as forces on obstacles and pressures, after calibrating the model appropriately.

6.6.2 Architecture

There are several methods of organizing the update computation.

1. One Processor per Site. This is the obvious method, using a hexagonal grid of processors and communication between them to deal with particle movement, but it is not practical for real models with as many as 4 million sites.

2. Single Phase. In this implementation the calculation consists of both particle movement and site computation. Enough memory is provided within the computation unit to store the values of all sites adjacent to those whose new values are now being computed. Each site takes the inputs for its computation from the memory corresponding to adjacent sites (converting arrows leaving the adjacent site in the "after" phase of the rule to arrows entering this site for the "before" phase). This method is very easy to use when only a single update processor is available, but the routing becomes complicated when several updates take place in parallel (because of the need to store "before" values for a given site after its new value is computed to allow adjacent nodes to perform their update).

3. Two Phase. In this approach [Clouq87] the memory subsystem is treated as several bit planes, and the values in the planes at a particular address correspond to the "before" data for the corresponding site. The computation unit performs the update and writes back the new "after" value as shown in Figure 6–37. After all sites have been updated, the memory subsystem manipulates bit-plane address offsets to perform a separate "movement" phase in which the bit planes are "realigned" so that in the next computation sweep, cells again have "before" values. For example,

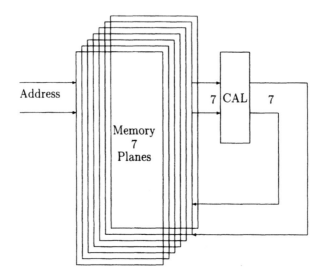

Figure 6–37. Basic lattice gas simulator architecture.

to move a bit plane "up," one would add an offset of the number of pixels in a row. This assumes that memory addresses 'wrap around' at the edge of the bit plane. Wraparound is actually very desirable in a cellular automaton system, since otherwise the fact that edge sites have no neighbors in one direction can distort the results. This approach is very easy to implement, involves almost no performance penalty, and simplifies the design of the update unit. We will assume the two-phase approach in this design, although because the circuitry is reconfigurable, it could also implement the single-phase method.

Performance Goals Before starting out on a design like this, it is important to consider the performance required. Supercomputer implementations of automata problems currently achieve 10^9 site updates per second, so we will take this as our goal and assume that we are working with 2048×2048 site lattices. Since 4M 7-bit words of memory are required for this size of model and 4096×4096 site models are already being suggested, we also require that the memory subsystem be implemented using cheap dynamic RAM.

Update Unit Implementation The first thing to consider is the best way to implement the site update computation with the CAL architecture. We note that the case where the "object" bit plane is 1 is very simple, since reflection simply involves a swapping operation on inputs. For use of a CAL with a read-only control store—a CAL-ROM—seems appropriate for the hexagonal-lattice-gas rules when no object is present. We can integrate the reflection unit with the CAL-ROM as shown in Figure 6–38. Note that for clarity the pipeline registers are not shown in this figure.

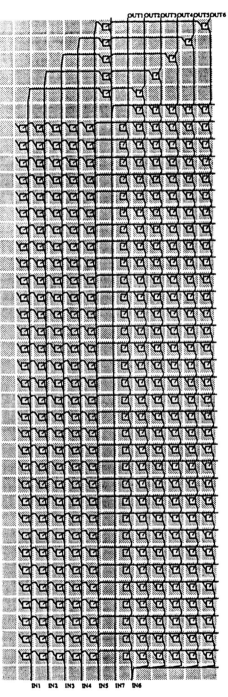

Figure 6-38. Layout of single update unit.

We have $n = 6, m = 6, p = 32$, so using the parameters for CAL256 delay given in section 6.3.3 and assuming 4 product terms per pipeline stage, the delay is $5 \times 10 + 5 \times 2.7 + 4 \times 10 = 103.5$ ns. There are eight pipeline stages in the ROM, plus one for the extra multiplexing. Use of dynamic memory suggests a pipeline tick of 120 ns to allow a memory access to occur and data be routed to the CAL in a single cycle. We will assume that 64×64 cell chips are being used: each CAL-ROM is 11 cells high and an extra line of cells is needed to route the seventh bit plane, giving a total height of 12 cells. This allows five units per chip. Assuming that the multiplexers use a fairly sparse layout 6 cells wide, we have a total width of 32 (product terms) + 6 (multiplexer) + 18 (pipeline registers) = 56 cells. We still have 4 spare rows and 10 spare columns of cells on each chip for any other circuitry we may want, for example, wiring channels to simplify off-chip routing. With 128 computation units (using 26 CAL chips) we can do 1.07×10^9 updates per second.

Memory Subsystem   In order to achieve the very high data rate ($6 \times 128 = 768$ bits every 120 ns) required, a special purpose memory subsystem is necessary. We will consider the design of one bit "plane"; all the bit planes can be identical. Each bit plane must provide 4M bits of RAM and deliver 128 bits every 120 ns. If we choose memory chips that output 4 bit words, then we need to access 32 chips. We also have to simultaneously write back information from the CAL into the bit-plane memory. Given these considerations, a single 4M bit-plane memory could be built from two banks of 32 cheap 16K $\times$ 4 (64K) dynamic RAMs (Figure 6–39). Larger 4096×4096 site models are already being suggested, so a version of the system with 64K $\times$ 4 memories is also worth considering.

The addressing circuitry required is shown in Figure 6–40. Note that we need to decrement the address from which data are being read by the number of stages in the pipeline to get the write address. Each bit plane is assumed to receive the current "site" address from a global controller. Naturally, all this control circuitry would be implemented using CAL chips to provide maximum flexibility.

6.6.3   Comparison with Previous Systems

The configurable logic architecture differs from previous special-purpose cellular automaton machines by having many processors and using configurable ROMs rather than lookup tables for calculations. The main disadvantage of the lookup technique is that the size of the RAM required grows as 2^n with the number of inputs n. RAM size and number of processors must also be fixed in advance—you do not get more processors when the rule is simple. Cellular automaton models with as many as 24 inputs have been suggested to increase the accuracy of the simulations. Naturally, if the rules were completely random functions of n variables, configurable logic could do no better than lookup tables: however, cellular automata rules for lattice gas equations

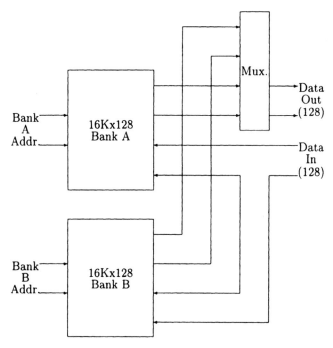

Figure 6-39. Architecture of single bit plane.

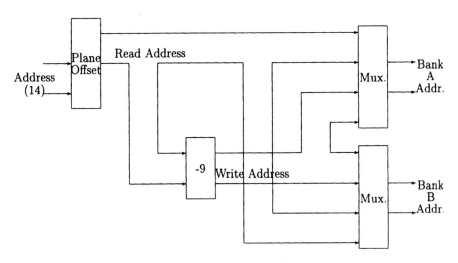

Figure 6-40. Memory addressing for one plane.

TABLE 6-7. Performance on Fluid Flow Simulations

System	(Site Updates/Second) $\times 10^6$
Cray X/MP	500
Connection Machine	1000
Single Princeton Chip	20
Princeton system	1000
Single 64 × 64 CAL	40
CAL system	1070

are very regular (this follows from basic properties of the physical model, such as symmetry and conservation of momentum). We can see the advantages of the configurable logic approach from the preceding example: if a RAM lookup table had been used, then the size of the RAM would be doubled by the seventh input bit. However, with the CAL implementation only a very small additional piece of logic is required. It is likely, therefore, that despite the number of inputs in the newer rules, an implementation using relatively few logic gates will be possible. The structure of this implementation will vary from rule to rule. In the lattice gas model of this example, rotation and reflection symmetry could be used to reduce the number of rules from 64 to 14 [Wayner88].

With a reasonable amount of hardware the configurable logic system can easily outperform any conventional computer on this problem: Table 6-7 compares the expected performance of the system with supercomputer implementations and custom chips. The first Princeton figure is a maximum per chip. There are 1500 chips in the present configuration. However, I/O considerations on the SUN-3 host limit the performance per chip to 2/3 million sites/second, giving an overall performance of 1000 million sites/second. This figure is disappointing for a custom chip and is a result of the method of organizing the computation to reduce I/O bandwidth and avoid the need for a special memory subsystem—75% of the Princeton chip area is taken up with a large shift register, and there are only two update units per chip. The Princeton chip uses 3-μm technology rather than the 1-μm technology needed for a 64 × 64 cell CAL. The Connection Machine and Princeton chip figures come from [Wayner88], and the figures for the Cray supercomputer are from [Shimom87]. The CAM-6 and RAP systems mentioned previously do not support enough lattice sites and have much lower performances because they have only one lookup table for site update calculation.

6.6.4 Conclusion

We can see that the CAL design is extremely cost effective, providing supercomputer performance from a system with fewer than 30 custom chips (even including control circuitry) and less memory than a low-end workstation. Even when the cost of a host computer to control and display the results of the simulations is included, the system is very attractive. The use of reconfigurable chips in the update and control units will allow this system to evolve as the models become more complex. Also, extra memory planes and larger update units are easily accommodated.

6.7 PLACE-AND-ROUTE ACCELERATION

The place-and-route subsystem of the Algotronix CAD software uses a simulated annealing algorithm to repeatedly generate and evaluate potential placements for a user's design. In the later stages of this process, the computer attempts to completely route the current placement. This step of the procedure is very computation intensive and results in long run times for the software. In this section we present a hardware acceleration tool for this application, which runs on the CHS2×4 board.

6.7.1 The Global Routing Algorithm

The global routing problem for CAL is to route a set of nets successfully, each of which has a single source and one or more destinations using the multiplexer routing resources of the CAL chip. The nets contend for multiplexer resources and the algorithm will fail if more than one net requires a particular multiplexer to route. In this case, the current placement will be rejected.

Each net is routed individually using a wavefront expansion algorithm, so the order in which nets are routed is of critical importance and it is usually necessary to rip up previously routed nets and retry nets in a different order to route a design successfully. The hardware accelerator described here allows the algorithm to very rapidly determine whether implementing the current net using a particular multiplexer will cause any of the currently unrouted nets to fail to route. That is, it answers the question: Given the present allocation of multiplexers, is it possible to complete a connection between cell (x1, y1) and (x2, y2)? Figure 6–41 shows a graphical representation of the output of the algorithm when run on the control CAL routing of Figure 4–27. The square marked "S" represents the source cell of the net, "." squares are reachable, and "U" squares cannot be wired to because of blocks caused by multiplexers assigned to other nets.

6.7.2 Hardware Architecture

Figure 6–42 shows the basic input and output connections to a CAL cell. Each output from the cell has a dedicated multiplexer that can select any of the other inputs to the cell or the function unit output. Figure 6–43 shows a circuit that can model the routing possibilities of the cell: if any of the cell inputs go high, then all the cell outputs go high. We can build an array of these blocks in one-to-one correspondence with the array of CAL cells we are attempting to route.

```
UUUUUUUUUUUUUUUUUUUUUUU.........        UUUUUUUUUUUUUUUUUUUUUUU.........
UUUUUUUUUUUUUUUUUUUUUUUU.........       UUUUS.....................
UUUUUUUUUUUUUUUUUUUUUUUU.........       UUUUUUUUUUUUUUUUUUUUUUUU.........
UUUUUUUUUUUUUUUUUUUUUUUU.........       UUUUUUUUUUUUUUUUUUUUUUUU.........
UUUUUUUUUUUUUUUUUUUUUUUU.........       UUUUUUUUUUUUUUUUUUUUUUUU.........
UUUUU........................          UUUUU........................
UUUU.........................          UUUU.........................
UUU..........................          UUU..........................
UU...........................          UU...........................
U.........................U....         U.........................U....
.........................U..            .........................U..
.........................UU.            .........................UU.
.........................U..            .........................U..
............................            ............................
...........................U            ...........................U
............................            ............................
..........................U...U          ..........................U...U
...........................UUU           ...........................UUU
...........................UUU           ...........................UUU
...........................UUU           ...........................UUU
...........................UUU           ...........................UUU
...........................UUU           ...........................UUU
...........................UUU           ...........................UUU
...........................UUU           ...........................UUU
.........U................UU              .........U................UU
.........U................UU              .........U................UU
.....U...S................UU              .....U....................UU
.....UU.....U.............UU              .....UU.....U.............UU
.....UU.......U...........                .....UU.......U...........
.....UU......UU...........                ............UU.............
```

Figure 6–41. Reachability data for control CAL.

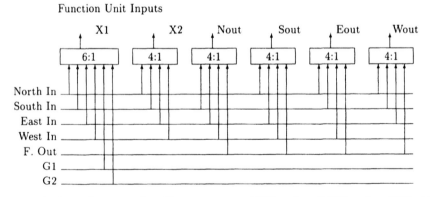

Figure 6–42. CAL cell routing. Figure courtesy of Xilinx, Inc. © Xilinx, Inc. 1991. All rights reserved.

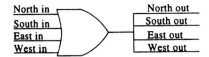

Figure 6–43. Hardware routing model of CAL cell.

If we think of logic 1 as representing "reachable" and logic 0 as representing "notreachable" and insert a single logic 1 into the array at the source point of the net of interest, then logic 1s will propagate to all reachable cells.

There are two remaining considerations:

1. It is necessary to force all the model circuit's outputs low before inserting the single logic 1. If there are any spurious logic 1s elsewhere in the circuit before starting the test, then these will propagate at the same time as the "real" 1, potentially resulting in unreachable cells being marked as reachable. Initialization is achieved by inserting an AND gate on the output of the OR gates with its input controlled by the global signal G1: thus when G1 is low, all outputs will be forced low.

2. The model at present represents an array prior to any configuration: we need to represent multiplexers currently assigned to the user's design. This is done by dynamically reconfiguring the logic within the blocks. We can represent a multiplexer assigned to another net by deleting the corresponding input to the OR gate in the adjacent cell. This is done by reconfiguring the function unit from OR to X1 or X2, or from X1 or X2 to constant ZERO, according to which input is to be deleted.

6.7.3 CAL Layout

The CAL layout for a single repeating block is shown in Figure 6–44. Since it is 4 cells wide and 2 cells high, we can model a single CAL chip on a 4-by-2 array of CAL chips contained on a CHS2×4 board. This layout is not optimized for density, since the goal was to model a single CAL device on the board and leaving extra space made some implementation details easier.

6.7.4 Software

The software required to implement the maze routing accelerator is in two parts:

1. A simple (30 line) *laura* program builds the array of cell models based on the basic repeating cell design described earlier.

2. Run-time software dynamically reconfigures the cells within the array to remove inputs to the OR gates where multiplexers are assigned to other

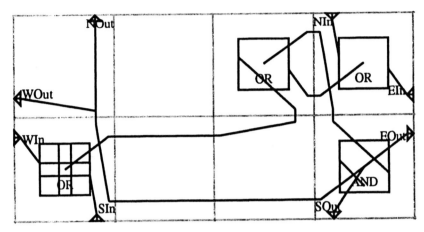

Figure 6–44. CAL layout for cell routing model.

nets. It also uses dynamic reconfiguration to insert a logic 1 at the trial net's source and to read back cell outputs to determine reachability.

6.7.5 Performance

The hardware architecture will propagate a signal across a cell in about 30 ns. This is sufficiently fast that performance is entirely limited by the program that accesses the board. This must calculate the memory addresses required, that is, to add the logic 1 at the net's source and read back whether its destinations have been reached. It is expected that integration of the hardware accelerator within the place-and-route system would result in substantial overall performance increases.

This example shows the potential benefits of a general technique where the FPGA logic is used to directly model the situation of interest, using direct access to the control store to set up initial conditions and read back results.

6.8 A FIELD-PROGRAMMABLE GATE ARRAY FOR SYSTOLIC COMPUTING

6.8.1 Introduction

Recent work [Gray89] [Gokhale91] [Bertin92] has shown that a handful of SRAM-based field-programmable gate arrays (FPGAs) wired together can achieve extraordinary levels of performance, often outperforming supercomputers at a tiny fraction of the cost. And, unlike ASIC solutions, these systems

Section 6.8 was contributed by Frederick Furtek and originally appeared in *Research on Integrated Circuits: Proceedings of the 1993 Symposium*, Gaetano Borriello and Carl Eberling, Eds. © 1993 Massachusetts Institute of Technology.

are general purpose and reprogrammable: they can be reconfigured in milliseconds to perform a completely new task.

The CLi6000 series of SRAM FPGA's from Concurrent Logic has evolved through several generations and is the product of two joint-development efforts, with Apple Computer [Furtek90] and National Semiconductor [Furtek92]. The original motivation for the technology, and still a key application area, is the acceleration of compute-intensive algorithms by exploiting the parallelism inherent in hardware. The capabilities of the technology are illustrated through a massively parallel algorithm for performing motion estimation, an especially compute-intensive algorithm used in digital video compression. The algorithm which determines the best estimate of how blocks of pixels move from frame to frame requires about 4,000 MIPS to perform in real time on a standard video signal.

The algorithm is implemented as a systolic array of 256 processing elements, each achieving 100% efficiency with no wasted clock cycles through pipelining, and a clever synchronization of input pixel streams. The CLi6000's high register count, NAND/XOR cell states, multiplexer states, fine-grained architecture, array symmetry, and high cell connectivity all work together in efficiently implementing the heavily pipelined, bit-serial arithmetic operations used in each processing element.

6.8.2 CLi6000 Architecture

At the heart of the CLi6000 architecture* is a symmetrical array of identical cells (Figure 6–45). Routing within the array is either by bus or by direct connection between neighboring cells (Figure 6–46). Direct connections are most useful in tight spaces and over short distances where maximum flexibility is required. Busses support fast, efficient communication over longer distances.

There are two kinds of busses: local and express. Local busses are the link between the array of cells and the bussing network. Express busses are not connected directly to cells and hence provide higher speeds. Connective units, called repeaters, spaced every eight cells, divide each bus both local and express into segments spanning eight cells. Repeaters can: isolate bus segments, connect local-bus segments, connect express-bus segments and provide local–express transfers.

The cell (Figure 6–47) is simple and small and yet provides many important and commonly used logic functions, including those most useful in pipelining and arithmetic: a D-type register, a NAND/XOR pair and a two-input multiplexer. The register is essential in pipelining, which is the most effective way to achieve high system throughput. The high register count of the CLi6000 architecture (there are 3,136 in the CLi6005) makes pipelining simple and efficient. The NAND and XOR, available simultaneously in a single cell, provide efficient implementation of full adders and other arithmetic functions. The mul-

---

*See [Conc92] for a more complete description of the CLi6000 architecture.

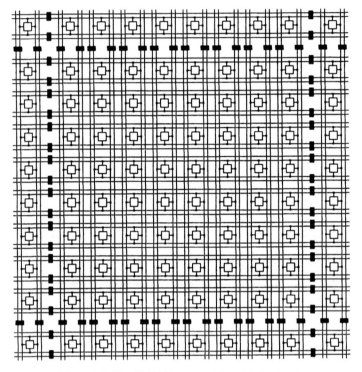

Figure 6–45. CLi6000 array (10 × 10 Section).

tiplexer, available by itself or feeding into a register, finds many uses in a broad range of circuits.

Because its four sides are functionally identical, each cell is completely symmetrical. Cell symmetry together with array symmetry, high cell connectivity, and a fine-grained architecture make the design of hard macros (circuits with fixed layouts) especially easy. More specifically, it facilitates the creation of bit-slice macros, hard macros in which the inputs/outputs on one side are aligned with the outputs/inputs on the opposite side. A larger circuit is constructed by simply abutting these bit-slice macros. The remainder of this section describes just such an approach in implementing a massively parallel algorithm.

6.8.3   Motion Estimation

Motion estimation is concerned with finding the best estimate of how blocks of pixels move from frame to frame in a video signal. For a block of pixels in the current frame (the current block), the object is to find the best match among search blocks the same size within a search window of the preceding frame. The best match is determined by finding the minimal error (distortion) between the current block and the search blocks. For a block C in the current frame and

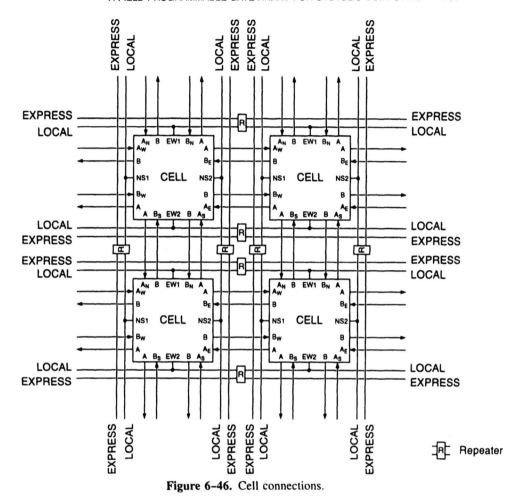

Figure 6-46. Cell connections.

a block P in the preceding frame:

$$\text{Error}(\Delta x, \Delta y) = \sum_{x=0}^{x-1} \sum_{y=0}^{y-1} |C(x, y) - P(x + \Delta x, y + \Delta y)|$$

where x and y are the horizontal and vertical displacements, respectively, of the search block relative to the current block, and X and Y are the horizontal and vertical dimensions, respectively, of the blocks being compared. The motion-estimation algorithm returns both the displacement vector x, y and $\text{Error}(x, y)$ of the best match. This calculation is repeated for each block in the current frame, which is assumed to be tiled with blocks except for an indentation around the edges to allow for the displacement of search blocks.

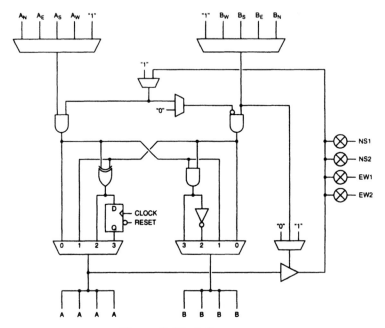

Figure 6–47. Cell structure.

We assume a standard video signal:

Frame rate: 30 frames/sec
Frame size: 360 pixels × 288 pixels
Pixel depth: 8 bits
Block size: 16 pixels × 16 pixels
Max hor. displ: −8, +7
Max vert. displ: −8, +7

The frame rate and frame size lead to a pixel rate of 3.11 MHz, which, in the bit-serial algorithm described here, means a bit rate and clock frequency of 24.88 MHz.

The algorithm assumes four bit-serial inputs:

- Preceding Frame: Upper Band
- Preceding Frame: Lower Band
- Current Frame
- Start of Block

The ordering of pixels in the first three inputs is by horizontal bands. Each

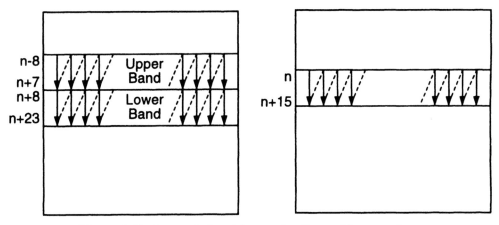

Figure 6-48. Input ordering: (*a*) preceding frame; (*b*) current frame.

band is 16 pixels high, and the pixels within a band enter serially by column, from top to bottom (Figure 6–48). The two bands in the preceding frame straddle the band in the current frame. The Upper Band is offset from the current band by 8 pixels, while the Lower Band is offset by +8 pixels. The scanning of all three bands starts at the same time.

Start of Block (SOB) signals the start of a new 16 pixel × 16 pixel block in the current frame. SOB is assumed to be active high, a high value coinciding with the first (8-bit) pixel of the new block. The first 16 × 16 block in a band of the current frame is indented by 8 columns to permit search blocks to be displaced by 8 pixels (Figure 6–49). Thereafter, blocks arrive every 16 columns. (In the algorithm described below, blocks need not abut, but they must not overlap.) Figure 6–50 illustrates the search window, containing 256 search blocks, corre-

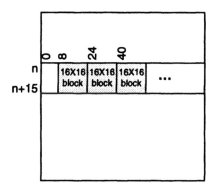

Figure 6-49. 16 × 16 blocks in the current frame.

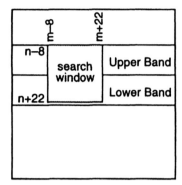 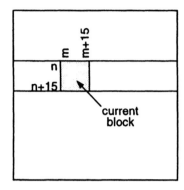

Figure 6-50. Current block and corresponding search window: (a) preceding frame, (b) current frame.

sponding to the current block. (The search window does not reach the bottom of the Lower Band because search blocks are displaced a maximum of +7 pixels.)

6.8.4 Algorithm Overview

The algorithm is bit serial and massively parallel. Figure 6-51 is a block diagram showing the heart of the algorithm: a linear array of 256 processing elements (PE's). The array, as well as each PE, has nine inputs:

- Current_Frame (CF)
- Select_Upper_Band (SUB)
- Select_Lower_Band (SLB)
- Upper_Band (UB)
- Lower Band (LB)
- Start_Of_Block (SOB)
- End_Of_Block (EOB)
- Error_Low_Order_Byte (ELOB)
- Error_High_Order_Byte (EHOB)

The Current-Frame pixel stream is supplied directly to the CF input of the linear array. The Upper-Band pixel stream, however, is delayed by 1024 clock cycles before being supplied to the UB array input. The delay retards the Upper-Band pixels by 8 columns relative to the current frame. (8 columns × 16 pixels/column × 8 cycles/pixel = 1024 cycles) The Lower-Band input is delayed by 1152 clock cycles, which retards the Lower-Band pixels by 9 columns relative to the current frame. (9 columns × 16 pixels/column × 8

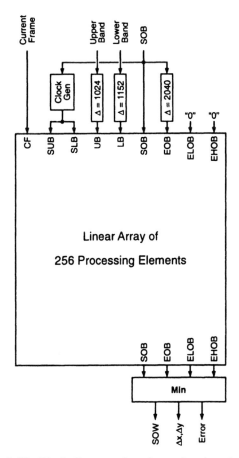

Figure 6-51. Block diagram of motion-estimation algorithm.

cycles/pixel = 1152 cycles) Clock Gen provides an 8-cycle high value every 128 clock cycles to both the SUB and SLB inputs of the array. Start of Block synchronizes Clock Gen so that this high value coincides with the first pixel of each column on the CF, UB, and LB inputs. Start of Block is also fed directly to the SOB input and is delayed by 2040 clock cycles to provide the EOB input. The values on the ERL and ERH inputs are immaterial since they are replaced by PE-supplied values. ERL and ERH are arbitrarily set to "0."

The array outputs SOB and EOB are each delayed by 2304 (9 × 256) clock cycles from the corresponding inputs. The 256 errors associated with the 256 search blocks appear serially on the ELOB and EHOB outputs. Min looks for the minimal error and supplies that error along with the corresponding displacement vector.

6.8.5   Processing Elements

Each processing element has nine outputs to match its nine inputs. The array of 256 PE's is formed by connecting the outputs of one PE to the matching inputs of the next PE, as shown in Figure 6–52. The computational demands of motion estimation are handled through massive parallelism: each PE computes the error between the current block and one of the 256 search blocks. Table 6–8 shows the correspondence between PE's and displacement vectors.

There are actually two slightly different types of processing elements: the one in Figure 6–53 is used for all PE's except for PE 0 and every 16th processing element thereafter that is, for all PE's except PE 0, PE 16, PE 32, PE 48, PE 64, ... These PE's are identical to the one in Figure 6–53 except that the SR

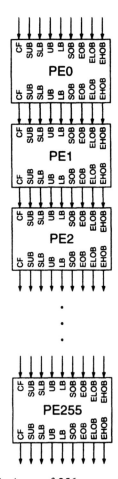

Figure 6-52. Array of 256 processing elements.

Table 6-8. Processing Elements and Associated Displacements

PE #	Displ.	PE #	Displ.
0	$\langle -8, -8 \rangle$	·	
1	$\langle -8, -7 \rangle$	·	
2	$\langle -8, -6 \rangle$	·	
3	$\langle -8, -5 \rangle$	237	$\langle +6, +5 \rangle$
4	$\langle -8, -4 \rangle$	238	$\langle +6, +6 \rangle$
5	$\langle -8, -3 \rangle$	239	$\langle +6, +7 \rangle$
6	$\langle -8, -2 \rangle$		
7	$\langle -8, -1 \rangle$	240	$\langle +7, -8 \rangle$
8	$\langle -8, +0 \rangle$	241	$\langle +7, -7 \rangle$
9	$\langle -8, +1 \rangle$	242	$\langle +7, -6 \rangle$
10	$\langle -8, +2 \rangle$	243	$\langle +7, -5 \rangle$
11	$\langle -8, +3 \rangle$	244	$\langle +7, -4 \rangle$
12	$\langle -8, +4 \rangle$	245	$\langle +7, -3 \rangle$
13	$\langle -8, +5 \rangle$	246	$\langle +7, -2 \rangle$
14	$\langle -8, +6 \rangle$	247	$\langle +7, -1 \rangle$
15	$\langle -8, +7 \rangle$	248	$\langle +7, +0 \rangle$
		249	$\langle +7, +1 \rangle$
16	$\langle -7, -8 \rangle$	250	$\langle +7, +2 \rangle$
17	$\langle -7, -7 \rangle$	251	$\langle +7, +3 \rangle$
18	$\langle -7, -6 \rangle$	252	$\langle +7, +4 \rangle$
		253	$\langle +7, +5 \rangle$
·		254	$\langle +7, +6 \rangle$
·		255	$\langle +7, +7 \rangle$
·			

latch and associated multiplexer are omitted, and just Upper-Band pixels are fed to the absolute-difference module.

At the heart of both types of processing elements is an absolute-difference module and an accumulator. The circuitry to the left supplies the absolute-difference module with two bit-serial streams of pixels. The circuitry to the right resets the accumulator at the beginning of a new block, and at the end of the block places the accumulated error both high- and low-order bytes† on busses that transport the values to the end of the PE array.

The left-side circuitry assures that the proper pixels for the current block and search block are supplied to the absolute-difference module. There is no problem with the current-block pixels they are constant for all PE's. The search-block pixels, however, must be synthesized from the Upper- and Lower-Band

---

† The accumulator has high- and low-order bytes because although the maximum difference between two pixels is 11111111 (255), the maximum accumulated error between two blocks is 1111111100000000 (256 × 255 = 65,280).

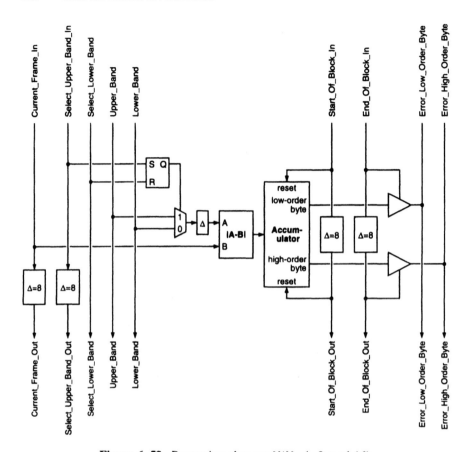

Figure 6-53. Processing element $N(N \neq 0 \mod 16)$.

pixels. The key to making this happen is the *fast-track/slow-track* technique pioneered by Dick Lyon in his serial multiplier designs (see Lyon [Lyon76] and Denyer & Renshaw [Denyer85]). The SLB, UB and LB signals are on fast tracks 0 clock-cycle delay per PE while the CF and SUB signals are on slow tracks 8 clock-cycle delay per PE.

To understand how the circuitry works, consider the pixel-alignments entering PE 0. The pixels in the Synthesized band, which are identical to the Upper-Band (UB) pixels, are displaced by $\langle -8, -8 \rangle$ relative to the Current (CF) pixels.‡ This is consistent with Table 6-8, which indicates a displacement of $\langle -8, -8 \rangle$ for PE 0.

Now consider the pixels entering PE 1. Because of the 8-clock-cycle delays

‡ The unit delay just before the A input of the absolute-difference module is only for pipelining Small delays on various array inputs, including CF, may have to be inserted to insure correct alignment.

on the Current Frame and the Select-Upper-Band (SUB) signal, the Upper and Lower Bands and the Select-Lower-Band (SLB) signal have been advanced by one pixel (8 clock cycles) relative to the Current pixels and SUB. SUB, which is always aligned with the Current pixels, sets the SR latch at the beginning of each new column of Current pixels. Setting the latch causes the Synthesized pixels to come from the Upper-Band until the latch is reset by SLB. SLB, which is coincident with SUB entering PE 0, is advanced by one pixel relative to SUB entering PE 1. The Synthesized Band therefore, takes only the 16th (last) pixel in each column from the Lower Band. The result of all this is that the Synthesized pixels are now displaced by $\langle -8, -7 \rangle$ relative to the Current pixels. In other words, the search block has dropped down one row. This pattern continues for PE 2 through PE 15, with each succeeding PE adding a row of pixels from the lower band.

The pattern is broken for PE 16 because we no longer want to move down one row but rather back to the top of the search window and to the right one column. This is accomplished by eliminating the Upper-Band/Lower-Band multiplexing logic, and simply reverting to the upper band. The pattern described above for PE's 0-15 now repeats for PE's 16-31, and for every succeeding group of 16 PE's.

On the right side of Figure 6–53, we again employ the fast-track/slow-track technique. The SOB and EOB signals are on slow tracks 8 clock cycles delay per PE to match the speed of the CF signal on the left side. The ELOB and EHOB signals are on fast tracks 0 clock cycles delay per PE so that the two errors from each PE fill unique *slots*.

The SOB signal is timed so that the low- and high-order registers in the accumulator are reset just as a new block begins.§¶ The EOB signal is timed so that the values in these two registers are placed on the two busses just as the last pixel error for the current block is accumulated. Note that no clock cycles are lost in the changeover from one block in the current frame to the next. Except at the left and right edges of the frame, the absolute-difference modules and the accumulators in all the PE's are always productively engaged.

Finally, notice that because ERL and ERH are on fast tracks while EOB is on a slow track, errors placed on the ERL and ERH busses by the n'th PE immediately follow the errors of the (n − 1)'th PE. The result is that errors appear at the output of the PE array in the order in which they are created. The 256 (high- and low-order) errors exactly fill the 256 slots available between Start-of-Block and End-of-Block.

---

§We are ignoring the latency in the absolute-difference module and the accumulator. Once these values are known, both the SOB and EOB signals will have to be delayed prior to PE 0 by an appropriate amount to compensate.

¶Because the accumulator is bit serial, the high-order byte is accumulated one word (8 clock periods) after the low-order byte.

6.8.6 Absolute-difference Module and Accumulator

At the core of each processing element are a bit-serial absolute-difference module and a bit-serial accumulator.

The task of performing the absolute difference is actually split between a subtracter module (Figure 6–54) and the low-order stage of the accumulator (Figure 6–55). Within the subtracter module is a bit-serial subtracter consisting of a full adder, two inverters, AND gate and unit delay. Employing a technique known as explicit subtraction (see [Denyer85] for a discussion of bit-serial operations), it takes A, B and Start_Of_Word as inputs and produces A-B. The register enabled by End_Of_Word latches the carry (borrow) at the end of each subtraction. A borrow of 0 indicates that A-B is positive and may be accumulated without modification. A borrow of 1, on the other hand, means that A-B is negative and must be negated when accumulated. The 8-unit delay aligns A-B with Sign. The low-order stage of the accumulator (top part of Figure

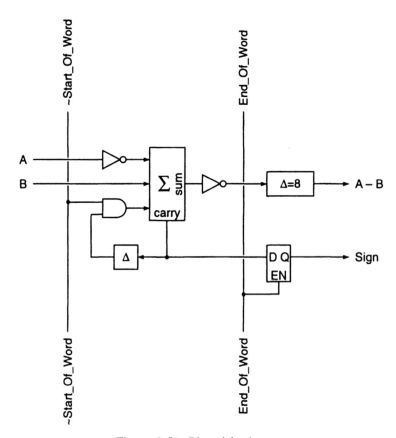

Figure 6–54. Bit-serial subtracter.

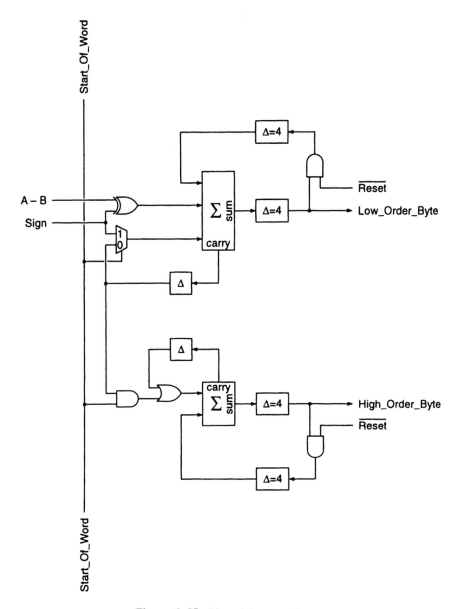

Figure 6-55. Bit-serial accumulator.

6–55) uses a full adder and recirculated 8-bit sums to accumulate the results of the subtracter module. If the Sign input is 0, then A-B enters the full adder unaltered and the carry input at the start of a new addition is 0. If, however, Sign is 1, then A-B is inverted and a 1 is supplied on the carry input at the start of a new addition, effectively negating A-B.

Overflow of the low-order stage of the accumulator is handled by the high-order stage (bottom part of Figure 6–55) which employs a half adder and acts as an incrementer. Whenever there is a carry out from the low-order stage at the end of addition, the value in the high-order stage is incremented by 1. (Since the high-order stage never overflows, the carry input at the start of a new operation is always 0.)

Both the low- and high-order stages make their results available and are reset at the midpoints of their 8-stage feedback paths. (The location is arbitrary and is made for the convenience of layout.)

6.8.7 Processing-element Layout

At the heart of the CLi6000 implementation of the motion-estimation algorithm is the layout for the processing-element macro. For both PE types, the CLi6000 requires just 72 cells arranged in a 2 × 36 rectangle. And because inputs and outputs on the macro's bottom side mate perfectly with the corresponding outputs and inputs on the macro's top side, an array of PE's can be formed by simply plugging macros together. Because it is more complex, we provide the layout (Figures 6–56 to 6–61) for the circuit (Figure 6–53) used for all PE's except those divisible by 16. Within each of these hard macros, there are approximately 285 equivalent gates contained in:

40 registers	2 NANDs
5 NAND/XORs	2 Inverters
3 Multiplexers	1 SR Latch
3 XORs	1 AND
2 Tri-state drivers	

Symbols for various cell states are explained in documentation for the CLI design environment.

6.8.8 Technology Comparisons

At 4000 MIPS, motion estimation of a standard digital video signal easily surpasses the performance of even the most energetic uni-processors. In fact, the work reported on here began at Apple Computer where a Cray XMP could achieve only about 1/10 the performance needed for real-time motion estimation.

Figure 6–56. Overview of PE layout.

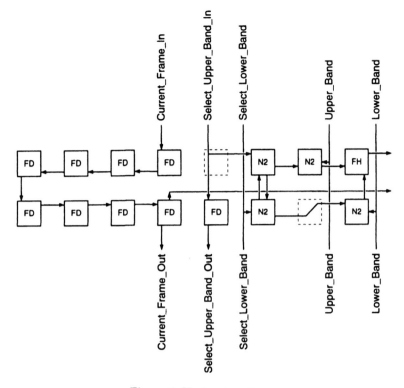

Figure 6-57. Input section.

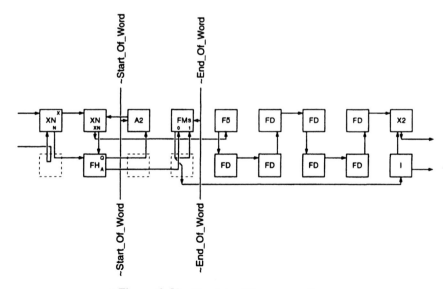

Figure 6-58. Absolute-difference section.

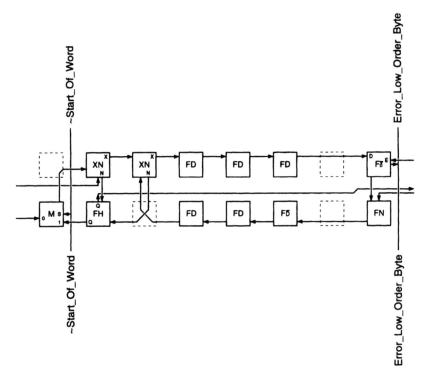

Figure 6-59. Low-order-accumulator section.

In Table 6–9, we provide comparisons of various technologies for implementing motion estimation. We make the following assumptions:

- We generously assume a performance level of 100 MIPS for the RISC microprocessor, but this is still a factor of 40 short of the 4,000 MIPS required.

- We assume that the FPGAs in the table implement the systolic array described earlier. Lower bounds for the Algotronix and Xilinx parts are based solely on register count.

- The CAL1024 SRAM FPGA from Algotronix requires two cells to implement a register and therefore at least three rows for each processing element, which has 40 registers.

- The XC3090 and XC4010 SRAM FPGAs from Xilinx provide two registers in each cell (CLB), and one 20-CLB row/column contains the 40 registers needed for a processing element.

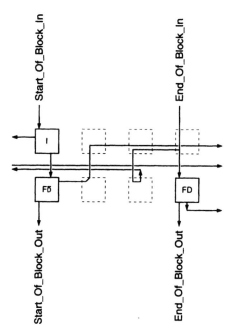

Figure 6-60. SOB & EOB section.

- The CLi6005 fits one 2 × 36 processing element in two rows. The CLi6010 available spring 1993 fits two 2 × 36 processing elements in two rows.

6.8.9 Conclusions

The CLi6000 series of SRAM-based field-programmable gate arrays provides features supporting efficient implementation of pipelined arithmetic circuits. These features are illustrated through a systolic array for motion estimation, an especially compute-intensive algorithm used in digital video compression. The CLi6000's high register count, NAND/XOR cell states, multiplexer states, fine-grained architecture, array symmetry and high cell connectivity all work together in efficiently implementing the systolic array's heavily pipelined, bit-serial arithmetic operations.

While only one example, this exercise suggests the suitability of the CLi6000* as a flexible alternative to hard-wired systolic arrays.

*Concurrent Logic Inc. was acquired by Atmel Inc. in 1993.

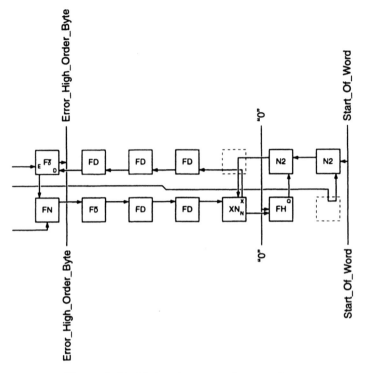

Figure 6–61. High-order-accumulator section.

PROBLEMS

Important Note: These problems explore the use of different FPGA architectures in regular structures, which would be useful in "custom computers," for example, special-purpose processors, on a scale from a 4-bit microcontroller in one FPGA, to a RISC microprocessor implemented with a number of FPGA chips. Ideally, the exercises should be carried out with suitable CAD tools to hand, but it is still possible to sketch feasible solutions, knowing the potential as well as limitations of the individual architecture, for example, tristate capability and routing capabilities. The examples should be in two different architectures chosen from the architectures with which you have become familiar. Note that these are feasibility studies, and sketches as well as complete, detailed solutions are useful. You should estimate the size of each solution, for example, number of cells or CLBs. Also, try to give a rough estimate of speed.

1. How would you implement a small pushdown stack (see figure), for example, 6 words of 4 bits? (*Hint:* The organization might be easier with a shift register rather than a counter.) The control signal and data locations,

TABLE 6-9. Technology Comparisons

Device	Size (Cells)	Devices Required
Cray XMP	—	≈10
RISC μP	—	≥40
CAL 1024	$32 \times 32 = 1,024$	≥24
XC3090	$16 \times 20 = 320$	≥16
XC4010	$20 \times 20 = 400$	≥13
CLi6005	$56 \times 56 = 3,136$	11
CLi6010	$80 \times 80 = 6,400$	4

that is, sides, are important considerations.

2. How would you implement a small scratchpad RAM (see figure), say 16 words of 4 bits? Again, assume the data and control signals are required as shown—you may change the order, but not the sides on which they appear.
(*Note:* It is not necessary to draw every cell in detail.)

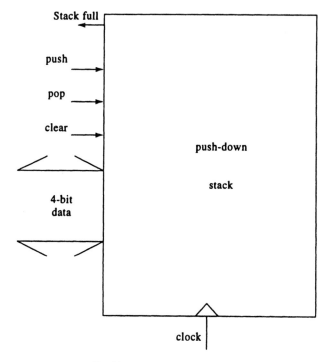

Problem 1. Pushdown stack.

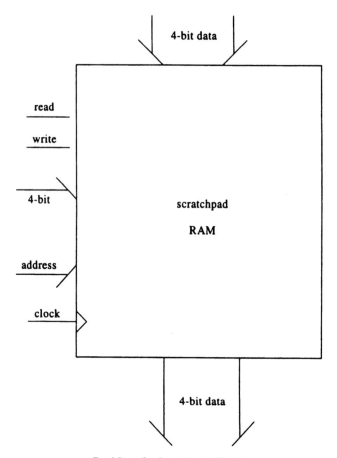

Problem 2. Scratchpad RAM.

BIBLIOGRAPHY

[Algo91]   Algotronix Ltd., *Configurable Array Logic User Manual*, Edinburgh UK, 1991.

[Altsch90]   Altschul, S. F., Gish, W., Miller, W., Myers, E. W., Lipman, D. J., "Basic Local Alignment Search Tool," *Journal of Molecular Biology*, Vol. 215, pp. 403–410, 1990.

[Aptix93]   Aptix Corporation, *Programmable Interconnect Data Book*, Aptix Corporation, San Jose, Calif., 1993.

[Arnold94]   Arnold, J. M., Buell, D. A., "VHDL Programming on Splash 2," in *More FPGAs*, (Moore, W., Luk, W., eds.), Abingdon EE & CS Books, U.K., 1994.

[Bertin89]   Bertin, P., Roncin, D., Vuillemin, J., *Introduction to Programmable Active Memories*, Digital Equipment Corporation, June 1989.

[Bertin89]   Bertin, P., Roncin, D., Vuillemin, J., "Introduction to Programmable Active Memories," *Systolic Array Processors*, J. McCanny, J. McWhirter, and E. Swartzlander, Jr., Eds., pp. 300–309, Prentice-Hall, 1989.

[Bertin92]   Bertin, P., Roncin, D., Vuillemin, J., "Programmable Active Memories: A Performance Assessment," FPGA92, *Proc. First International ACM/SIGDA Workshop on FPGA's*, Berkeley, Calif., 1992.

[Clouq87]   Clouqueur, A., d'Humieres, D, "RAP1, A Cellular Automata Machine for Fluid Dynamics," *Complex Systems*, Vol. 1, pp. 584–596, 1987.

[Conc92]   Concurrent Logic, "CLi6000 Series Field-Programmable Gate Arrays," Concurrent Logic, Inc., May 1992.

[D'Amour89]   D'Amour, M., Sample, S., Payne, T., *ASIC Emulation Cuts Design Risk*, High Performance Systems, October 1989.

[Denyer85]   Denyer, P., Renshaw, D. *VLSI Signal Processing: A Bit-Serial Approach*, Addison-Wesley, pp. 151, 196, 303, 1985.

[Furtek90]   Furtek, F., Stone, G., Jones, I., "Labyrinth: A Homogeneous Computational Medium," presented at the 1990 Custom Integrated Circuits Conference, May 1990.

[Furtek92]   Furtek, F., "An FPGA Architecture for Massively Parallel Computing," presented at the 2nd International Workshop on Field-Programmable Logic and Applications, August 1992.

[Furtek93]   Furtek, F., "A Field-Programmable Gate Array for Systolic Computing," *Research on Integrated Systems*, MIT Press, Cambridge, Mass., pp. 183–200, 1993.

[Gokh91]   Gokhale, M., et. al., "Building and Using a Highly Parallel Programmable Logic Array," *IEEE Computer Magazine*, January 1991.

[Gray89]   Gray, J. P., Kean, T. A., "Configurable Hardware: A New Paradigm for Computation." *Proc. Decennial Caltech Conference on VLSI*, Pasadena, Calif., March 1989.

[Heeb92]   Heeb, B., Pfister, C., "Chameleon: A Workstation of a Different Color," Proceedings of 2nd International Workshop on Field-Programmable Logic and Applications, Vienna, Austria, September 1992.

[Hoang93]   Hoang, D. T., "Searching Genetic Databases on Splash 2," *Proc. IEEE Workship on FPGAs for Custom Computing Machines*, pp. 185–199, April 1993.

[Hoorn84]   Hoornaert, F., Goubert, J., Desmedt, Y., "Efficient Hardware Implementation of the DES," Advances in Cryptology, *Proc. Crypto 84*, Springer-Verlag, 1984.

[Hoorn88]   Verbauwhede, I., Hoornaert, F., Vandewalle, J., "Security and Performance Optimisation of a new DES Data Encryption Chip," *IEEE Journal of Solid-State Circuits*, Vol. 23, pp. 647–656, June 1988.

[Kean89]   Kean, T. A., "Configurable Logic: A Dynamically Programmable Cellular Architecture and Its VLSI Implementation," Ph.D. Thesis CST-62-89, University of Edinburgh, Dept. Computer Science, 1989.

[Konh85]   Konheim, A. G., *Cryptography, a Primer*, Wiley, 1985.

[Lipton85]   Lipton, R. J., Lopresti, D. P., "A Systolic Array for Rapid String Comparison," in *1985 Chapel Hill Conference on VLSI*, (Fuchs, H., Ed.), Computer Science Press, pp. 363–376, 1985.

[Lyon76]   Lyon, R., "Two's Complement Pipeline Multipliers," *IEEE Transactions on Communications*, pp. 418–425, April 1976.

[Masek83]   Masek, W. J., Patterson, M. S., "How to Compute String-Edit Distances Quickly," in *Time Warps, String Edits, and Macromolecules: the Theory and Practice of Sequence Comparison*, (Sankoff, D., Kruskal, K., eds.), pp. 337–349, Addison-Wesley, 1983.

[NBS77]   National Bureau of Standards, *Data Encryption Standard*, Fed. Inf. Process. Stand. Publ. 46, January 1977.

[NBS80]   National Bureau of Standards, *DES Modes of Operation*, Fed. Inf. Process. Stand. Publ. 81, December 1980.

[Oldfield91]   Oldfield, J. V., Kappler, C. J., "Implementing Self-Timed Systems: Comparison of a Configurable Logic Array with a Full-Custom VLSI Circuit," *FPGA's: Proceedings of the International Workshop on Field Programmable Logic and Applications*, (Moore, W., Luk, W., eds.) Abingdon EE & CS Press, 1991.

[Prest84]   Preston, K., Duff, M., *Modern Cellular Automata*, Plenum, New York, 1984.

[Shimom87]   Shimomura, T., Doolen, G. D., Hasslacher, B., Fu, C., "Calculations Using Lattice Gas Techniques," *Los Alamos Science* (Special Issue), 1987.

[Stormon90]   Stormon, C., *Rapid Genome Analysis on a Workstation with an Associative Coprocessor*, Phase I Final Report for the U.S. Department of Energy, Coherent Research Inc., Syracuse, N.Y., April 1990.

[Suther89]   Sutherland, I. E., "Micropipelines," *Communications of the ACM*, Vol. 32, No. 6, pp. 720–738, June 1989.

[Tanenb81]   Tanenbaum, A. S., *Computer Networks*, Prentice-Hall International, 1981.

[Thomae91]   Thomae, D. A., Petersen, T. A., Van den Bout, D. E., "The Anyboard Rapid Prototyping Environment," *Advanced Research in VLSI 1991*, University of California at Santa Cruz, Santa Cruz, pp. 356–370, 1991.

[Toffoli87]   Toffoli, T., Margolus, N., *Cellular Automata Machines*, MIT Press, 1987.

[Tse92]   Tse, K. W., Yuk, T. I., Chan, S. S., "Implementation of Data Encryption Standard Algorithm with FPGAs," *Proceedings of 2nd International Workshop on Field-Programmable Logic and Applications*, Vienna, Austria, September 1992.

[Wayner88]   Wayner, P., "Modelling Chaos," *Byte*, pp. 253–258, May 1988.

[Wolfram86]   Wolfram, S., *Theory and Applications of Cellular Automata*, World Scientific, Singapore, 1986.

CHAPTER 7

BUSINESS DEVELOPMENT

The purpose of this chapter is to:

- Show the interdependencies of a technology-oriented business
- Show the pioneering role and dynamics of start-up companies
- Speculate on the future shape of products, markets, and companies
- Discuss how novel designs can be protected

7.1 TECHNOLOGY PUSH OR MARKET PULL?

Dramatic changes in the semiconductor industry have been a consequence of both "technology push" and "market pull." These processes usually work in tandem and result in new products and business ventures. New methods and tools often develop as a by-product of scientific research in an underlying technology. Frequently, the engineer or scientist has to convince potential users of the value and benefit of the new technology. The phenomenon is referred to as *technology push* as opposed to *market pull*, where the need for a product or tool is commonly understood, but no widely accepted solution currently exists.

Does the development of the field-programmable gate array (FPGA) fit either categorization? In the mid-1980s, the FPGA emerged as a novel solution offering quick design and reduced time-to-market in the highly competitive arena of custom-designed chips for high-performance electronic systems.

This chapter contains substantial contributions by Mary Haas-Wendel.

It increased the productivity of the designer, particularly for system prototyping with the aid of accurate performance simulation. The advent of the FPGA was recognized as a means of shortening the product development time for complex- and high-performance digital systems, such as those used in telecommunication applications, specialized computer peripheral equipment, industrial instrumenta- tion, and control systems, along with military and aerospace applications where space and power are at a premium.

The concepts of reprogrammability were formulated in the 1960s [Min- nick64] but ineffectual until the 1980s, which saw the arrival of silicon com- plementary metal-oxide semiconductor (CMOS) technology and fabrication with adequate density and multilayer metalization. Higher density components reduced the cost of printed-circuit design and manufacture, assembly, and test, as well as overall size. The FPGA entered as an almost universal digital building block enabling faster prototyping, thereby solving a commercial problem of shortening the time to market for complex electronic systems in a sphere of intense worldwide competition and rapid product obsolescence.

7.2 THE PIONEERS

An idea for a FPGA as distinct from the programmable logic device (PLD) was developed by Ross Freeman, an engineer with Zilog, Inc., a small semiconductor-chip-making subsidiary of Exxon Corporation. Freeman's idea was not warmly received by the executives of the parent company and as a result three individuals, Bernard Vonderschmitt, Ross Freeman, and James Bar- nett left Zilog, raised $4.25 million in venture capital from Hambrecht & Quist and Kleiner Perkins Caufield and Byers, among others, to form Xilinx, Inc., in 1984. The previous year, Altera Corporation was founded to provide fuse- programmable alternatives to mask-programmable gate arrays, and was first in the market. However, Xilinx's patented static-random-access-memory-based (SRAM) FPGA architecture was a more radical development and soon outpaced the Altera product. At the same time, two additional companies were founded: Atmel Corporation (1984) and Actel Corporation (1985), both manufacturers of programmable semiconductor components. Atmel Corporation designs and manufactures PLDs and FPGAs, as well as mask-programmable gate arrays. Actel Corporation became the leader in the development of FPGAs based on antifuse switching elements. In 1994 Actel was the world's leading antifuse FPGA producer and held number two market position in FPGAs, just behind Xilinx.

FPGAs were originally introduced to the marketplace by start-up compa- nies rather than established semiconductor suppliers. This was consistent with the pattern for earlier components, such as memory, microprocessors, and pro- grammable logic. Indeed the parallel with the microprocessor "revolution" in the late 1970s is particularly relevant. As a rule, large organizations have diffi- culty introducing new components. Often they are unwilling to take the speculative risks required even though new product development may enhance sales of existing components and systems. As with Xilinx and Actel, the role of venture capital has been critical, particularly for start-up companies in the United States, along with the commitment of individual engineers willing to risk career and family security, and devote the effort required to transform a laboratory brainchild into a successful commercial product.

Several factors enabled the FPGA to become a successful asset to system designers. From the outset, the FPGA had to be supported by proven CAD software, as well as provide competitive solutions to existing implementation problems. At the same time, the emergence of electronic CAD (ECAD) as a business in its own right, allowed the entrepreneurial FPGA companies to use existing design entry software and to concentrate on perfecting the hardware. The reshaping of the integrated-circuit (IC) industry into specialist operations, for example, memory companies and "Silicon foundries" providing reliable fabrication of FPGAs as well as application-specific integrated circuits (ASICs), also served to pave the way for the FPGA. Other factors that aided the success of FPGAs included:

- Widespread availability of powerful, yet inexpensive personal computers and engineering workstations.
- Development of electronic CAD for IC technologies and design styles, including placement, design-rule checking, partitioning, routing, and simulation.
- Development of systematic approaches to digital design, including finite state machines, datapath design, and timing disciplines.

7.3 FPGA MARKET AND START-UP COMPANIES

The FPGA market has progressed through several evolutions, beginning with logic replacement and rapid prototyping to an emerging technology allowing dynamic reconfiguration. The market has consistently grown due the advantages of the device and the continuing development of new applications. In 1990 worldwide sales of FPGAs were $108 million, expanding to $187 million in 1991 [Willett92]. By 1992 U.S. sales of FPGAs reached $247.6 million, representing a 56.7% growth rate for the FPGA within the U.S. programmable logic market. According to In-Stat, Inc., the U.S. FPGA market grew 42.9% from 1992 to 1993. In-Stat, Inc., has projected the U.S. FPGA market will grow from $353.9 million in 1993 to $998.6 million by 1998; a compounded annual growth rate of 23.1% [Rohl94] (see Figures 7–1 and 7–2).

The FPGA enabled companies in telecommunications, cable, medical device development, among others, to move products to market more efficiently. There are distinct phases of application development, as designers and managers see the potential of a new approach, ranging from initial, hesitant steps to

US $ Millions	1992	1993	1994	1995	1996	1997	1998
Simple PLD:	566.4	576.1	605.3	630.4	644.3	651.7	652.2
Bipolar	275.9	225.8	205.3	187.7	175.5	165.3	156.7
CMOS	287.2	337.2	383.5	424	448.3	464.1	472.1
BiCMOS	3.3	13.1	16.5	18.7	20.5	22.3	23.4
Complex PLD:	156.4	254.6	358.2	468.5	602.4	739.8	879.2
FPGA:	247.6	353.9	472.1	599.4	732.8	861.7	998.6

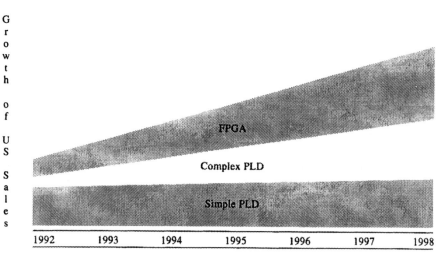

Figure 7-1. Programmable logic market, 5-year forecast as of April 1994. Derived from data provided by In-Stat, Inc.†

major paradigm shifts, that is, exploiting the new device for its unique capabilities.

7.3.1 Rapid Prototyping

Due to the user-programmable feature of the FPGA, new designs could be created more efficiently and quickly. Testing and modification of new designs became possible with lower nonrecurring engineering (NRE) costs.

7.3.2 Logic Replacement

Printed-circuit-board design, fabrication, and component insertion costs can be reduced, since much logic can be compressed into a single FPGA package. In

† Market forecasts are revised on a six month basis.

Sales in Millions	1993 sales	mkt. share		1992 sales	mkt. share
Xilinx, Inc.	231.2	65.30%		161.7	65.30%
Actel Corporation	54.6	15.40%		45	18.20%
AT&T Micro	33.5	9.50%		17.5	7.10%
Texas Instruments	28.6	8.10%		18.8	7.60%
QuickLogic	3	0.80%		2	0.80%
Crosspoint Solutions	2	0.60%		2	0.80%
Atmel Corporation	1	0.30%		0.5	0.20%
GEC Plessey	0	0.00%		0.1	0.00%
Total	353.9	100.00%		247.6	100.00%

1993 FPGA Market Share by Company

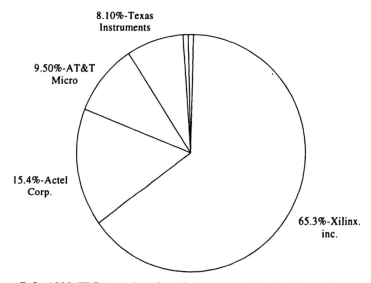

Figure 7–2. 1993 FPGA market share by company. Derived from data provided by In-Stat, Inc. as of April 1994.

addition, this improves the reliability and often, but not always, the speed of a digital system. Designs may exploit FPGA reconfiguration, for example, in an instrument that changes major functions or applicable standards, for example, European (PAL, or SECAM) TV measurements compared with U.S. (NTSC) TV. System upgrades, whether due to design error or improved performance, can be carried out particularly easily compared with older implementations that require printed-circuit or component changes.

7.3.3   Arrays of FPGA Chips

The term *custom computing* refers to the creation of special-purpose, often highly parallel, computer systems for specialized tasks, such as genetic string distance evaluation and cryptography, the subject of Chapter 6. The performance must be orders of magnitude greater than conventional computers (including parallel ones) to make this worthwhile. More importantly, the fraction of the task must be substantial. For example, if the FPGA array reduces, say, 50% of the task to virtually zero time, the overall application is only accelerated by a factor of 2, and the user may well prefer to wait for the next "winner" of the reduced instruction set computer (RISC) microprocessor race!

7.3.4   Dynamic Reconfiguration

Only RAM-based FPGAs, like the ones discussed in this book, can be changed quickly enough (< 10 ms) for in-system reconfiguration. Erasable-programmable-read-only-memory-based (EPROM) FPGAs must be removed to an external ultraviolet erasure device and a device programmer. But most of the present-day FPGAs are configured in a serial fashion, that is, by sending a string of bits via a single input pin. Thus a single change requires shutting-down the application and totally reloading the on-chip RAM. A few FPGAs, notably Algotronix, Atmel (Concurrent Logic), and Pilkington allow the configuration memory to be addressed at run-time, and so an individual bit may be changed. This is a highly novel, even hazardous type of computing, changing the logic while the data remains in place. There are few convincing applications yet, but this feature represents a major paradigm shift that will probably be exploited in the next decade.

Start-up FPGA companies opted to devote financial and human resources to research and development, and consequently produced novel architectures such as fine-grain fuse-programmable transistor arrays (Crosspoint Solutions), a relatively fine-grain SRAM-based architecture (Concurrent Logic), and coarse-grain antifuse architecture (QuickLogic). Start-up companies also relied upon third-party providers of "front-end" CAD software, for such tasks as schematic entry and simulation, while providing their own "back-end" software for the architecturally dependent aspects, such as technology mapping, placement, routing, and configuration. Even the back-end will not remain a monopoly of the FPGA vendor, since electronic CAD companies are developing rival software capable of mapping to a variety of architectures (e.g., Minc, NeoCAD, etc.). This trend will be furthered by electronic system designers who prefer to work with alternative FPGAs, rather than be locked into a particular vendor. The "front-end" software is also being extended toward higher levels of system specification, for example, VHDL, a standard language for specifying digital systems. VHDL has a particular merit of reusability, for building blocks of earlier systems expressed in VHDL can be incorporated into new systems without concern for FPGA architectural details.

7.3.5 Do You Need a Fabrication Facility?

The semiconductor industry is in a state of rapid change, both organizationally as well as technically. It has evolved from a few vertically integrated companies with high-volume in-house wafer fabrication, to a more diverse industry with silicon foundries serving low- to medium-volume demand, as well as bulk fabricators of memory and microprocessor products. Start-up FPGA companies have benefited from worldwide availability of state-of-the-art fabrication facilities.

In reviewing the state of the U.S. computer industry, Andrew Rappaport and Shmuel Halevi [Rappaport91] point to the advantage of defining and controlling a computing environment, as distinct from delivering raw computing horsepower. They contrast the success of Microsoft with its Windows operating system, which provides a distinct computing paradigm for vast numbers of computer users and software developers, with the proliferation of marginally differentiated producers of personal computers and workstations. They suggest that the primary, strategic goal of U.S. computer companies should be "to create persistent value in computing," rather than to build the hardware on which computer applications run. Are there parallels here for the programmable semiconductor industry? Rappaport and Halevi point out that semiconductor value is now largely a function of design specialization rather than processing, and the overabundance of advanced processing facilities is becoming more pronounced.

"Commodity" semiconductors are high-volume components, which are largely interchangeable, and for which competitive advantage is based on price and performance (e.g., memory, simple microprocessors, and controllers.) Prices are often driven down by aggressive worldwide competition. In contrast, highly differentiated components such as FPGAs can be produced in lower volumes with higher profit margins due to their distinctive purpose. Applying FPGAs in products allows design-oriented-system companies to concentrate on delivering and controlling value. The utilization of flexible, programmable integrated circuits and superior design tools will enable competitive electronics companies to add value to their product stream via continuous improvements. To quote from [Rappaport91], "Maximize the sophistication of the value you deliver; minimize the sophistication of the technology you consume."

7.4 THE MPGA AS AN ALTERNATIVE TO THE FPGA FOR LOW-VOLUME PRODUCTION

The mask-programmable gate array (MPGA) is a well-established alternative to the FPGA for designs that go into production, assuming sufficient quantities are required. Consideration of time-to-market strategy affects the choice between MPGA and FPGA technology [Xilinx92].

As discussed in Chapter 1, MPGAs are arrays of transistors that are configured into the logic required by metal interconnections made in the final stages of fabrication. Partially completed wafers can be stockpiled, ready to be customized for a particular design that takes three weeks or less, compared with 16 to 18 weeks for the full-custom process, assuming a couple of design and fabrication iterations. MPGAs are available in a range of sizes and may have more than 100,000 gates, with typical utilization figures of 80–90% for small arrays and 40–60% for the largest. There are approximately 24,000 gate array designs initiated each year worldwide, and the annual volume in 1990 was reaching $3.5 billion. Nearly half the designs require 10,000 or fewer gates, and consequently FPGAs offer an alternative in many cases.

An MPGA design will typically occupy about one-third the area of an equivalent FPGA design since it does not require configuration storage. In consequence, volume quantities (5000 plus) tend to be cheaper than for the FPGA. At the same time, there are certain fixed costs in producing the MPGA design, referred to as NRE charges, which are independent of the volume to be produced. NRE charges provide for:

- Interfacing with the MPGA vendor.
- Adapting the design for the selected MPGA.
- Design verification, including simulation.
- Production of the custom metalization and contact cut masks required.
- Prototype samples.
- Devising a suitable testing strategy.

Not all designs are successful at the first attempt and it is prudent to allow for a second run.

In contrast, taking the FPGA design into production will incur few if any NRE charges, particularly if it was prototyped as an FPGA. If, however, a second-source MPGA is required, there will be additional NRE charges for the alternative, while for an FPGA, a second-source is often available. The MPGA design will require a set of test vectors, or possibly improving the original design for test. In contrast, SRAM-based and antifuse-based FPGAs are fully tested by the vendor. The point at which the MPGA becomes more economical will vary, depending on design complexity and market conditions, but typically might be in the range of 12,000 to 15,000 units.

A less concrete, yet highly significant factor is the intensely competitive market technology companies such as computers and peripherals, telecommunications, military electronics, and industrial control, must endure. Under unrelenting pressure to design and produce products in a timely manner in order to create competitive advantages, companies face unpredictable production volumes and may confront frequent design modifications to adapt products quickly to new markets. The ability to be innovative and anticipate changes in the marketplace and subsequently introduce products quickly while still maintaining quality is often a formula for success.

A typical electronic product may be obsolete within 24 months after it is developed. Short time-to-market is a key reason more and more manufacturers of electronic systems are turning to FPGAs. The companies require the advantages of production flexibility along with the speed and density achieved with current semiconductor technology. With FPGAs, companies can manufacture many electronic systems with only three types of high-volume standard components: microprocessors, memory, and FPGAs. While FPGAs can perform functions similar to many custom gate arrays, they also can be simply and quickly programmed by the user. Unlike gate arrays that are customized during the manufacturing process, FPGAs are customized by the design engineer on-site using a workstation or personal computer running a combination of standard computer-aided engineering (CAE) software and development system software. This software makes it possible to complete multiple design iterations within a day. Furthermore, once a design is released to manufacturing, production quantities are readily possible since FPGAs are standard off-the-shelf products.

Many designs can be quickly and economically prototyped with static-memory-based, or antifuse-based FPGA devices, reducing the costs and risks of development. The key issue for success, however, is time to market, not time to prototype.

One common strategy is to begin production with FPGAs immediately after prototyping, and then switch to a lower cost custom ASIC device when it is available. Many manufacturers now choose to begin production with the same FPGA technology used during prototype development, thereby getting their products to market quickly while decreasing ASIC design risks. As fabrication processes improve and minimum-feature sizes are reduced, both MPGA and FPGA vendors can improve their products, both in density and speed. While field-programmability carries a higher overhead in silicon area and restricts speed compared with MPGAs, there is probably a greater incentive for the FPGA manufacturer to move to the latest processes, because of the higher volumes required. Figure 7–3 is a snapshot of the limits of FPGA single-chip applications at one point in time, but it is evident that the operating frequencies and gate-counts will continue to increase.

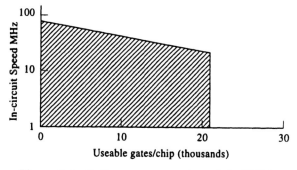

Figure 7–3. Performance parameters of the FPGA.

7.5   INTELLECTUAL PROPERTY

Intellectual property refers to a body of rights relating to works of authorship, inventions, trademarks, masks, designs, and trade secrets. There are two broad areas: industrial property (inventions, trademarks, industrial design, and protection of trade secrets) and copyrights.

Society at large acknowledges that without some form of protection, invention will be stifled. Legal frameworks for the protection of intellectual property across a wide range of creative work from art to engineering have been established. Naturally laws vary from country to country, and while this treatment is written from a U.S. perspective, the broad principles are similar. However, it is important to investigate the laws of a particular country to ensure proper analysis of the legal safeguards.

In the context of FPGAs, both novel FPGA applications as well as novel forms of architecture or device engineering represent intellectual property, and design engineers as well as corporations need to protect their investment of time, effort and resources.

7.5.1   Patents

A patent allows its owner to control the exploitation of an invention, either directly or by licensing to others, for 17 years from the time a patent is awarded. (In many other countries a patent is offered for a period of 20 years from the time of application for the patent.) A patentable invention must have some tangible implementation, which now includes algorithms as implemented in software and microprograms, as well as architecture and circuit techniques.

7.5.2   Copyrights

In the United States a copyright gives the owner exclusive right to reproduce the work, prepare derivative works, distribute copies, or perform or display the work publicly. Copyright protection originated from the printed word, but now includes *artwork* such as layouts for integrated circuits.

7.5.3   The Semiconductor Chip Protection Act of 1984

The Semiconductor Chip Protection Act of 1984 provides a special method of legal protection for original mask works and allows mask sets for ICs to be deposited with the Library of Congress. Protection is provided for a term of 10 years, subject to registration by the Copyright Office.

Prior to the Act, there were several cases in which ICs appear to have been replicated by stripping off the layers of an existing IC by selective chemical processing, using microphotography to create new masks and fabricating the rival product. In some cases, the "new" masks included portions of company symbols ("logos") that were irrelevant to the functioning of the original circuit! The Semiconductor Chip Protection Act provides a useful deterrent to the copyist.

7.5.4 Trade Secrets

Trade secret legislation allows an employer, partners, or parties to any business relationship to prevent disclosure by a private contract. Trade secrets can protect inventions, ideas, principles, formulas, and functions, within the provisions of individual contracts (see the model nondisclosure agreement, Figure 7-4).

7.5.5 Reverse Engineering

The U.S. Supreme Court defines reverse engineering as:

> Starting with a known product and working backwards to divine the process which aided in its development or manufacture.

When is reverse engineering legitimate and when is it not? (See Table 7-1.) First, the law makes a clear distinction between copying and the application of intellectual effort in discovery. The different forms of protection vary in their attitude to reverse engineering. With patent law, the basic concept encourages reverse engineering by its extensive disclosure requirements. It is legitimate to deconstruct a patented article, although it is generally wrong to construct another copy identical to it. Since a patent is broader than the implementation and protects the underlying ideas, principles, circuits, and so forth, to avoid a challenge of infringement any new product must be substantially dissimilar.

Copyright protection covers more than matching appearance, particularly for IC maskworks. Reverse engineering is permitted for the purposes of teaching and research, which are defined as "fair use," but not a part of product development. It would be relatively straightforward to transform a given integrated circuit layout to an alternative realization with an identical underlying circuit, but physically different in appearance. For highly regular structures such as FPGAs, there may be a limited number of methods for producing a significant key element, such as a functional block.

How can one distinguish a copy from an independent creation? During the progress of legislation and court challenges, the concept of "clean-room technology" has emerged. This does not refer to the clean rooms required in IC manufacture, but to an organization arrangement in which the team producing a new product is isolated from details of the existing product. The team is provided with a functional specification of what is required and then develops its own implementation. The team must maintain a "paper trail" of abundant documentation to prove, if need be, that their creative work has required intellectual effort, including significant decision making along the path to the new product.

Copyright cannot protect against works that were genuinely created independently, or implement a basic idea, or require a set way of implementing

**MODEL
CONFIDENTIALITY AND NON-DISCLOSURE AGREEMENT**

AGREEMENT dated as of the   day of   , 1994, by and between
                    , located at   (hereinafter referred to as the
"Disclosing Party"), and   (hereinafter referred to as
"You" and "Your").

W I T N E S S E T H:

WHEREAS, the Disclosing Party wishes to deliver to you certain information and data
deemed proprietary and confidential and relating to their operations and products, and
financial condition, (hereinafter referred to as the "Property"), and you wish to review such
information and data, in connection with your business.

NOW, THEREFORE, the parties hereto agree as follows:

1. CONFIDENTIAL INFORMATION.

For purposes of this Agreement, "Confidential Information" shall mean written infor-
mation and data received by you from the Disclosing Party which has been marked
"Confidential" by the Disclosing Party. Notwithstanding the foregoing, information and
data disclosed by the Disclosing Party to you shall not be deemed to be Confidential
Information, and you shall have no obligation to treat such information and data as
Confidential Information, if such information and data:

(a) was known by you at the time of such disclosure; or

(b) was known to the public at the time of such disclosure; or

(c) becomes known to the public (other than by act of you) subsequent to such disclosure; or

(d) is disclosed lawfully to you by a third party subsequent to such disclosure by the
Disclosing Party; or

(e) is approved in writing by the Disclosing Party for disclosure by you; or

(f) is required by law to be disclosed by you provided that you give to the Disclosing
Party prior written notice of such required disclosure.

2. CONFIDENTIALITY.

Commencing on the date hereof, you shall not disclose, directly or indirectly, in whole
or in part, to any third person, firm or corporation any Confidential Information which
it receives from the Disclosing Party, except that you may disclose any such information to your employees, agents or advisors in connection with your investigation of the
Property or the preparation of an offer to acquire the Property to the extent that you

Figure 7–4. Model nondisclosure agreement.

Property to the extent that you reasonably determine such disclosure to be necessary. You shall use the same degree of care in safeguarding the Confidential Information as you use for your own confidential and proprietary information.

You shall not prototype, manufacture, sell, patent, or otherwise use the Confidential Information in any way whatsoever, including but not limited to, facsimile copies, adaptation, imitation, re-design, or modification of the Confidential Information provided.

3. TRADE SECRETS.

You understand that all Confidential Information disclosed to you shall be considered a trade secret belonging to the Disclosing Party, whether or not it is labeled "confidential." You therefore will neither divulge nor discuss with third parties matters relating to the Confidential Information without written permission of the Disclosing Party, since doing so without such permission would cause irreparable damage. Thus, money damages would not be adequate reparation.

4. IRREPARABLE DAMAGE.

You understand that (i) the unauthorized disclosure or use of any Confidential Information may cause irreparable injury to the Disclosing Party. In the event of a violation of any of your obligations hereunder, the Disclosing Party may be entitled to seek to enforce each such obligation by temporary or permanent injunctive or mandatory relief, reasonable attorney's fees, reasonable expert witness fees, and reasonable costs of suit and expenses, in addition to any other relief to which the Disclosing Party may be entitled without prejudice to any other rights or remedies which may be available at law or in equity; (ii) money damages may not be a sufficient remedy for any breach of this Agreement by you or your Representatives and that, in addition to other remedies which may be available, the Disclosing Party may be entitled to specific performance and injunctive relief as a remedy for any such breach.

5. OWNER OF INFORMATION.

All Confidential Information shall be and remain the property of the Disclosing Party.

6. SCOPE OF AGREEMENT.

You have no other obligation to the Disclosing Party aside from this confidentiality and non-disclosure requirement.

7. TERMINATION.

Either party hereto may terminate this Agreement at any time by delivering written notice of termination to the other party. Upon termination, at the request of the Disclosing Party, you shall either destroy or return to the Disclosing Party all copies of the Confidential Information and all other materials furnished to you by the

Figure 7-4. (*Continued*)

Disclosing Party in connection with the aforesaid investigation, in the possession of its employees, agents or advisors. Notwithstanding such termination, the restrictions on disclosure and use of Confidential Information arising under this Agreement shall continue to be effective for three (3) years after the date of termination.

8. AMENDMENT; WAIVER.

This Agreement may not be amended or any provision hereof waived in whole or in part except by a writing signed by both parties hereto.

9. GOVERNING LAW.

This Agreement shall be governed by and construed in accordance with the laws of the State of _____.

IN WITNESS WHEREOF, the parties hereto have caused this Agreement to be executed as of the date first above written.

[Disclosing Party]   _____

By: _____   By: _____
Title: _____   Title: _____
Date: _____   Date: _____

lh-0021

Figure 7-4. (*Continued*)

some function. There have been several cases in which the introduction of some redundant feature has revealed a copyist rather than an independent inventor. For example, this occurred in a microcode instruction set that happened to contain the originator's initials! Since maskwork legislation specifically permits reverse engineering and does not allow commonal-garden circuits to be protected, any infringement case in which reverse engineering had occurred, would have to be based on an extremely high degree of similarity for either the whole circuit or its major building blocks.

Intellectual property legislation continues to evolve. At the same time, progress in semiconductor processing has increased the sophistication of fabrication technology. No longer is mere copying likely to provide circuits of adequate performance. Reverse engineering, however, has become easier with electron-beam inspection, which allows both the layout of a working chip to be examined and its internal workings probed as if with a high-performance oscilloscope.

TABLE 7-1. Comparison of Reverse Engineering under Different Types of Intellectual Property

Type of Property	Activities	Results
Patent	Reverse Engineering Encouraged	Broad Protection of Invention
	Enabling disclosure Best mode practice Patent Office records	Equivalent elements Independent creation Applied ideas Functions
Copyright	Reverse Engineering Difficult	Narrow Protection of Copyright Work
	Copying prohibited (except under limited circumstances) Source = object code Disassembly	No protection for: Ideas Functions Original creations Fair use
Trade Secret	All Types of Reverse Engineering Permitted	Misappropriation, Not Infringement
	Only limited by contract duty of confidence	Can be found in portion of product or process No overall similarity required
Mask Work	Reverse Engineering Expressly Allowed	Two Standards for Infringement:
	Only requirement: Documentation Commercial development expected	If reverse engineered, Substantial identity; If not, substantial similarity

Adapted from Theodore Hagelin, Syracuse University College of Law, 1989.
Copyright 1989 Ted Hagelin.

7.6 SOURCES FOR CAPITAL

A traditional method of obtaining start-up funds to bring a design to market has been through venture capital. This was the source Xilinx, Inc. and other FPGA companies initially used to get started. A lengthy process of "courtship" between the venture capitalists and the team who is proposing the new venture is necessary and may not result in success. It is projected that venture capital will become less available during the 1990s [Bell91]. However, during the 1980s, sources of government funding have become available in the United States to stimulate small business growth and also to encourage the collaboration between university-based technological research and commercial development.

7.6.1   Small Business Innovation Research

Small Business Innovation Research (SBIR) was established by an act of the U.S. Congress in 1982 to allocate research and development (R&D) funds solely to stimulate small business. The purpose was to both benefit small businesses and to meet R&D needs of federal agencies. The Act was reauthorized in 1992 with legally mandated step increases in the allocation of funds through 1997. Eleven federal agencies participate in SBIR; Department of Agriculture, Department of Commerce, Department of Defense, Department of Education, Department of Energy, Department of Transportation, Environmental Protection Agency, Department of Health and Human Services, National Aeronautics and Space Administration, National Science Foundation, and Nuclear Regulatory Commission.

The Small Business Administration (SBA) sets overall guidelines regarding the SBIR program. Information relative to the requirements for application, proposal procedures, and so forth, can be obtained from the SBA.

7.6.2   Small Business Technology Transfer Program

The Small Business Technology Transfer Program (STTR) came into existence in October 1992. This program is intended to exploit commercially promising ideas that originate in universities, federally funded research and development centers, and not-for-profit research institutions. Five federal agencies are participating in the STTR program; Department of Defense, Department of Health and Human Services, National Aeronautics and Space Administration, Department of Energy, and National Science Foundation.

As with any new and promising idea, seeking advice and obtaining funding to allow for the commercialization of the proposed product is not only beneficial to the designer but also to industry. The semiconductor industry has grown as a result of the creative thinking of engineers and their willingness to take risks and follow an entrepreneurial spirit.

BIBLIOGRAPHY

[Baker92]   Baker, S., "Many Winding Roads for PLD Progress," *Electronic Engineering Times*, p. 62, December 7, 1992.

[Bell86]   Bell, C. G., "A Surge for Solid State," *IEEE Spectrum*, pp. 71–74, April 1986.

[Bell91]   Bell C. G., McNamara, J. E., *High-Tech Ventures—The Guide for Entrepreneurial Success*, Addison-Wesley, 1991.

[Bell93]   Bell, G., Mead, C., "The Way Things Really Work: Two Inventors on Innovation," VHS Videotape, University Video Communications, Stanford, Calif., 1993.

[Bursky93]   Bursky, D., "Denser, Faster FPGAs Vie For Gate-Array Applications," *Electronic Design*, pp. 55–75, May 27, 1993.

[Freeman91]   Freeman, R., "User-Programmable Gate Arrays," *IEEE Spectrum*, pp. 32–35, December 1988.

[Goering92]   Goering, R., "AT&T Aims to Bite Xilinx with Orca FPGA," *Electronic Engineering Times*, p. 4, April 27, 1992.

[Jenkins90]   Jenkins, J., "PLDs Take on Gate Array Issues," *Electronic Engineering Times*, pp. 51, 75, September 3, 1990.

[Minnick64]   Minnick, R. C., "Cutpoint Cellular Logic," *IEEE Transactions on Electronic Computers*, Vol. EC-13, pp. 685–698, December 1964.

[Mohsen88]   Mohsen, A., "Desktop-Configurable Channeled Gate Arrays," *VLSI Systems Design*, pp. 24–33, August 1988.

[Morris93]   Morris, C. R., Ferguson, C. H., "How Architecture Wins Technology Wars," *Harvard Business Review*, pp. 86–96, March/April 1993.

[Rappaport91]   Rappaport, A. S., Halevi, S., "The Computerless Computer Company," *Harvard Business Review*, pp. 69–119, July 1991.

[Rauch93]   Rauch, J. G., "The Law on Reverse Engineering," *IEEE Spectrum*, pp. 47–48, August 1993.

[Rohl94]   Rohleder, R., *FPGA Market Research*, In-Stat, Inc., 1994.

[Small90]   Small, C. H., "FPGA vendors race to upgrade products," *EDN*, pp. 57–66, September 17, 1990.

[Small92]   Small, C. H., "FPGA Conversion," *EDN*, pp. 107–116, June 4, 1992.

[Sprack92]   Sprackland, T., "Semiconductor Vendors Pray for 10," *Electronic Business*, pp. 41–42, January 13, 1992.

[Stas90]   Stasaitis, D., "PLDs Tackle Heat, Ground Bounce," *Electronic Engineering Times*, pp. 54, 75, September 3, 1990.

[Tomasko93]   Tomasko, R. M., *Rethinking the Corporation: The Architecture of Change*, Amacom, New York, 1993.

[Tuck91]   Tuck, B., "Claims by FPGA Tool Vendors Bury Reality in Noise," *Computer Design*, pp. 52–55, November 1991.

[Waller92]   Waller, L., "How Partnerships Go Awry," *ASIC & EDA*, pp. 44–45, July 1992.

[Willett92]   Willett, H., "FPGA Market Booms, but Too Many Vendors could Sink Profits," *Electronic Business*, pp. 113–116, May 18, 1992.

[Wilson92a]   Wilson, R., "FPGAs are Closing in on Gate Array Business," *Electronic Engineering Times*, pp. 1, 98, October 26, 1992.

[Wilson92b]   Wilson, R., "Crosspoint eyes FPGA lead," *Electronic Engineering Times*, p. 14, November 9, 1992.

[Xilinx92]   Xilinx, Inc., "A Cost of Ownership Comparison," in *The Programmable Gate Array Data Book*, Xilinix, Inc., San Jose, Calif., pp. 111–119, 1992.

CHAPTER 8

RECENT DEVELOPMENTS

The purpose of this chapter is to allow the reader to:

- Become aware of new developments and trends in field-programmable gate array (FPGA) architectures

- Understand the relevance of field-programmable *interconnection* and its applications

- Examine the impact of developments and trends in CAD support

8.1 INTRODUCTION

During the course of writing this text we have seen significant developments in FPGA architectures, applications, and also the business side of the industry itself. Inevitably there will be novel developments and business rearrangements during the course of book production, but it seems useful to bring out distinctive features of new developments, rather than leaving the reader with an outdated view of the FPGA industry and marketplace. The sections given here have largely been contributed by the companies responsible, with strict editorial limits on size. Further details can readily be obtained from the companies concerned. Our list is not comprehensive, and there is no slight intended to companies that have been left out.

8.2 NEW ARCHITECTURES

The chapter opens with some new FPGA architectures for *reprogrammable* FPGAs. We have deliberately excluded fuse- and electrically programmable FPGAs. Readers may note the wide range of approaches at both ends of the spectrum from fine- to coarse-grain, and the importance of wire delays—dynamic reprogrammability does not come for free. It is interesting to note that "dynamic" includes the possibility of reconfiguration while FPGA logic is active. Until recently virtually all manufacturers chose a serial loading process which implied that any change required a total reconfiguration, even for a single bit. Clearly most present-day applications do not require truly dynamic reconfigurability, but new applications may well exploit it, and this will require total reconsideration of CAD support and the host environment in cases where the FPGA is interfaced to a host computer.

8.2.1 Altera FLEX

Altera has developed four generations of complex programmable logic devices (CPLDs). The various families of devices are Classic, MAX 5000, MAX 7000, and FLEX 8000. While there are many differences in architectural details of these three families, there are some significant similarities as well. The similarities are a rich (nonblocking, local/global) interconnection scheme, and a coarse-grain/fine-grain logic architecture (groups of logic elements in clusters called logic array blocks (LABs)). The following is a brief description of the FLEX 8000 family.

FLEX 8000   The FLEX 8000 family is fabricated using a standard complementary metal-oxide semiconductor (CMOS) technology. Static random-access memory (SRAM) bits are used as the programming element. Semiconductor technology aside, there are other details of the FLEX architecture that are different from the earlier Classic and MAX families. However, the common heritage of LABs (fine-grain/coarse-grain logic architecture) interconnected by a hierarchical interconnect structure is apparent.

Dual Granularity   A macroscopic view of the FLEX architectures is shown in Figure 8–1. Logic elements (LEs) are grouped in clusters of eight to form LABs. Within a LAB, the output of every LE is available as an input to every other LE by means of a completely nonblocking local interconnect scheme (Local FastTrack). The grouping of LEs into LABs enables the FLEX 8000 devices to exhibit the high-speed characteristics of coarse-grained architectures together with the high logic utilization of fine-grained architectures.

Section 8.2.1 was contributed by Robert Hartman of Altera, Inc.

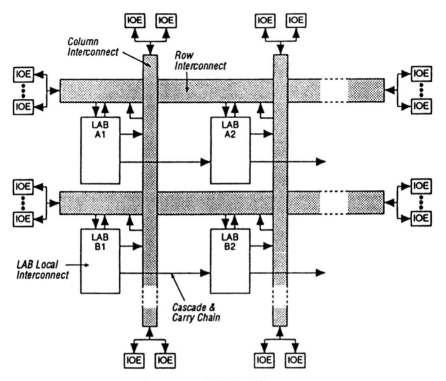

Figure 8-1. FLEX architectures.

Logic Array Block LABs communicate with other LABs by means of row and column interconnect buses called FastTrack. These are continuous metal lines that span the chip, horizontally and vertically, eliminating the highly variable, cumulative delays of the segmented interconnect structure commonly found in FPGAs. The FastTracks are also used to carry signals to and from the input/output elements (IOEs).

Signals enter a LAB from the Row FastTrack. Signals generated by a LAB are output to both the Row and Column FastTrack. Figure 8-2 shows a typical LAB in greater detail. There is a LAB Local Interconnect consisting of 24 lines selected from the Row FastTrack and 8 lines fed back from the output of each of the LEs within a LAB. In addition, there are 4 other inputs that provide clock, clear, and reset signals to the LE.

Logic Element The Logic Element, shown in Figure 8-3, is the smallest unit of logic in the FLEX 8000 architecture. Each LE contains a 4-input lookup table (LUT), a programmable flip-flop, a carry chain, and a cascade chain. For a purely combinational function, the flip-flop can be bypassed. The carry chain provides a very fast (<1 ns) carry-forward function between adjacent LEs. This feature allows implementation of high-speed counters and adders.

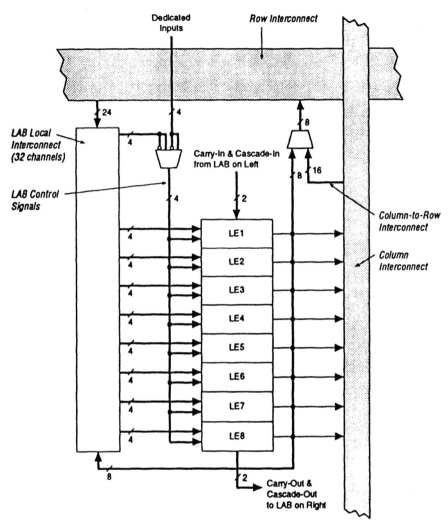

Figure 8-2. FLEX 8000 LAB architecture.

The cascade chain allows implementation of functions requiring wide fan-in (wider than the four inputs of the LUT). Adjacent LUTs can be used to compute portions of the function in parallel; the cascade chain serially connects the intermediate values. Outputs of adjacent LUTs can be combined with either an AND or an OR function. Each additional LE provides four more inputs to the effective width of the function with a delay of approximately 1 ns per LE.

Input/Output Element Figure 8–4 shows the IOE block diagram. Signals

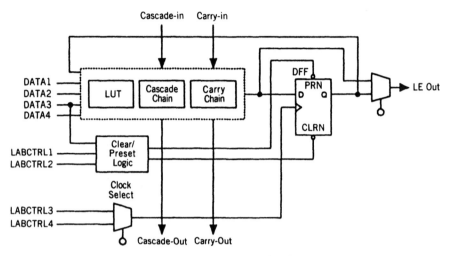

Figure 8–3. FLEX 8000 logic element.

enter the FLEX 8000 device from either the input/output (I/O) pins that provide general-purpose input capability or the four dedicated inputs that are typically used for fast, global control signals. The IOEs are located at the ends of the row and column interconnect.

I/O pins can be used as input, output, or bidirectional pins. Each I/O pin has a register that can be used either as an input register or as an output register. A programmable inversion option is provided to invert signals from the row and column interconnect when required. The output buffer also has an adjustable output slew rate that can be configured for low-noise or high-speed performance.

The Clock, Clear, and Output Enable controls for the IOEs are provided by a network of I/O control signals. These signals can be supplied by either the dedicated input pins or internal logic. The IOE control signal paths are designed to minimize the skew across the device. All control signal sources are buffered onto high-speed drivers that drive the signals around the periphery of the device. The I/O control signals can be configured to provide up to ten Output Enable signals, and up to two Clock or Clear Signals.

The FLEX Family The current family of FLEX 8000 products is shown in Figure 8–5. The FLEX family brings high register counts and high performance together in one programmable logic family. The FLEX 8000 family consists of devices in six logic densities that range from 2500 to 16,000 usable gates. Total flip-flops in the device family range from 282 to 1500. In addition, a variety of pin count options, from 84 to 304 leads per device, are well-suited for a wide range of I/O intensive applications.

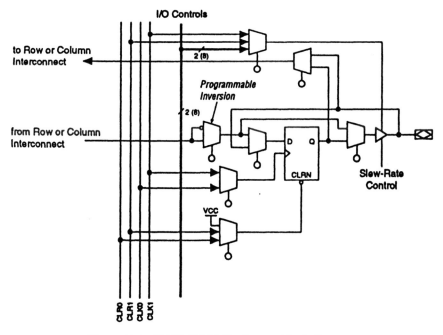

Figure 8–4. FLEX 8000 I/O element block diagram.

The FLEX 8000 family builds on Altera's previous innovations found in the Classic, MAX 5000, and MAX 7000 families of programmable logic devices. The result is a logic family that combines the high speed, predictable timing, and ease of use of EPLDs, with the high register counts, low power consumption, and in-circuit reconfigurability normally associated with FPGAs.

	EPF8282	EPF8452	EPF8636	EPF8820	EPF81188	EPF81500
Logic Elements	2##	###	5##	6##	1,###	1,###
Flip-flops	2##	452	6##	82#	1,###	1,###
User I/O	7#	12#	13#	152	1##	21#
Maximum Pins	1##	16#	2##	2##	2##	3##
Usable Gates	2,5##	4,###	6,###	8,###	12,###	15,###

Figure 8–5. FLEX 8000 family of products.

8.2.2 Pilkington (Motorola/Plessey/Toshiba)

The PMeL FPGA architecture is currently in its fourth generation. This development process has taken place over a 6-year period. During this time PMeL has gained a wide body of experience in the techniques required to obtain the high performance and capacities needed from a leading-edge FPGA and an understanding of the users' requirements from such devices, particularly in the field of autolayout software. This is an area often neglected, especially for fine-grain architectures where the problem may be difficult. The focus of the development effort has been to produce an architecture that works in sympathy with the autolayout software to produce a complete design system. Advanced architecture development tools have allowed the architecture and autolayout algorithms to be developed simultaneously. The Pilkington FPGA architecture is currently under license to Motorola Inc., Toshiba Corporation, and GEC Plessey Semiconductors.

The Pilkington Micro-electronics Architecture The Pilkington architecture is based on a sea-of-gates structure. All function elements (cells) directly abut, unlike the more common channeled-FPGAs (e.g., Xilinx, Actel) where there are routing channels separating the cells. The close proximity of functional cells allows fast direct connections between neighboring cells, enabling the user to combine cells to form compact local functions. A hierarchical routing network runs over the top of the array, making highly efficient use of the available silicon area. All cells implement only simple functions, allowing the basic cell to be optimized for performance.

The Array Structure A key feature of the Pilkington array is its provision of a hierarchy of resources, both for function and interconnect. Although it is modeled on a sea-of-gates type, a flat array of this type was found to be an inefficient target for autolayout. It forces the tools to treat autolayout as one simultaneous and very complex problem. A better solution is to break the problem into simpler subproblems. This is achieved by partitioning the array into 100 cell zones (see Figure 8–6). Each zone can then be treated as a separate autolayout problem. A zone can be considered as a separate array with the port cells forming an interface between the zone interconnect and the global interconnect, see Figure 8–7. The global interconnect joins individual zones together to form the larger array. There is also a hidden clock network which distributes very low skew clocks throughout the array, directly into cells that have clocked registers.

The Interconnect The structure of the interconnect also follows a strict hierarchy of resources. At the lowest level the fast local connections (see Figure 8–8), are used to join local cells to form macros. These efficiently implement

Section 8.2.2 was contributed by Gareth Jones of Pilkington Microelectronics Ltd.

**User I/O Cells
50 per Side**

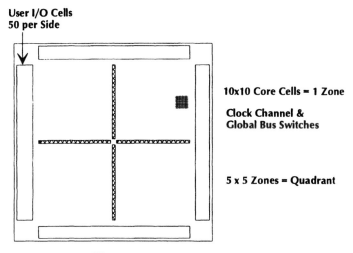

10x10 Core Cells = 1 Zone

**Clock Channel &
Global Bus Switches**

5 x 5 Zones = Quadrant

Figure 8-6. A 10,000-cell array.

small functions, such as a counters, comparators, and complex combinatorial functions. These functions are then combined, using the medium interconnect within the zone and the higher level global interconnect throughout the array, to construct the complete layout. The short range of the local connections and their limited loading means that they are very fast. As a result of this there is negligible overhead in building local function from individual cells. Additionally there is no redundancy in the cells used to construct the functions.

The partitioning introduced into the array enforces a hierarchy onto the routing resources, with the port cell separating the zone routing resource and

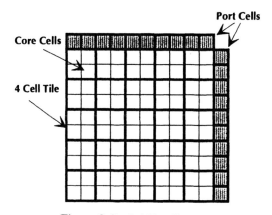

Figure 8-7. A 100-cell zone.

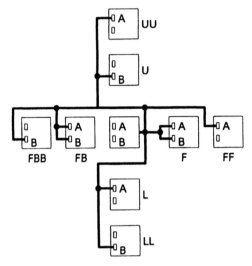

Figure 8-8. Local routing resources.

the global routing resource, see Figure 8–9. This separation enables the global and zone routing phases to be completed independently. The separation of the two layout phases allows the global partitioning and routing to be completed before any detailed zone-level layout has been done. This is a particular advantage when applying timing-driven autolayout algorithms to the array. Once the

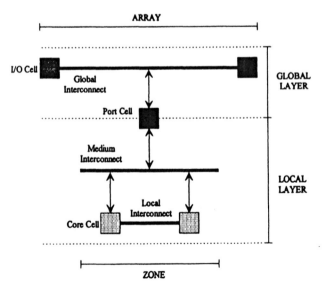

Figure 8-9. Resource hierarchy.

global layout phase has been completed an accurate estimate of the final layout performance can be made. This estimation allows realistic target delays to be assigned to the zone-level net while still obtaining the best possible performance from the array. Setting reasonable target delays for the zone-level layout results in consistent autolayout completion rates and shorter run times.

The hidden clocking structures provide an extra layer of interconnect which can be ignored by the autolayout process, further simplifying the task.

The Cell   Another difference between this architecture and the current dominant architectures is the functionality of the cell. The cell used has a very low level of functionality, providing only a small set of two input functions. Using a conventional channeled routing structure, such a cell would be very inefficient with a high routing overhead between each level of logic; however, using a hierarchical routing structure, these small cells can be very efficiently combined into macros with negligible routing overhead. This combination has two main advantages: first, there is no redundancy; if a cell is only used to perform a simple function, there is no unnecessary capability in the cell to be wasted. Second, the simple cell can be very highly optimized, as the critical paths through the cell are limited in number.

The function of the cells on the array is no longer homogeneous, but varies over a group of four cells. This group of cells (a tile, see Figure 8–10) is then repeated uniformly over the array. The functions within each cell are simple fixed functions. All cells have a basic AND function along with a subsidiary function such as an XOR or D-type flip-flop. These subsidiary functions are available in the ratios found in typical gate array designs and are arranged in such a way as to allow the construction of very high performance hard macros. The tile is repeated uniformly across the array. The sharing of all the essential functions over a tile of four cells results in a significant improvement in the overall silicon efficiency, without any reduction in the gate count supported by the array. This is largely due the careful choice of the function ratios. The addi-

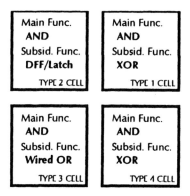

Figure 8–10. The 4-cell tile.

tion of a programmable inversion on the inputs to the cell extends the functions available and removes the need to consider net sense during the autolayout.

The Benefits   The fine-grained structure of this architecture lends itself well to automated design and layout, and has been designed specifically with this in mind. The low-level nature of the basic element results in good performance across a broad range of applications, since there are no special complex structures. Where arrays use larger basic elements the performance is directly related to the ability of the design tools to map the application efficiently to the array elements. Inevitably this process will be more successful for some applications than others, leading to unpredictability in performance. This architecture is a particularly good target for synthesis tools, supporting all the fundamental functions required. As single levels of logic are supported within the cell, all nodes in a circuit are accessible. This gives the tools far greater flexibility, allowing areas to be optimized without compromising performance.

Dynamic Reconfiguration   Any array programmed using volatile means can be used for dynamic reconfiguration in its basic form, that is, where the entire array is reprogrammed. However, the overhead required for this, that is, large data sets for each configuration and long configuration times, means that this form is not suitable for a large number of applications. The obvious enhancement is to partially program the device, thus reducing the size of the configuration data used and hence the time taken to reprogram it. When using a device in this mode there will be several independent functions resident on the array simultaneously. These functions will communicate with each other or the I/O. In either case if one of the functions is changed it must not alter the existing functions or their associated global routing. This is particularly a problem, since a complete rectangular area of the array must be programmed in order to use an efficient addressing mechanism.

The hierarchy of the Pilkington architecture directly supports the isolation of areas suitable for partial reconfiguration. As stated earlier the zone can be treated as an independent array and similarly, several zones can be grouped and treated as an independent area. By defining ports on this area, the layout inside can be swapped without affecting any of the existing global routing in the remainder of the array or interacting with any other existing function. A further advantage is that layouts defined in this way are position-independent, since all zones are identical.

8.2.3   Xilinx XC4000 Family

The XC4000 family of Field Programmable Gate Arrays is Xilinx's third-generation static-memory-based FPGA architecture. As with the earlier XC2000

Section 8.2.3 was contributed by Bradly Fawcett of Xilinx, Inc. Section courtesy of Xilinx, Inc.

and XC3000 families, the architecture is based on three major configurable elements: a matrix of configurable logic blocks (CLBs), a perimeter of input/output blocks (IOBs), and programmable routing resources. The third generation XC4000 family extends this architecture, with a yet more powerful and flexible logic block. I/O block functions, interconnection options, and integration features have also been enhanced with each successive generation, further extending the range of applications that can be implemented with FPGA technology.

Configurable Logic Blocks   A number of architectural improvements contribute to the XC4000 family's increased logic density and performance levels. Principal among these is a more powerful and flexible configurable logic block (CLB) surrounded by a rich set of routing resources, resulting in more "effective gates per CLB". Figure 8-11 is a block diagram of the principal elements within the XC4000 CLB.

Each CLB contains three combinatorial function generators, two flip-flops, and their associated control logic. Thirteen CLB inputs and four CLB outputs provide access to the function generators and flip-flops from the programmable interconnect lines surrounding the block. Four independent inputs are provided to each of two lookup-table-based function generators (F' and G'). A third function generator, labeled H', can implement any Boolean function of its three inputs: the functions F' and G' and a third input from outside the block (H1). In addition, each CLB contains dedicated arithmetic logic for the fast generation of carry and borrow signals (not shown in Figure 8-11); this logic is used in conjunction with the F' and G' function generators to implement high-performance arithmetic functions. The two storage elements in the CLB are edge-triggered D-type flip-flops with common clock (K) and clock enable (EC) inputs, a third common input (S/R) that can be programmed as either an asynchronous set or reset signal, and programmable clock polarity.

The flexibility and symmetry of the CLB architecture facilitates the placement and routing of a given application. Since the function generators and registers have independent inputs and outputs, each can be treated as a separate entity during placement to achieve high packing densities. Inputs, outputs, and the functions themselves can freely swap positions within a CLB during placement and routing operations.

CLBs and On-Chip Memory   The XC4000 family FPGAs are the first programmable logic devices to include on-chip static memory resources, further increasing system integration levels. An optional mode for each CLB allows the memory look-up tables in the F' and G' function generators to be used as either a 16×2 or 32×1 bit array of read/write memory cells. Groups of CLBs can be used together to form a memory array of the desired length and width. Configuring the CLB's function generators as read/write memory does not affect the functionality of the other portions of the CLB, with the exception of the redefinition of the control signals.

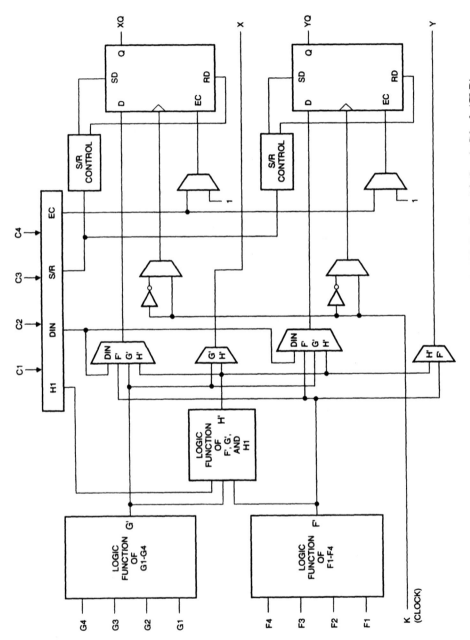

Figure 8–11. A simplified block diagram of the XC4000 Configurable Logic Block (CLB).

288

Input/Output Block   User-configurable I/O Blocks (IOBs) provide the interface between external package pins and the internal logic (Figure 8–12). Each
IOB controls one package pin and can be defined for input, output, or bi-directional signals. Input signals can be routed to an input register that can be programmed as either an edge-triggered flip-flop or a level-sensitive transparent
latch. Optionally, the data input to the register can be delayed to compensate
for the delay on a clock signal that first passes through a global buffer before
arriving at the IOB, thereby eliminating any hold time requirement on the data
at the external pin.

Output signals can pass directly to the pin or be stored in an edge-triggered
flip-flop. Optionally, an output enable signal can be used to place the output
buffer in a high-impedance state, allowing three-state outputs or bi-directional
pins. The output (O) and output enable (OE) signals can be inverted, and the
slew rate of the output buffer can be controlled to minimize power bus transients
when switching non-critical signals.

Programmable pull-up and pull-down resistors are useful for tying unused
pins to Vcc or ground to prevent unnecessary power consumption. Separate
clock signals are provided for the input and output registers; these clocks can
be inverted, allowing either falling-edge or rising-edge triggered flip-flops. As
with the CLB's registers, a global set/reset signal can be used to set or clear
the input and output registers whenever the RESET net is active.

Embedded logic attached to the IOBs contains test structures compatible

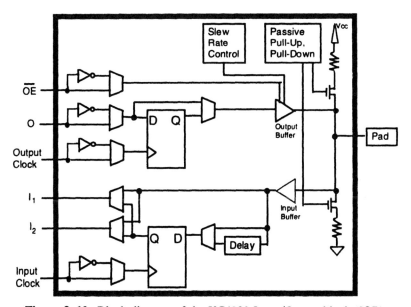

Figure 8–12. Block diagram of the XC4000 Input/Output block (IOB).

with IEEE Standard 1149.1 for boundary scan testing, permitting easy chip and board-level testing of FPGA-based applications.

A master three-state control, when active, places all the I/O blocks in a high-impedance mode. Such a function often is useful during board test operations, or to put the FPGA in a passive, low-power state in battery-driven applications.

Programmable Interconnect All internal connections are composed of metal segments with programmable switching points provided to implement the desired routing. A rich amount and variety of routing resources was chosen to allow efficient automated routing. Routing is scaled to the size of the array, that is, the number of routing channels increases with array size. The CLB's inputs and outputs are distributed on all four sides of the block, for added routing flexibility. In general, the entire architecture is more symmetric and regular than the previous generations, and is more suited to well-established placement and routing algorithms developed for conventional mask-programmed gate array design.

The routing scheme was designed to minimize the resistance and capacitance of the average routing path, resulting in significant performance improvements. There are three main types of interconnect, characterized by the relative length of their segments: single-length lines, double-length lines, and long lines. The single-length lines are a grid of horizontal and vertical lines that intersect at a "Switch Matrix" between each block. The number of possible connections through the Switch Matrix has been streamlined compared to the previous generations of FPGA architectures, in order to reduce capacitive loading to minimize routing delays and increase performance. However, a much richer set of connections between the single-length lines and the CLB's inputs and outputs more than compensate for this reduction in Switch Matrix options, resulting in overall increased "routability." Double-length lines, as implied by their name, run past two CLBs before entering a Switch Matrix, for efficient implementation of intermediate length interconnections. Long lines run the entire length or width of the array, and are intended for high fan-out control signals. Each vertical long line has a programmable "splitter switch" at its center, allowing the long line to be used as two independent routing channels that each run half the height of the array. Automated routing software uses this hierarchy of routing resources to achieve an efficient implementation of a given application.

Eight low-skew global buffers are provided for distributing clocks and other high fan-out control signals throughout the device. Overall skew on these global nets is less than 2 ns, even in the largest devices. An internally-generated clock signal also is available to the user.

Three-State Buffers and Edge Decoders Associated with each CLB in the array are a pair of three-state buffers that can be used to drive signals onto the nearest horizontal long lines above and below the block. Additional three-state buffers are located near each I/O Block along the right and left edges of the array. These buffers can be used to implement multiplexed or bi-directional busses on the horizontal long lines. Programmable pull-up resistors attached to these long lines facilitate their use for wide wired-AND logic functions.

Fast decoding is a requirement in many high-speed microprocessor systems. When the width of the decoding function exceeds the fan-in of the logic block in the FPGA, the use of multiple levels of logic blocks can result in unacceptable performance delays. The XC4000 architecture addresses this need with 16 dedicated "edge decoders," four along each edge of the chip. These "wired-AND" circuits accept inputs from nearby IOBs and CLBs; for example, each edge decoder in the XC4010 accepts up to 40 inputs from adjacent IOBs and 20 inputs from on-chip, and generates a decoded output in 11 ns.

The XC4000 Family   The XC4000 family is at the time of writing the broadest available family of FPGAs, ranging from the 2,000-gate XC4002A to the 25,000-gate XC4025 (Table 8-1). For applications requiring many I/O pins but modest logic capacity, the XC4003H and XC4005H feature about twice as many I/O blocks as the base family members; these devices do not include registers in the I/O Blocks. This breadth of product offerings allows designers to select the FPGA device that is most cost-effective for the target application.

8.3 FIELD-PROGRAMMABLE INTERCONNECT

This section is concerned with a simpler concept, that of field-programmable interconnect, that is, an FPGA without its on-chip logic. This type of chip allows much more flexibility in assembling systems composed of multiple FPGA chips, possibly with other components such as random-access memory. The chips

TABLE 8-1. The XC4000 Family of FPGAs

Device	Typical Gate Count	CLB Matrix	Number of CLBs	Number of IOBs	Number of Flip-Flops
XC4002A	2000	8 × 8	64	64	256
XC4003A	3000	10 × 10	100	80	360
XC4003H	3000	10 × 10	100	160	200
XC4004A	4000	12 × 12	144	96	480
XC4005A	5000	14 × 14	196	112	616
XC4005	5000	14 × 14	196	112	616
XC4005H	5000	14 × 14	196	192	392
XC4006	6000	16 × 16	256	128	768
XC4008	8000	18 × 18	324	144	936
XC4010	10,000	20 × 20	400	160	1,120
XC4013	13,000	24 × 24	576	192	1,536
XC4025	25,000	32 × 32	1,024	256	2,560

required are conceptually crossbar switches, that is, they permit any signal to enter the chip and be broadcast to any number of other signal pins. This additional flexibility in interconnection *from chip-to-chip* gives flexibility in partitioning designs across multiple FPGA chips, and is important in keeping down the cost of design iterations at the printed-circuit-board level. It also has practical advantages in locating errant signals at debugging time.

8.3.1 Aptix Field-programmable Interconnect

The System Verification Bottleneck Over the last several years board-level system complexity has dramatically increased, largely due to the fast-paced evolution of advanced integrated circuits. Such advances in silicon inevitably provide products with improved function, performance, integration, and cost. However, they have also forced the system verification process to become a significant bottleneck in the development cycle. As verification methodologies, printed-circuit-board (PCB) prototyping and simulation both have their benefits, but neither can provide the revolutionary change needed to support the increasing time-to-market emphasis of today's electronic products. Aptix Corporation provides a solution to the system verification challenge and beyond, through a new technology called *programmable interconnect*.

Prototype Form and Function Conventional prototyping offers a verification vehicle with the form and function of the final PCB design. This allows a hands-on debug approach that often uncovers real-world problems too difficult or time-consuming to find through simulation. Prototyping also makes possible replicate copies for other purposes in the development process, including software integration, test, and customer evaluation. Due to these attributes, it is rare to bypass a PCB prototype before a final production version is committed to. However, advances of today's high-density microprocessors, peripheral/support chip-sets, application-specific integrated circuits (ASICs), FPGAs, and complex programmable logic devices (CPLDs), have forced initial system verification away from prototyping and more toward simulation. Factors such as high-density surface-mount packaging, higher interconnect complexity (pins/square inch) and greater functional complexity make gathering and observing data, and making design modifications, much more difficult with a physical prototype than in a computer-aided engineering (CAE) simulation environment.

Simulation Flexibility System simulation offers the key verification benefit of flexibility allowing for easy experimentation, extensive observability, and quick changes, all in an environment fully integrated with design entry tools. But as powerful and convenient as simulation tools are, they are only as effective as the test vectors and simulation model parameters provided. Creating

Section 8.3.1 was contributed by Dr. Amr Mohsen of Aptix, Inc.

vectors for all possible cases can be very time-consuming, adding significant time to the verification process. Even if a thorough set of vectors is created, there will always be variations between the real world and the simulated environment, making physical prototyping inevitable. Additionally, when long simulation efforts are conducted, other development tasks, like software integration, must stay on the side lines waiting for a physical prototype.

Programmable Interconnect: The Missing Link   This comparison of simulation and prototyping is not to state that one methodology is better than the other, but to point out that both have a place in system verification. Unfortunately, one is in a CAE environment and the other is in the laboratory. The ideal solution would offer the flexibility of simulation, the form and function of a physical prototype, and a link between the CAE and laboratory environments.

As the next logical step in the evolution of programmable devices, Field-programmable interconnect components (FPIC),* bring the benefits of programmability to the system level by enabling totally "programmable hardware." FPIC devices, combined with the design tools and hardware that support them, offer a development and verification vehicle with true form, function, and flexibility. The end result is faster and more thorough verification, earlier product integration, and accelerated time to market (see Figure 8–13).

Field-programmable Interconnect Components   Continuing the evolution started by programmable memory and programmable logic (see Figure 8–14),

*FPIC is a trademark of Aptix Corporation.

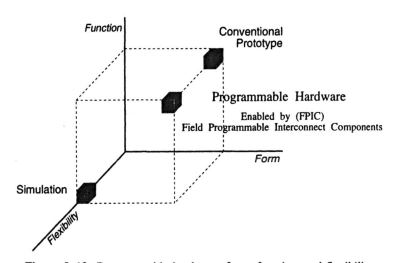

Figure 8–13. Programmable hardware: form, function, and flexibility.

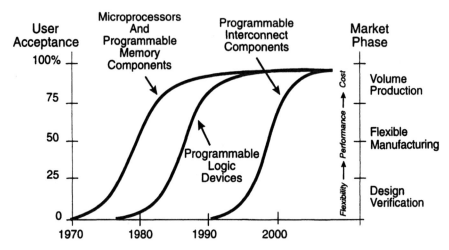

Figure 8–14. The programmable hardware evolution.

programmable interconnect holds the key to complete system programmability. History has shown that programmable technologies initially are used in a laboratory environment, enhancing development and ease of experimentation. As experience by more users is accumulated, and component prices are reduced, applications rapidly expand into final manufactured products. With similar benefits of programmable predecessors, FPICs provide the high-density interconnect architecture, performance, and packaging needed to make programmable interconnect a reality.

The first two members of the FPIC family include the FPIC AX1024D (FPIC/D) and the FPIC AX1024R (FPIC/R). Each has 1024 pins arranged in a 32 × 32 pin matrix. The vast majority of these pins are passive path bidirectional I/Os (typically 120 ohms, 20 pF) that can be interconnected to any pin or group of pins through a programmable routed-array architecture. Rich in routing resources, the unique FPIC architecture achieves 100% routability for most applications. Designed in an advanced 0.8-μ CMOS technology using over 1M transistors, FPIC devices deliver high-speed I/O interconnects as fast as 5 ns. Interconnect programming elements based in CMOS SRAM allow the architecture to be quickly reprogrammed in the system through a high-speed serial interface. The FPIC/D and FPIC/R are designed for interconnection of signal ranges from 0 V to 5 V.

Sporting equivalent routing and performance capabilities, the primary difference between the two FPIC devices has to do with their packaging and functional utility. The FPIC/D is optimized for development and is housed in a screw-mount removable 1024 gold button socket. Protruding from the socket is a 64-pin diagnostic cable providing an observability window for selectively accessing any of the pins. The diagnostic capabilities, explained in more detail later, make the FPIC/D ideal for initial prototype development and verification. The FPIC/R complements the FPIC/D by providing an interconnect solution geared toward replication and stand-alone operation. It is housed in a lower-cost surface-mount pin-grid-array (PGA) package, allowing permanent attachment. Of the 1024 pins on FPIC devices, approximately 20 are used for the programming interface and power, 64 are reserved for diagnostics (FPIC/D only), and 940 are available for user-defined programmable interconnect purposes.

Programming of FPIC devices is handled through serial interface. For the FPIC/D, this interface is typically controlled externally through a connection to a PC or workstation. For the FPIC/R the interface may optionally be configured using a stand-alone memory/interface circuit that initializes the FPIC/R upon power-up. The configuration data used for programming FPIC devices can be generated using the Aptix Development System.

Applications for the FPIC devices address a broad spectrum of interconnect needs, including system prototypes and breadboards; user-specific/configurable PCBs; application configurable processors; test interfaces; as well as programmable connector and switching matrix applications. Using FPIC devices for system prototyping, in conjunction with other programmable components (PLDs, FPGAs, microprocessors, micro controllers, digital signal processors (DSP), and programmable memory), can further enhance the design verification process, allowing faster, more flexible, and thorough product integration.

Field-programmable Circuit Boards Field-programmable circuit boards (FPCBs)† are unique PC boards designed to take full advantage of the high-density interconnect and observability of FPIC devices. FPCBs provide an ideal vehicle for system prototyping by utilizing FPIC/D devices for development and FPIC/R devices for replication. Programming FPIC devices is handled through a connector on the FPCB that interfaces to a PC or workstation via a cable and host interface module.

Unlike conventional PCBs, all FPCB component pin traces are routed to a centralized matrix of pads where an FPIC device provides for pin-to-pin interconnect (see Figure 8–15). FPCBs can have one or more FPIC device for interconnection, depending on the pin density required. A single FPIC device on an FPCB can provide up to 940 user interconnect pins. When higher pin densities are needed, multiple FPIC regions are used. Interconnections between FPIC regions are supported through assigned "global" interconnect pins that enable a direct link between FPIC devices. For example, Figure 8–16 shows an FPCB in an AT form factor with three FPIC regions of approximately 750 component pins and 200 global pins. To connect one pin of a device to another pin, the signal is routed through the local FPIC device, and if necessary, through the global pins to another FPIC region for final connection to a component pin. In this scheme signals will travel through a maximum of two FPIC devices.

---

† FPCB is a trademark of Aptix Corporation.

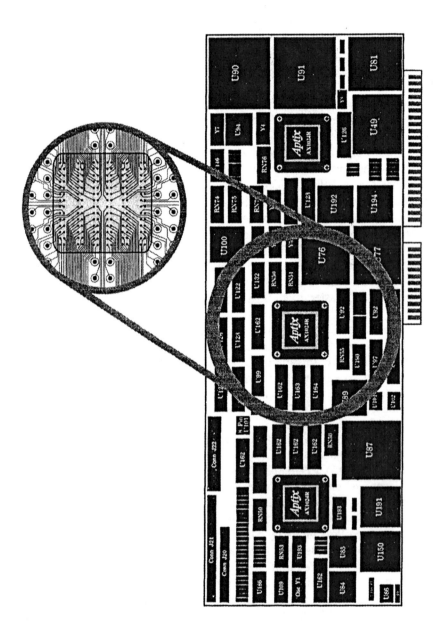

Figure 8–15. All FPCB component pins connect to a matrix of pads located under the FPIC device.

Figure 8–16. Each FPIC support regions of component pins that connect to other regions through global pins.

The through-hole pattern on an FPCB is arranged with repeated rows spaced at 100 mil, 300 mil, 100 mil, 300 mil, and so on. This industry standard pattern not only directly supports insertion of standard 300-mil DIP components, but allows adaptation of a wide variety of larger through-hole and surface mount components through the use of socket adapters. FPCBs are equipped with pin sockets in each through-hole location, allowing components to be easily inserted and removed.

Between each 300-mil row of pins are power or ground pads that provide direct access to every pin for connecting component power supplies, decoupling capacitors or pull-up/pull-down resistors. Additional user-supplied voltages (outside the 0 to +5-V supply range) can be accessed on the perimeter of the FPCB hole pattern. Pin densities of the FPCB pattern are approximately 50 pins/in^2, which is currently above industry PCB averages of 32 pins/in^2.

FPCBs from Aptix come in a variety of standard form factors, the first of which includes a general-purpose FPCB, along with two for standard busses, an AT-FPCB and a VME-FPCB. These initial FPCBs will satisfy a large number of general development applications; however, for those with more specific needs, the Aptix FPCB compiler software makes it possible to create user-customized FPCBs. Per user specification, the FPCB compiler creates Gerber plots for the FPCB hole pattern and its unique routing architecture. The Gerber plots can then be integrated with existing PCB layout software, allowing company-specific form factors, connectors, and special circuitry to be maintained while providing the interconnect flexibility of an FPCB with FPIC devices.

The Aptix Development System   The Aptix Development System provides everything needed to effectively implement FPCB prototypes using FPIC devices (see Figure 8–17). The system lets system designers do front-end design with existing PC or workstation-based schematic capture software. When the design is ready for prototyping, a netlist is created for use by the Aptix Development System software.

Within the software there are five primary stages in creating an FPIC/FPCB design. These stages are setup, partitioning, placement, routing, and programming. In the initial setup stage several preliminary design issues are addressed, including FPCB board selection, netlist importation, package assignment (if not already assigned via the netlist), and critical net prioritization. After setup is complete, the components can be automatically and/or manually partitioned between multiple FPIC regions. Components on the FPCB can then be placed using either automatic or manual placement methods or a combination of both. Once this is accomplished the actual component interconnections from the netlist are automatically routed for programming into the FPIC. All automatic partitioning, placement, and routing operations are guided by critical net priorities, resulting in the fastest routes for the most critical nets. After the board is populated with the design components, the routed FPIC programming file can be downloaded to the FPIC device via the serial port and host interface module. Throughout the development process the Aptix software provides

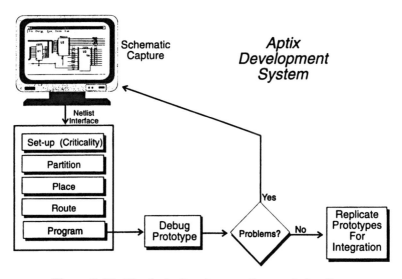

Figure 8-17. The Aptix Development System design flow.

flexible design file management, detailed design statistics and information, and assembly documentation to ease the FPCB prototype process. Initial platforms supported by the Aptix Development System are SUN SPARCstations using X-Windows and on 386/486 PCs operating under Windows.

The FPIC/FPCB Development Environment Once an FPIC programming pattern is downloaded to an FPCB, debugging takes on an entirely new form compared to conventional prototyping. For example, although all the components may physically reside on the FPCB, the software allows components to be electrically removed or isolated through selective placement and routing. This makes possible a step-by-step debug approach whereby incremental blocks of logic can be analyzed in a fast and interactive way. If actual component interconnections need to be altered or added, such changes can be made in the original schematic and then imported for incremental rerouting and programming. This prototyping method removes the need for cuts, jumps, or marked-up schematics, and results in a proven schematic and netlist when finished.

   To further aid in the debugging process, special diagnostic options can greatly enhance signal observability. The diagnostics software and hardware provide a direct link between the 64-pin cable of each FPIC/D and a logic analyzer (initially the HP16500 family, with others to follow). The diagnostic functions are fully controlled via the PC or workstation being used, allowing any FPCB pins to be quickly routed to the analyzer, sampled and reviewed. The system also automatically sets up the analyzer for displaying the signals in a predetermined pattern that is fully-annotated with part and pin numbers, obviating the need for tedious probe-clip setups, since every pin can be quickly routed by software in seconds. Besides using logic analyzers, diagnostic options are also useful for analysis with oscilloscopes, allowing probes to be stationary while hard-to-get signals are routed to the oscilloscope as needed.

Figure 8–18 shows the typical FPIC/FPCB development environment when using a logic analyzer diagnostics option. Included is a PC or workstation, a host interface module, an FPCB (in this case an FPCB-AT), and multiple FPIC/D devices with logic analyzer pods connected to a logic analyzer. The programming files are downloaded from an RS-232 serial interface to the host interface module, which handles the programming interface for FPIC devices on the FPCB. Once programmed, the 64-pin diagnostics cable on each FPIC/D provides a high-speed wide-path connection to the logic analyzer via an analyzer pod. Another RS-232 port from the PC or workstation supports the link for automatically setting up and organizing the analyzer waveforms as well as uploading of captured data for observing within the CAE system.

Once the initial system prototype is fully debugged, stand-alone replicate FPCBs can be created using FPIC/R devices (see Figure 8–19). Replicates provide a key time-to-market benefit by allowing the designer's newly debugged prototype to be put quickly in the hands of the other members in the development team. This means software integration, test generation, customer evalu-

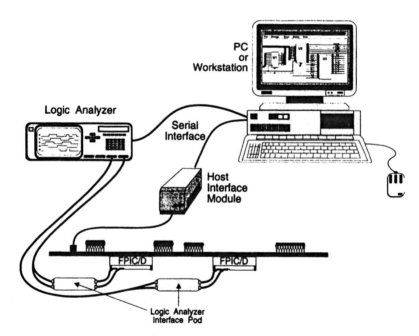

Figure 8–18. The development configuration for system prototyping with the Aptix FPCB Development System.

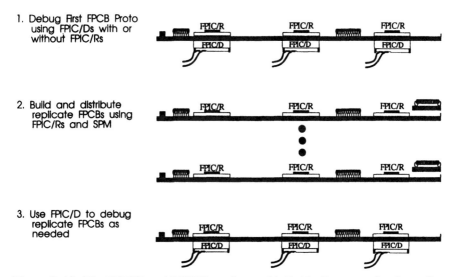

1. Debug First FPCB Proto using FPIC/Ds with or without FPIC/Rs

2. Build and distribute replicate FPCBs using FPIC/Rs and SPM

3. Use FPIC/D to debug replicate FPCBs as needed

Figure 8-19. The FPIC/D and FPIC/R can be used individually or together depending on the function required.

ation, and demonstrations can all occur weeks to months ahead of the normal prototype process. If by chance the FPIC/R-based FPCBs need to be analyzed, the FPIC/D can mount directly under the FPIC/R to provide the diagnostic link to the analyzer.

The Benefits of Programmable Interconnect Today's system design teams are faced with the conflicting challenges of greater system complexity and shorter development cycles. Aptix FPIC and FPCB provide designers with an effective solution that results in company-wide benefits:

- Instant prototypes from schematic.
- Quick changes allow experimentation/innovation.
- Full signal observability and automated debugging aids.
- Consistent documentation.
- Faster design verification.
- Early system and software integration.
- Quicker time to market.

System and ASIC Prototyping FPIC devices and FPCBs are not limited to component-based system prototyping. They are also quite effective for ASIC prototyping minimizing the time and cost risks associated with such designs. Figure 8–20, for example, shows a typical FPCB-based ASIC prototype using

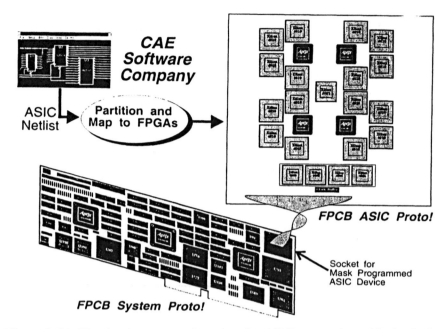

Figure 8-20. The development configuration for ASIC prototyping with the Aptix FPCB Development System.

FPGAs for the logic, an FPIC device for the interconnect, and a connector and cable that adapts to a target socket. In this scenario the designer enters the ASIC design, then partitions and maps the logic to the desired FPGA or high-density PLD. The Aptix Development System provides the interconnect routing for the fastest possible performance between FPGAs and the target socket. Since the FPIC device is providing all the pin-to-pin interconnects, the I/O assignments of the FPGAs can be optimized purely for performance, resulting in an even faster ASIC prototype solution. Of course, the FPCB ASIC prototype could actually plug into an FPCB system prototype, thus bringing the benefits of programmable interconnect to the entire design effort.

8.3.2 I-Cube IQ160 Description

I-Cube's family of field-programmable interconnect devices (FPIDs) is available in a variety of I/O densities, ranging from 96 to 320 usable ports. This family employs a second-generation architecture, resulting in increased performance and architectural flexibility. The FPIDs are manufactured with a 0.8 μ CMOS SRAM process, and are available in a variety of industry standard packaging options.

Section 8.3.2 was contributed by Shrikant Sathe of I-Cube, Inc.

These devices are designed for use in programmable switching, interfacing, and wiring applications. In switching applications, these devices are used to dynamically switch or multiplex a large number of signals. When used in interfacing applications, FPIDs allow a common board or system to satisfy different interfacing requirements. In wiring applications, these devices emulate a trace on a PCB and can be used to change point-to-point connections between components on a board or signals on the backplane.

At the heart of the FPID is a nonblocking, globally connected crossbar switch, allowing total flexibility in routing signals. Every signal in the crossbar switch can be connected to one or more other signals. Each I/O port is identical and can be programmed as input, output, or bidirectional. The FPID devices support either flowthrough or clocked signal flow. The delays through the devices are identical and predictable, thereby simplifying hardware design.

The crossbar array connections are programmed and the I/O port attributes are configured by storing data in the internal SRAM cells and registers. These devices (Figure 8–21) permit in-system configuration, thereby making them suitable for applications that require static or dynamic (on-the-fly) reconfigu-

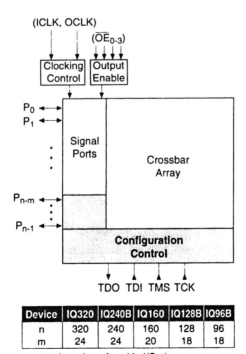

Device	IQ320	IQ240B	IQ160	IQ128B	IQ96B
n	320	240	160	128	96
m	24	24	20	18	18

n = total number of usable I/O pins
m = I/O pins used for RapidConnect

Figure 8–21. Architecture.

rations. Also, they offer two different configuration modes: JTAG-based serial mode for static connections, and a RapidConnect mode for fast configuration changes. The crossbar connections can be programmed incrementally in either mode.

The FPID devices support an industry standard JTAG (IEEE 1149.1) interface for board-level testing. A full functional test of these devices can be done using this interface. The same JTAG protocol is used for loading the configuration bit stream into the device in the serial configuration mode.

Architecture External signals pass to each device through its I/O ports. The crossbar switch array is used internally to connect the I/O ports to one another, thereby establishing connections between the external signals.

The JTAG-based configuration controller decodes the incoming configuration bit stream and stores the data into internal SRAM and registers to establish the desired configuration. Additionally, by switching the device to RapidConnect mode, one can directly access the internal crossbar SRAM to make or break crossbar connections incrementally in under 40 ns.

Enhanced Crossbar Array The enhanced crossbar array is an array of pass transistor switches, each programmable with an SRAM cell. Each switch, when programmed to be in the ON state, connects a unique pair of signal lines in the array. The external I/O signals are connected to the lines in the crossbar array.

A connection between two I/O ports is made by closing the transistor switch at the intersection of the crossbar signal lines. The array is globally connected, and therefore a connection can always be made between any two I/O ports. Moreover, only one transistor switch needs to be closed in order to make a connection between two I/O ports. This arrangement provides a nonblocking, architecture offering 100% utilization, guaranteed connections, and uniform and predictable delays.

This enhanced crossbar architecture supports connecting more than two I/O ports together for multicasting/broadcasting operation. A new connection can be made or an existing connection can be broken without affecting other connections, allowing incremental reconfiguration of the crossbar array.

I/O Ports Figure 8–22 shows the general arrangement. The attributes of each I/O port are individually programmable. The attributes include its I/O function, output voltage level, and pull-up current. The various programming attributes are shown in Figure 8–22. Each I/O port is buffered to provide low-capacitive loading (in input mode) and low-impedance and high current drive (in output mode). The I/O buffer is tristatable, using an OutputEnable control signal.

> **IOB Function:** Figure 8–23 shows the different IOB functions that can be programmed and are described in the following section.
>
> **Input (IN):** In this mode, the external signal at the I/O port pin is connected to the corresponding crossbar line through a buffer.

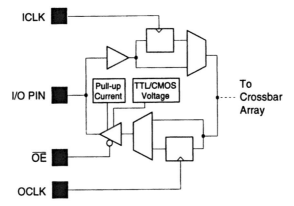

Figure 8–22. Programmable I/O buffer.

Registered Input (RI): In this mode, the external signal at the I/O port pin is connected to the corresponding crossbar line through a register. The register is controlled by an external clock signal.

Output (OP): In this mode, the corresponding crossbar line is connected to the I/O port pin through a buffer.

Registered Output (RO): In this mode, the corresponding crossbar line is connected to the I/O port pin through a register. The register is controlled by an external clock signal.

Output Force 0 (F0): In this mode, the I/O port pin is forced low (logic 0), regardless of the state of the signal on the corresponding crossbar line.

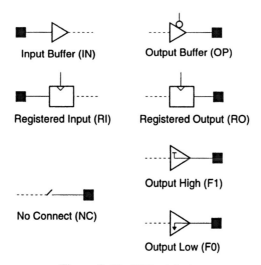

Figure 8–23. IOB attributes.

Output Force 1 (F1): In this mode, the I/O port pin is forced high (logic 1), regardless of the state of the signal on the corresponding crossbar line.

Bus Repeater (BR): This mode is used for connecting two external signals that are bidirectional, but the direction control signal for them is not available. When in this mode, the device automatically detects the driving port and passes the signal to the receiving port. Figure 8–24 shows the circuit.

No Connect (NC): In this mode, the I/O port pin is isolated from the crossbar array.

In the four output (OP, RO, F0, and F1) and the BR modes just described, the active and high impedance states are controlled by the OutputEnable signal.

Output Voltage Level   When the I/O port is programmed to be in one of the output modes, the output (high) voltage level can be programmed as transistor–transistor logic (TTL) or CMOS.

Pull-up Current   For those I/Os programmed for CMOS output levels, an additional pull-up current of 3 mA or 20 mA can be programmed. The normal pull-up current is 8 mA.

Configuration Control   The FPID device is programmed using the JTAG (IEEE 1149.1) serial bus. The JTAG serial bus uses four pins: Test Data In (TDI), Test Data Out (TDO), Test Clock (TCK), and Test Mode Select (TMS). TCK is used to clock data in and out of TDI and TDO. TMS, in conjunction with TDI implements a state machine that controls the various operations of the JTAG protocol. In addition, the reset signal (TRST*) is used to reset the FPID device.

The FPID device, the I/O attributes, and the crossbar connections can be programmed using the JTAG serial bus. Additionally, a special mode called

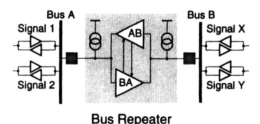

Bus Repeater

Figure 8–24. Bus repeater.

RapidConnect described below in the following subsection, can be enabled or disabled using the JTAG serial bus.

RapidConnect   The RapidConnect mode is used for real-time switching applications, where crossbar connections need to be altered dynamically within the user's system. In this mode, a designated number of I/O ports are used to directly address the internal crossbar SRAM for writing, allowing contents of the crossbar SRAM to be changed very quickly, resulting in fast connection changes.

Configuring FPID Devices

Bitstream Generation   The configuration bitstream generation can be done off-line or in real time in the target system (see Figure 8–25). Software available from I-Cube automates this process.

For applications that do not require FPID devices to be dynamically reconfigured in system, users can generate the required configuration bitstreams off-line. The software used for off-line generation accepts a text file describing the desired configuration connections between different I/O ports and functional attributes of each I/O port, and generates a file containing the bitstream. The software guarantees 100% utilization and 100% completion in a single pass. This software is a part of the development system available on PCs and Sun SPARC Workstations.

For applications requiring dynamic reconfiguration of FPID devices, I-Cube offers users a license to C source code libraries and routines. This allows the user to embed I-Cube Development Software into a target system, for in-system, dynamic bitstream generation and downloading (see Figure 8–26).

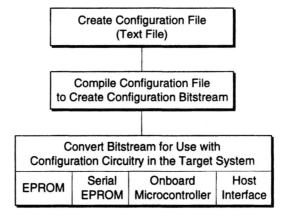

Figure 8–25. Off-line bitstream generation.

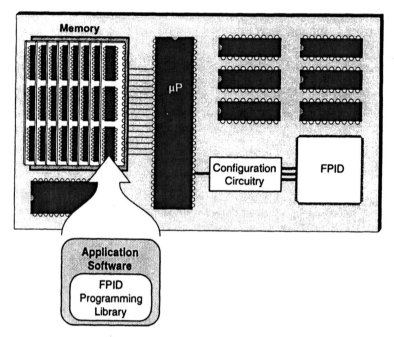

Figure 8–26. Embedded bitstream generation.

Bitstream Downloading   The bitstream can be downloaded into the FPID device(s) using several different hardware schemes. The choice depends on the end application. All these schemes use the standard JTAG protocol and timing.

If the target hardware is controlled by a computer such as a PC, the parallel port on the computer can be used to download the bitstream. I-Cube provides a software utility to do this downloading. Under this scheme, the necessary data for TDI and TMS pins as well as the (software generated) TCK clock signal are sent over the parallel port.

An on-board erasable programmable read-only memory (EPROM) or EEPROM, in either bitwide or bytewide configuration, or a serial EPROM can be used to store the bitstream. Using minimal external logic, the bitstream stored in one of these devices can be downloaded into the FPID device(s) over the TDI and TMS pins, with the TCK pin used for synchronization. The clock signal for the TCK pin is generated by the external logic.

If the target system has an on-board microcontroller, the bitstream data can be read from memory (either an EPROM or SRAM) and downloaded into the FPID device(s) using three I/O pins on the microcontroller to generate the required TDI, TMS, and TCK signals. For real-time applications, the microcontroller/microprocessor will generate the bitstream and download it into the FPID device(s) in a single operation.

8.4 CONFIGURABLE LOGIC ARRAYS AND PROTOTYPING BOARDS

In Chapter 6, we saw how regular arrays of FPGAs could provide a high-performance custom-computing environment. The Algotronix CHS2×4 board took advantage of an unusual feature of the CAL architecture, that is, chips can be cascaded in any of the four principal directions, without much concern to effects at chip boundaries.

8.4.1 The XESS RIPP Board

The RIPP is a PC-based reconfigurable system containing up to eight Altera FLEX 8000 FPGAs or I-CUBE FPIDs on a single card. The FPGAs and FPIDs can be used interchangeably, thus allowing the user to trade off logic and I/O resources for a given application. The RIPP also has four 512K × 8 RAMs for data storage and another FLEX FPGA, which manages the interfaces between the RIPP, the PC, and the external world.

Fundamental Components   The Altera FLEX81188 packs 12,000 logic gates into a 17 × 17 pin-grid array (PGA) package. So if all eight sockets are loaded with FPGAs, the RIPP can support applications needing up to ≈100,000 gates.

The IQ160 FPID described in more detail earlier in this chapter has a 160 × 160 crossbar architecture that can realize any interconnection pattern without the need for complex routing. Since the IQ160 and the FLEX81188 have roughly the same amount of I/O (160 pins versus 184 pins), a single socket can support either device via the use of an adapter.

RIPP ***Internal Architecture***   The bussing arrangement that interconnects the eight RIPP sockets is shown in Figure 8–27. The underlying interconnection pattern is a bipartite graph with sockets $\{1, 3, 6, 8\}$ in one partition and sockets $\{2, 4, 5, 7\}$ in the other partition. Each socket has a separate 32- or 46-bit local bus going to every socket in the other partition, but sockets within the same partition not directly connected. If communication within a partition is necessary, it can be passed through one of the FPGAs or FPIDs in the other partition. Each FPGA or FPID can also send and receive data over a 36-bit global bus that connects to all eight FPGA/FPID sockets.

A RAM resides between each of the following pairs of sockets: $\{1, 2\}, \{3, 4\}, \{5, 6\}, \{7, 8\}$. The RAM and the pair of FPGA/FPIDs are connected by a 46-bit local bus. All 46 wires of this bus can be used to transfer data between the FPGA/FPIDs, or 30 of the bus lines can be used to access the 512K × 8 static RAM (the other 16 wires are still usable for FPGA/FPID data

Section 8.4.1 was contributed by Dr. David E. Van den Bout of XESS Corporation.

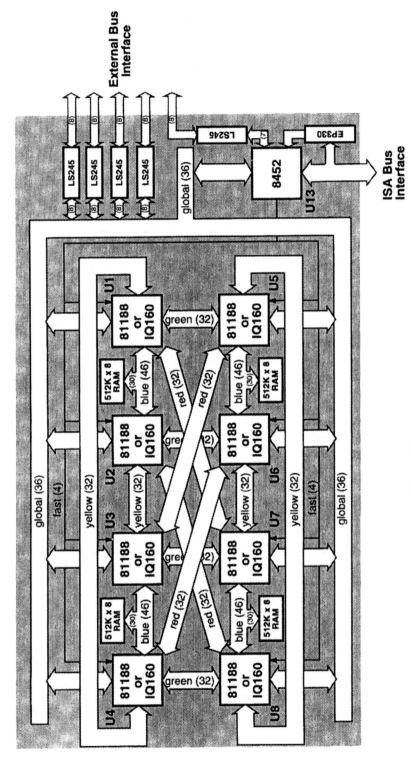

Figure 8-27. RIPP bussing and interfaces.

310

transfers). Either or both FPGA and FPIDs can generate the address and control signals, and either or both FPGA and FPIDs can use the RAM data. With this interconnection scheme, the RAMs could also be replaced by other types of chips that the FPGA and FPIDs might use for special-purpose applications.

The IQ160 FPID has fewer I/O pins than the Altera FLEX81188, so when an FPID is placed in one of the sockets it only connects to 18 lines of the 36-bit global bus. This is a small loss, since the global bus already interconnects all the FPGAs, and rerouting these connections using an IQ160 has few benefits. But, by connecting the IQ160 to the full 46-bit local bus, it becomes possible for a FPGA to access RAMs in other elements by routing address and data signals through the IQ160. This adds another level of flexibility to the RIPP.

RIPP *External Interfaces*   There are two interfaces to the RIPP: one to the outside world and one to the host PC. An Altera FLEX8452 FPGA controls the passage of data through each of these interfaces.

The interface to the outside world goes through an 80-pin nanoconnector. Forty of these signal lines are grounded and the other 40 lines are organized into five individually controlled banks of eight bits each. Four of these byte-wide signal banks connect to the global bus and can be either inputs or outputs. The remaining byte-wide bank is connected to the FLEX8452 and is used to manage the transfer of data over the external interface.

The RIPP resides in the I/O address space of the PC host. The FLEX8452 FPGA can be programmed to support polled, interrupt, or DMA types of operations over the Industry Standard Architecture (ISA) bus of the host PC.

Reconfiguring the RIPP   Loading an application into the RIPP through the ISA bus requires the following main phases:

1. Configuring the FLEX8452 with the standard downloading interface
2. Configuring the FLEX81188s
3. Configuring the IQ160s
4. Reconfiguring the FLEX8452 with the custom interface required by the application (optional)

Because each application may need a specialized interface to the host PC, the FLEX8452 has no fixed configuration EPROM. Instead, a small Altera EP330 PLD on the RIPP serves as a "boot loader" that manages the configuration of the FLEX8452 over the ISA bus. By writing to addresses in the range 0x31C-0x31F, the PC can program the FLEX8452 to act as a downloading interface for the FLEX81188s and IQ160s on the rest of the RIPP. Once configured, the FLEX8452 accepts configuration data from the ISA bus and uses it to configure any FLEX81188 FPGAs on the RIPP via the global bus. Next, the FLEX8452 takes configuration data for any IQ160 FPIDs on the RIPP and programs them through their JTAG interface. Once the main array of FPGA/FPIDs is configured, the FLEX8452 can be reconfigured to support any type of specialized interface needed by the application.

RIPP **Applications** For applications with very regular interconnection structures, such as signal processing or neural networks, an RIPP loaded only with FPGAs is often suitable. The RIPP bus arrangement supports a simple data pipeline, mesh, or torus, among others. The 36-bit global bus provides sufficient bandwidth for transmitting global data and/or control signals to the processing elements residing in the FPGAs.

Many applications, such as an emulated microprocessor, have less regular communication paths. A microprocessor emulator can be built by assigning the microsequencer, arithmetic logic unit (ALU), register set, and memory manager to individual FPGAs and interconnecting them through FPIDs loaded in the remaining sockets. Because of the interconnection topology, each FPID is connected to each FPGA through a wide 32- or 46-bit bus. This provides ample control lines from the microsequencer to each of the other sections. The other sections are equally well connected so that data can be exchanged between the register set and the ALU, for example. In addition, the RAMs can be used to hold microprograms, windowed register sets, and to emulate system memory.

Conclusion The RIPP is an attempt to bring reconfigurable systems to a larger audience. It uses a commonly available host computer, possesses a bus structure applicable to many applications, allows trade-offs to be made between logic density and signal routing, and has a very reconfigurable I/O interface.

8.5   CAD SUPPORT

We have seen that the designer's requirements can range from virtually automatic design, in which the user simply desires that the logic be packed into a given FPGA chip, and to run at the speed desired for the application, to more sophisticated ones, in which the user needs to control the detailed organization of a cell in, say, a systolic array. CAD support can be effective at many stages, including minimization steps, which are sensible for any implementation, that is, they are *technology-independent*.

8.5.1   NeoCAD Foundry

NeoCAD, Inc., based in Boulder, Colorado, has a unique strategy toward delivering an open FPGA design environment, which it refers to as FPGA Foundry. As an independent FPGA CAD tool supplier, NeoCAD provides a single set of high-performance tools supporting the many different architectures

Section 8.5.1 was contributed by Carle Churgin of NeoCAD Inc.

offered by a growing number of FPGA vendors. This focused strategy enables technology–transparent design, allowing the engineer to optimize cost and performance as the design progresses. Development tools include the Timing Wizard for timing and frequency-driven design, the Prism logic partitioning system, the HYDRA client/server place-and-route engine, and CAE tool integration.

The FPGA design process using FPGA Foundry is shown in Figure 8–28. Traditional schematic capture tools or logic synthesis tools can be used to create the FPGA design file in all popular formats. CAE tool integration includes Synopsys, Mentor Graphics, ViewLogic, and Exemplar Logic. The FPGA Foundry supports many reprogrammable FPGA devices, including Xilinx XC3000, XC3000A, XC3000L, XC3100, XC4000, XC4000A; Motorola MPA 1000 family; AT&T's 3000 and ORCA families.

Vendor Independence   FPGA design tools have traditionally been supplied by the FPGA vendors, and every vendor developed its own unique set of tools. Even different families of devices from a single vendor may require different design tools. This inhibits design engineers from using new devices due to the learning curve associated with a new vendor or a new family of devices.

NeoCAD's vendor-independent approach eliminates the learning curve problem, freeing the designer to choose the FPGA device that best suits the price and performance requirements of the design. The designer can become highly proficient in one FPGA design toolset and apply that proficiency to many different FPGA devices.

The implementation of NeoCAD's vendor-independent data structures enables a single software solution to support multiple unique device architectures while providing full support for device-specific features.

Technology-transparent Design   The FPGA Foundry enables technology-transparent design—the ability to design without targeting a specific device architecture in advance. Designers no longer need to identify the target architecture during the schematic capture phase of design. Technology-transparent design also allows easy migration to new FPGA architectures as they become available.

With the combination of device independence and technology transparency, the designer can accurately meet the requirements of the application by delaying final selection of the vendor and the architecture until design capture and functional verification are complete.

Timing and Frequency-driven Design   NeoCAD provides a proprietary capability for frequency-driven placement and routing called Timing Wizard. The designer simply provides the desired operating frequency of the device with input and output offset preferences and the Timing Wizard automatically generates the specific path delays and skew requirements for all critical nets. User preferences are provided as input using a simple ASCII format called the

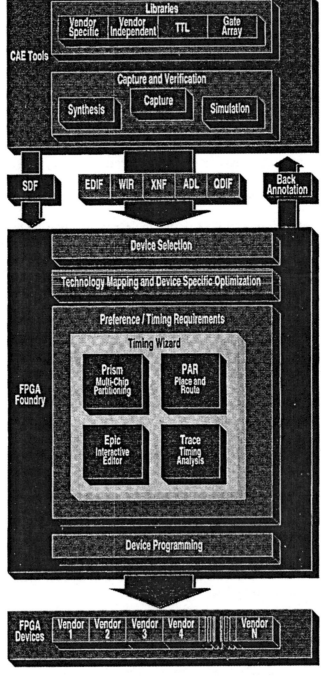

Figure 8–28. FPGA Foundry—design process flow.

NeoCAD Preference Language. In addition to offset, frequency, and physical constraint information, secondary timing information may be specified by the designer.

Four interactive modules comprise NeoCAD's timing-driven placement tools as shown in Figure 8–29. Auto Placement, the Delay Predictor/Scoring Function, Delay Calculator Timing Analysis and Auto Routing. The Delay Predictor/Scoring Function interacts with Auto Placement to yield a placement that has the best chance of conforming to the frequency/timing constraints. The results of placement and delay prediction feed the Auto Routing and Delay Calculator Timing Analysis modules to complete the design with maximum conformance to frequency and timing information.

A variety of proprietary placement algorithms are used in parallel with the delay estimator. As placement proceeds, the delay estimator calculates anticipated wire and component delays. The delay estimator is customized for each FPGA family, since each family is constructed with different component

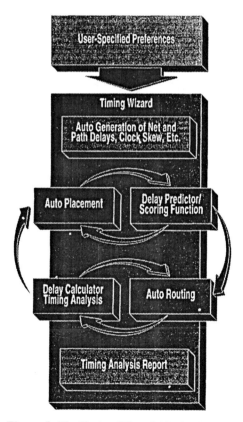

Figure 8–29. Timing Wizard–block diagram.

choices and routing resources. The scoring function then augments the information from the delay estimator and from the initial preferences file by calculating several weighted judgments for factors such as path delays, slack, density, alignment along routing resources, and total connection length. The scoring function operates in parallel with the placement algorithms and the delay estimator.

Timing Wizard determines the acceptability of a particular placement using inputs from the preferences list, the delay estimator, and the scoring function. A complete timing analysis is created based on actual delays of the routing paths chosen during placement. Timing analysis is conducted on two levels within the Timing Wizard: as a basis for placement and routing and as a stand-alone tool for postrouting analysis. Because the Timing Wizard comprehends frequency and timing constraints in the placement and routing process, most timing problems can be avoided.

The timing analysis package within Timing Wizard, called TRACE, is optimized for FPGAs. All the essential data for complex FPGA designs is provided, while irrelevant and extraneous information from typical timing analysis charts is edited for more efficient analysis by the designer. FPGA users can establish their own timing preferences as a filter, allowing TRACE to provide error reports for all results that do not meet the timing specifications. The error reports explicitly depict the path or net locations where problems exist, allowing quick identification and correction.

Partitioning When an FPGA design exceeds the capacity of even the largest device available, the design must be partitioned into multiple FPGA devices. Partitioning may also be required for cost or performance reasons. There are two categories of users who require the ability to partition their logic designs into more than one FPGA device—board-level designers and system-level ASIC designers—each with their own unique needs.

Unlike the traditional approach of dividing the design at the schematic capture level, PRISM partitions after technology mapping, allowing it to be truly timing driven, meeting user-specified operating frequencies and maximum point-to-point path delays. This is shown graphically in Figure 8–30. The tool operates within FPGA Foundry, providing a complete, integrated implementation environment. This is important, because timing-driven partitioning between devices cannot be effective without timing-driven place-and-route within each device.

PRISM is useful for both board-level designers and system-level ASIC designers. For those designing at the board level with multiple FPGAs, PRISM obsoletes the manual process by automatically generating a partition optimized for utilization and timing performance. Although PRISM can be used with little more than the desired operating frequency as input, the ability to manually specify numerous constraints or preferences, such as signals to split, signals not to split, and assignment of specified logic into target devices (floorplanning) is also fully supported. Even with careful manual partitioning, this level of optimization has not previously been possible.

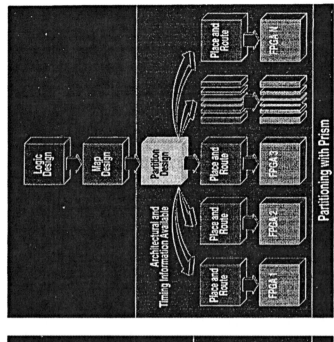

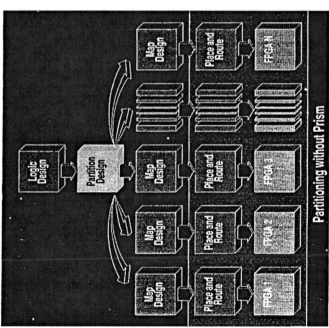

Figure 8-30. PRISM – pre- and post-mapped partitioning.

For system-level ASIC verification prototyping, PRISM not only eliminates the need for manual partitioning but also improves time-to-market for ASIC systems. This is because system-level ASIC verification can run in parallel with the later stages of design, verification, and fabrication. Since the prototype is designed and built by the designer, multiple copies can be made inexpensively. Further, PRISM's timing-driven postmapped approach yields prototypes that run at optimum speed with less chance of internal timing problems. If major changes are made to the design, PRISM will determine if a new partition needs to be made and, if necessary, repartition while still adhering to timing requirements. PRISM supports incremental partitioning, which prevents it from repartitioning the entire design if only a small change is made.

PRISM is invoked after completing technology mapping of the logic design (see Figure 8–30). The user provides PRISM with timing requirements and a list of the devices in which to implement the design (e.g., two Xilinx 3090s and a 3042). The user may select switches to control features such as incremental partitioning and the level of effort PRISM exerts, trading execution time for solution optimization.

PRISM then draws on technology-specific algorithms to determine the best partitioning solution for the design. PRISM uses an iterative loop of the following activities to develop the solution: generating a partition; evaluating it on the basis of the timing requirements, the number of interconnections, utilization of each device, and adherence to user-specified preferences or constraints; then improving the partition based on these results. This iterative loop is fully automatic, requiring no intervention from the user. Once the partition is generated, the resulting designs are ready for the remainder of the FPGA implementation tasks provided by FPGA Foundry.

PRISM is also fully integrated with Timing Wizard, NeoCAD's advanced timing-driven tool that provides the user with complete control over timing requirements and operating frequencies during the implementation of FPGA designs. This integration from mapping and partitioning, through place-and-route, is crucial to providing a timing-driven solution that works. Since each of these functions contribute to the ability to meet the desired operating frequency, it is important that they all work from the same data, and that each software module is capable of meeting the user constraints and timing requirements delivered from the module preceding it. Working together, these automated tools can produce results equivalent to those of a dedicated, knowledgeable engineer, but in a fraction of the time.

HYDRA Client/Server Place-and-Route Engine   The iterative placement and routing algorithms used by NeoCAD can optimize designs simply by allowing the process to run for longer periods of time. Multiple alternatives can also be explored to find the best solution to an FPGA design, including single- and multiple-chip designs. This process is computer-intensive and tends to consume substantial computer time.

HYDRA was designed to utilize the computing power available on networks that are typically not used during "off hours." The two components of HYDRA, HYDRA Manager and HYDRA Place and Route, enable multiple, simultaneous placement and routing of FPGA designs to improve design completion rates and decrease overall implementation time. The HYDRA Manager provides automatic distribution of the place-and-route process to available network CPUs and serves as the control point. The user specifies the design parameters and available CPUs, and the HYDRA Manager allocates the design processing to appropriate CPUs. The HYDRA Place and Route modules accept mapped or previously placed and routed designs as input to explore alternatives that might yield improved designs.

CAE Tool Integration NeoCAD's FPGA Foundry is fully integrated with CAE tools for design capture, logic synthesis, and simulation. Designers are free to choose the best front-end tools for their needs and to use the vendor-independent FPGA Foundry for their FPGA designs.

NeoCAD has adopted the industry-standard library of parameterized modules (LPM) as a standard library for FPGA design. This library includes both primitive and block-level functional components, and features parametric design specification to offer designers broad flexibility in creating designs. FPGA Foundry supports hardware description language (HDL) design and synthesis tools with architecture-specific logic optimization capabilities, timing-constraint interfaces to and from logic optimization and physical place-and-route, and hard-macro integration, both through automatic inference from HDL descriptions and explicit user instantiation. FPGA Foundry provides full simulation support with postlayout back annotation for accurate timing models.

8.6 FUTURE OUTLOOK

While the concept of truly dynamic reconfiguration has been known for some time, there have so far been few applications that justify its complexities. Rapid reconfiguration increases the number of pins that must be totally dedicated to this purpose.

Several companies, including Atmel and PMeL, have announced their intention to exploit dynamic reconfiguration. For example, the Atmel Cache Logic* concept allows newly required functions to be loaded into an FPGA while inactive functions are kept in an adjacent memory.

Clearly, the gate count of FPGAs will continue to increase as finer detailed very-large-scale integration (VLSI) processes continue to develop. FPGAs have the same attraction as memory to fabricators, that is, they are highly regular and the end application is of little concern. But there are differences as well as

---

*Cache Logic is a trademark of Atmel.

similarities, and the provision of a routing network that is generous enough for all applications and yet fast is a particular challenge.

MANUFACTURER'S ADDRESSES

ALTERA CORPORATION
2610 Orchard Parkway
San Jose, CA 95134

APTIX CORPORATION
225 Charcot Avenue
San Jose, CA 95131

I-CUBE, INC.
2328-C Walsh Avenue
Santa Clara, CA 95051

PILKINGTON MICROELECTRONICS LTD.
Sherwood House
Gadbrook Business Center
Rudheath, Northwich, Cheshire CW9 7TN, U.K.

XESS CORPORATION
2608 Sweetgum Drive
Apex, NC 27502

XILINX INC.
2100 Logic Drive
San Jose, CA 95124

AFTERWORD

It is interesting to ask software people what they like about their work. Most say that intellectual stimulation is foremost. But if that is the case, then why wouldn't proving mathematical theorems be just as stimulating? Surely that exercise requires the same type of intellectual activity? But theorem-proving lacks the feeling of creation that accompanies the writing of a program. Both are logical constructions in particular formal systems—but the theorem simply "is," while the program (eventually!) "runs."

Those who prefer hardware to software often point to the absence of constraints as the basis of their choice. They are free to create *ab initio* a machine that solves a problem optimally, rather than merely programming a suboptimal solution on an arbitrary machine. But to date, hardware has lacked the immediacy—instant gratification—of software.

This book has shown how the field-programmable gate array (FPGA) has brought hardware and software closer together. An FPGA would be virtually useless without extensive CAD support, including algorithms that represent some of the toughest challenges to software engineers and scientists. The act of programming an FPGA captures some of the immediacy of software design along with some of the freedom of hardware design.

From a systems perspective, FPGAs are often thought of as a replacement for "glue logic," or for application-specific integrated circuits (ASICs), which have a longer design and fabrication cycle. But there is a potential for FPGAs to have a profound effect on how systems are designed at the fundamental level. The fact that an FPGA can be quickly reprogrammed in system means that one can design into a system a component whose functions change as the need arises. Like the microprocessor before it, the FPGA may replace hundreds of single-function components with one programmable part.

A system can be built with FPGAs and random-access memory (RAM) with instructions on how to configure the hardware, interleaved with other instructions on how to process data. Such a system is reminiscent of a living organism, in which the DNA codes the arrangement of basic building blocks needed to create the proteins that will make the organism function. This book points the way toward the next generation of systems with even higher levels of integration and functionality than ever before, with FPGA structures at the core.

CHARLES D. STORMON

President and Chief Scientist
Coherent Research Inc.
East Syracuse, New York

GLOSSARY

Antifuse An initially open switch between two points, which may be closed by electrical selection of the location, using a nonreversible process activated by a higher-than-normal voltage. There is a variety of proprietary technologies.

ASIC Application-specific integrated circuit. This term is used to distinguish integrated circuits for specialized applications, from commodity components.

CAE Computer-aided engineering. Software tools for use by engineers.

CBIC Cell-based integrated circuit. An IC mostly composed from a library of proven, pre–designed cells.

CLB Configurable logic block. Proprietary term describing the internal element used in field-programmable gate array architectures developed by Xilinx, Inc.

CMOS Complementary metal-oxide semiconductor. The fabrication process used for field-programmable gate arrays.

Commodity component A widely used type of integrated circuit that is produced in high volume and is readily available from different manufacturers with virtually–identical specifications.

DIL Dual-in-line integrated circuit package. Common form of packaging with two rows of pins typically spaced by 0.1 inch.

CAL Configurable Array Logic. Proprietary term describing the architecture employed by Algotronix Ltd.

DRAM Dynamic random-access memory. A volatile semiconductor memory that requires periodic refresh cycles to maintain its contents.

EPROM Erasable programmable read-only memory. A nonvolatile semiconductor memory, usually with floating gates, that in normal system operation can be read electrically. It must be removed from the system: for erasure by exposure to ultraviolet light, and for reprogramming. It cannot be erased selectively, that is, every bit must be rewritten even if only one needs to be changed.

EEPROM Electrically erasable programmable read-only memory. A semiconductor memory that can be erased electrically, otherwise similar to an EPROM.

EPLD Electrically programmable logic device. A regular assembly of logic components whose functions and connections can be specified electrically and remain nonvolatile.

FPGA Field-programmable gate array. A regular array of logic components and an interconnection network, both of which can be configured at the point of application.

FPLA Field-Programmable Logic Array. A Programmable Logic Array structure which can be configured at the point of application.

GAL Gate array logic. Proprietary term of Lattice Semiconductor Inc.

"Glue" Logic After choosing the major components, the extra logic that "glues" everything together, that is, that integrates the system into a whole. Often used derogatively to apply to a mass of small- and medium-scale integrated components supporting a few very large-scale integrated components.

HDL Hardware description language. A formal language for describing digital systems in hardware terms. Examples include VHDL.

LCA Logic cell array. Proprietary term of Xilinx Inc.

LSI Large-scale integration. Generally applied to integrated circuits with between 200 and 20,000 transistors.

MOSFET Metal-oxide semiconductor field-effect transistor. Transistor type used in FPGA circuits.

MSI Medium-scale integration. Generally applied to integrated circuits with between 20 and 200 transistors.

PAL Programmable array logic. Proprietary term of American MicroDevices Inc.

PCB Printed circuit board.

PLA Programmable logic array. Used to describe specific two-level arrangement with an AND plane feeding an OR plane.

PLD Programmable logic device. An integrated circuit with a regular pattern of logic elements that can be configured for a particular application.

    Simple PLD LSI component comprising a programmable AND plane followed by a fixed set of logic functions.

    Complex PLD A collection of simple PLDs on a single die with a global interconnection network.

Real Estate Colloquial term referring to the area taken up by some function or resource of an integrated circuit.

RAM Random-access memory. Memory with no preferred sequence of addresses.

SRAM Static random-access memory. Preserves its contents without refresh, provided power supply is maintained.

Switchbox A general-purpose interconnection network that aids in routing signals from one part of an FPGA to another.

SSI Small-scale integration. Refers to integrated circuits with fewer than 20 transistors.

Systolic Architecture   A computing structure with many identical processing elements that are composed in an array, and for which the flow of data is highly regular.

VLSI   Very-large-scale integration. Usually restricted to integrated circuits with over 20,000 transistors.

INDEX

Lightning Source UK Ltd.
Milton Keynes UK
UKOW04n2200211014

240438UK00001B/41/A